TOXIC FEAR

TOXIC FEAR

Pollution Anxieties in the American 1980s

Michael Egan

THE UNIVERSITY OF GEORGIA PRESS | ATHENS

Athens, Georgia 30602
www.ugapress.org

Set in Sans and Arno Pro by Westchester Publishing Services

Printed digitally

EU Authorized Representative
Easy Access System Europe—Mustamäe tee 50, 10621 Tallinn, Estonia, gpsr.requests@easproject.com

Library of Congress Control Number: 2026008559
ISBN: 9780820377346 (paperback)
ISBN: 9780820377339 (hardback)
ISBN: 9780820377353 (ebook)
ISBN: 9780820377360 (PDF)

For Susanna's granddaughters
For Jordan & Meredith's grandmother

CONTENTS

Love Song for the Hazmat Suit

They say the dose makes the poison, an assertive Paracelsian piece of iatrochemical wisdom from the alchemical early modern world before petrochemical production saturated landscapes with materials that do not break down—that defy the processes of nature—so there's always more of them, but when they say the dose makes the poison—which they said more and more in the 1980s, and an unimpeachable truth to which they clung in these not early but most postmodern times—they are bounding the debate, because if it is the quantity that determines a poison there is no room to acknowledge that the correct or best amount of any persistent organic pollutant in living tissue is zero: They (and who is they?) don't want to talk about that, because it would shift attention toward why these chemicals need measuring in landscapes outside of the factory, and remind publics that the presence of any of these hazards was a choice imposed by industrial interests who saw in innovation an opportunity for better living; it's better to assure wary, anxious publics that "the dose makes the poison" to evade pointed questions about the provenance of (and responsibility for) those hazardous, uncertain, and invisible pollutants—especially because chemistry was unquestionably responsible for a more affluent post–World War II United States, and access to good and cheap materials was a boon, an addictive boon (there's no going back now), not least to companies and their stockholders, so good at outsourcing risks and externalizing costs, so that when spills, or leaks, or the problem of disposing/storing these chemicals does occur, they do not show up on the balance sheet, are left for concerned residents, who wonder why their children are sick and how scared they should be and look to underfunded health agencies, whose representatives (taking measurements on obscure devices) are hidden behind impermeable protective suits—necessary for trained professionals, but less so for permanent inhabitants of contaminated communities, until such time as the risks can be ascertained—these hazmat suits, quintessential costume, heartbeat, of the 1980s—from Three Mile Island to Love Canal to communities the length and breadth of the United States, but also in *Star Wars* (stormtroopers and Darth Vader), *Ghostbusters*, and *E.T.*—that climactic scene terrified me as a child (how violent, invasive) and it wasn't until I was an adult, when I had the courage to watch that movie again with my own children, that I realized that it wasn't actually a hazmat suit but a spacesuit, made, of course, from the same DuPont materials (Tyvek or PVC or Teflon) as the public health and environmental monitors who wore them in the background in every newsreel of contamination events—design the problem, design the solution: the dose makes the poison: avoid that question of choice, bound the debate—but that suit, that hazmat suit, masked and anonymous voice of expert authority in measuring, weighing, evaluating, mitigating risk—the dose of which . . . —and hazard in places where lived experience counts for less in environmental decision-making than corporate stock options, or hazmat-suited acceptable levels of exposure, or clinically derived body burdens, and this is all the price of progress, the price of modernity, which Walter Benjamin, who warned about modernity's storm of progress—catastrophe—was tragically swept up and killed by, that storm, saw with such clarity, and who wrote about history as fire alarm: history as premonition of fears and catastrophes, the better with which to address them in good time. But history as the hazmat suit—prolegomenon to an accounting of pollution fears and anxieties in the 1980s—is tacit recognition of history's failure to warn or to be heard, and if there is to be a love song for the hazmat suit, it is also a song to the future—one already mortgaged by the optimism of a chemical industry that championed potential over consequence and considered only the positive lines in the balance sheet, where the profits made the poisons and the rest is shunted, dumped, confined in fifty-five-gallon barrels, vats, drums.

TOXIC FEAR

The Eighties Almost Killed Me

This is a book about fear and the state and the ways in which feelings and concerns became imprinted in law, literature, politics, and society. It seeks to enliven the cultural dimensions of risk perception and how danger and hazard were interpreted among lay publics during the American 1980s.[1] In a nutshell, my argument is this: In the 1980s, Americans were frightened by the ubiquity of toxic pollution and its potential to rear up in their homes; this chemical anxiety constituted a blatant expression of the disconnect between popular risk aversion and the administration of public health—and it transformed the nature of American environmental politics.

During the 1980s, Americans became especially attuned to and concerned about the proliferation of chemicals in the environment; the hazards associated with chemical pollution unlocked a deluge of fear and anxiety across American society. Toxic contaminants—real and imagined—provoked fear "in new and special ways," observed the sociologist Kai Erikson. They "elicit an uncanny fear in us," he argued, that constituted "a new species of trouble."[2] The psychologist Paul Slovic found that chemical hazards frightened Americans more gravely than natural hazards.[3] Chemicals contaminated rather than merely damaged. Their poisons penetrated human tissue and caused invisible, indirect harm in the body. In most cases, the threat from chemical exposure was not strictly acute, but slow, chronic, latent, deferred, uncertain, and enduring. New and alarming smells—metallic or sweet, sharp or musty—triggered anxiety in households and communities.[4] Such exposures are part of a family of catastrophes that scholars have come to call "slow disasters": troubles that frequently lack a flashpoint and/or linger—fester—invisibly. A slow disaster is especially sinister because its threat and impact take on an ahistorical or anachronistic quality that gives the impression that its presence is not a function of past cause and event. By the end of the 1980s, for example, an emerging understanding of what had become known as hormone-disrupting chemicals reinforced the potential for real harm. The chronological separation between their release into the environment (in growing quantities after World War II) and their discovery as serious human health risk (with growing popular awareness only decades later) introduced these contaminants as a clear and present danger, and separated the nature of the public health hazard from the industrial regimes that had for many years been the source of the slow disaster. The emotions these kinds of slow threats aroused remain critical to understanding the contemporary environmental narrative, and they demand new historical frameworks for engaging with environment and society.

The distinction between popular and expert readings of this new species of trouble is an important one to which I will return frequently: Public understandings of risk and "expert" risk analysis, which drives policy, are two fundamentally different things. The 1980s showed that the assertion of scientific or technical expertise could not subdue a frightened public. To that end, the breadth of toxic fear across the American population—regardless of whether people considered themselves environmentalists or not—suggests that environmental issues were a much bigger and more central facet of American political life in the 1980s than previously believed. That notion and its consequences require more careful understanding. Put another way, popular fear is an important and underrepresented chapter in the history of American environmentalism. To engage with policy, social activism, and environmental destruction and not take the emotional pulse of the country as a whole offers little more than a siloed reading of environmentalism's larger significance. Environmental health, this book suggests, is not only an economic or biological or political phenomenon but also a sociocultural measurement of the people, by the people, and for the people. And toxic fear—as expressed in small communities and nationwide—is a component of that environmental health.[5]

* * *

One of the underlying propositions of this book is that it is important to take fear and the expression of fear seriously. Emotions are not a character weakness but an aspect of lived experience, and fear contends with how individuals and groups interpret the potential outcomes and threats of the unknown.[6] I need to be clear, though: I do not consider fear to be an expression of passive victimhood.[7] My reading of pollution anxieties is not an exercise in silencing or dismissing or ridiculing the agency of people who were frightened.[8] I want to make an important distinction between the two kinds of chemophobia—a fear of chemicals and a term that entered the popular lexicon—present in the American 1980s. The first chemophobia (which receives discussion in chapter 6) was a pejorative, promoted by the chemical industry that suggested the hysteria was unwarranted; the term crescendoed toward the end of the 1980s and denigrated fear by referring to people who were afraid of chemical pollution as hysterical dupes or practitioners of an antimodernist luddism. This first chemophobia treats fear as a subject that abdicates agency from its actors. In the case studies presented in this work, one could read whole communities of people as passive victims in an industrial history of poison. That does not strike me as particularly interesting or accurate, especially when subsequent studies determined that so many of these communities were justified in their concerns about the pollutants in their communities. This first definition of chemophobia is typically a tool of the conservative, industrial, antienvironmental lobby. It implies that we live in a rational world, and those who *exhibit* fear are overly emotional, prone to hysteria. That women were prominent at the vanguard of community grassroots groups who opposed chemical contaminants imposes an ugly gender stereotype into this rhetoric. It reads the popular response to chemicals as a kind of paranoia. In this context, fear, as the novelist and essayist Marilynne Robinson has observed, "operates as an appetite or an addiction. You can never be safe enough."[9] Modernity has no place for emotions—and that is a critical social problem that transcends a history of environmental fears.

I am more interested in a second definition of chemophobia, which is a more active expression of how individuals and communities responded to perceived threats to their health. Upon learning of unanticipated hazards and risks, in the absence of good information, they were afraid. A fear of uncertain hazards is a normal response: biological, even. Their fears manifested themselves in different ways, and they prompted different actions, but during the 1980s toxic fears were a transformative catalyst in American environmental politics. Indeed, an important part of this book's argument is to stress that fear can be an active, rather than passive, emotion and that the historical agency of Americans who were afraid of chemicals radically transformed recent environmentalism and American environmental policy. Fear is an intrinsic part of the human condition and part of our evolutionary makeup, but fear also has a history.[10] In his investigation of the history of political fear, the political scientist Corey Robin acknowledges that "few elements of the human experience seem less amenable to the strictures of the intellect or of history" than fear. "It has no history."[11] To wit, Robin invokes the sociologist Raymond Aron's assertion that fear "is a primal, and so to speak, subpolitical emotion."[12] Robin's work turns that notion on its head, however, to examine the manner in which fear is recruited as a political tool, often used to fill the vacuum created by a lack of positive politics in the American system. In this framework, fear is derived from a top-down approach to social control. The anthropologist Joseph Masco concurs: "Existential terror . . . not only empowers the most radical actions of the security state; it also creates ideological barriers to dealing with a vast set of everyday forms of suffering and vulnerability that Americans experience."[13] Where Robin explores a more abstract reading of political fear, Masco is predominantly interested in "existential terror" as a tool to impose national security measures—specifically in response to the atomic bomb after World War II, and weapons of mass destruction after 2001. Both works are convincing, but it can be difficult to read chemical anxieties with a similar deep state perspective or as a function of a top-down public discourse. Toxic fear feels different, even if its public expressions work within similar kinds of emotional regimes. Fears of pollution escaped the carefully contrived narratives of political and cultural control that enlivened other forms of social fear. They seem a pushback against that impulse. Toxic fear undermined rather than confirmed social order. In a lot of ways, chemophobia might be better understood as a popular fear without a specific author. By every measure, it appears as though the popular reaction to chemical pollution caught government and industry wholly by surprise.

* * *

Chemical exposure has been described as "contact between misplaced matter and flesh."[14] Put another way, chemical harm is the presence of pollution "in the wrong quantities, to the wrong place, at the wrong point in time, and for the wrong duration."[15] Misplaced chemicals—whatever their potential harm—are a tinderbox for toxic fear. But pause a moment to consider "misplaced matter." A big part of the modern toxic legacy is precisely the process of how new and hazardous chemicals escaped an array of Pandora's boxes—the factory, the laboratory, and the landfill (where they belonged)—and infiltrated workplaces, homes, and bodies. Misplaced also implies a lack of control and a concomitant lack of understanding: of unanticipated consequences. In many instances, the chemical transgressions that provoked such fear in the 1980s were the culmination of manufacturing and dumping practices from the 1950s and 1960s—long since forgotten—when the magnitude of chemical risk was less well known.

By the 1980s, chemical contaminations and the environmental anxieties they provoked were widespread. From the late 1970s into the 1980s a growing tsunami of incidences of industrial chemicals spilling, leaking, emitting, and escaping from laboratories, factories, and disposal sites—and turning up in air, soil, and water systems—saturated mainstream political discourse. In 1980, U.S. Surgeon General Julius Richmond reported to the Senate that Americans would "confront a series of environmental emergencies" related to human-made toxic pollution, which "are adding to the disease burden in a significant, although as yet not precisely defined, way."[16] The authority of the office impressed the gravity of the message. "The public health risk associated with toxic chemicals is increasing, and will continue to do so until we are successful in identifying chemicals which are highly toxic and controlling the introduction of these chemicals into our environment."[17] Only a couple of years earlier, Representative John E. Moss (D-Calif.), chairman of the House Subcommittee on Oversight and Investigations, had declared that "toxic chemical waste may be the sleeping giant of the decade."[18]

"Hardly a day goes by," one *Los Angeles Times* reporter asserted in 1980, "without a new story about toxic exposures, radiation leakage, poisoned land and poisoned people. Like thousands of sleeping monsters, toxic-waste dumping grounds are now awakening to horrify entire communities throughout the country."[19] In September 1980, the *Time* cover extolled "The Poisoning of America." The story within outlined the national scope of toxic pollution; no American was safe from the contaminants that had spread across the country.[20] More ink was devoted to chemical pollution and the fears it provoked in the 1980s than in the previous two decades combined.[21]

It's not as though there was a shortage of toxic reference points. Contaminated communities such as Love Canal in New York—the site of a particularly famous contamination of an entire community at the end of the

1970s, where a Niagara town was built on top of an old landfill—along with poisoned water in such diverse places as Woburn, Massachusetts, Toone County, Tennessee, and Salinas and McFarland, California, served as catalysts for a growing popular fear of chemicals. The abandonment of Times Beach, Missouri, a community exodus from widespread dioxin contamination in 1983, sent shockwaves across the United States, as did the relocation of many of Love Canal's inhabitants. These led to worries about toxic waste disposal sites in Emelle, Alabama; in Warren County, North Carolina; in Seymour, Indiana; throughout New Jersey. The popular perception was that Everytown, USA, could be at risk. During the 1980s, the swelling number of places given Superfund designation—sites requiring large-scale remediation from hazardous wastes—gave Americans pause. New chemical names saturated not just air, soil, water, and food systems, but also media reporting and popular imaginations. Dioxins, PCBs (banned from production, but turning up everywhere in the 1980s), benzene all became household names, even if their chemical constitution and hazards were not fully understood by the public. Nevertheless, that American public was attuned to respond negatively to any polysyllabic chemical name based on the litany of historical events in which chemicals from kepone to dioxins to PCBs to ethylene dibromide to trichloroethylene had poisoned people and landscapes. And the number of chemical threats continued to grow by the year. Consistent across the reams of literature and government documents on chemicals and public health was an overriding uncertainty on the number of human-made chemical substances in the environment, but according to a 2008 study in the *Annals of the New York Academy of Science,* roughly 80,000 new commercial synthetic chemicals had been released into the environment since World War II.[22] Quantities increased on a similarly inconceivable scale. "In 1941," *Time* informed American readers in 1980, "the American petrochemical industry produced 1 billion lbs. of synthetic chemicals. By 1977 that rate had soared to 350 billion lbs."[23]

That problem, the problem of a modern society drowning in its own poisons, is the environmental tragedy of the late twentieth century and early twenty-first. Chemicals are the enduring artifacts of the modern world. They are the products of the industrial chemical revolution that began at the end of the nineteenth century and proliferated in the marketplace in the years immediately following World War II. They are instrumental to our contemporary well-being. They are the medicines that preserve us and the materials that make up the world around us. The innovations and creations of the chemical industries have quite literally transformed everything. There is hardly any product or process that has not been directly influenced by this history. But at a price. Inasmuch as the history of chemical manufacturing can be interpreted as one of unparalleled progress, it needs to be counterbalanced with an unseemly account of technological hubris and unanticipated consequences. Outside the laboratory—and beyond the factory—some of these chemicals have precipitated new problems. Synthetic pesticides, plastics, dioxins, and PCBs defy environmental degradation. They persist. As a result they pose considerable risks to human and environmental health because they tend to magnify up the food chain and accumulate in human and animal tissue. They have become an ominous part of the global toxic story—as carcinogens and endocrine disruptors—that continues to haunt contemporary society. My study of toxic fear puts the cultural response to this problematique under the microscope.

* * *

But a book without a conspiracy isn't very interesting. And while it is easy to suggest that less government oversight of chemicals likely produced more public uncertainty and anxiety, I think this oversimplifies the relationship between social fear and the neoliberal project, which fostered a cult of individualism that galvanized anxieties and undermined a public sense of security. Neoliberalism is the logical extension of uncontrolled markets and the concomitant belief that prosperity is best achieved through individuals being free to pursue their own self-interest. As an idea, it proposes a model for improving the world, but those improvements must not disrupt the underlying structures of economy and power. That means less government and (more significantly) less government intervention, lower taxes, and fewer controls. In practice, neoliberalism meant "deregulation, privatization, and withdrawal of the state from many areas of social provision."[24]

The 1980s witnessed neoliberalism's most ardent champions in power on the western side of the Iron Curtain. Just as toxic chemicals became a prominent feature of the American social and physical landscape in the 1980s, the traditional forms of state oversight designed to provide security for its people were eroded. Within the context of environmental concerns, neoliberalism encouraged industry to self-monitor its practices and the safety of its own products. These voluntary checks were regularly less stringent than Americans might have wished for.

The 1980s marked the ascendancy of neoliberalism and conservative politics, both of which constituted a departure from the last remnants of the Great Society. In their place, free trade and smaller government championed personal freedoms and permitted the market to dictate the direction of flows and services. Michael Douglas playing Gordon Gekko playing Ivan Boesky would affirm in the 1980s that "greed . . . is good."[25] Social problems were outsourced. They became individual problems: Their solutions required individual fixes.[26] Safety (security), long held as a defining feature of the implicit contract between the state and its people, evolved from social safety to the safety of the individual. Further, the onus of responsibility moved from government and government agencies to a public that had in the previous decade abdicated environmental oversight and the necessary scientific literacy to experts no longer equipped for the job. If uncertainty excited toxic fears, then, it was aided by deregulation and the cuts in social spending that curtailed government agencies tasked with monitoring environmental health. In the absence of funding, fewer tests were conducted and more public questions and concerns about local water and air quality went unanswered. Deregulation in American federal politics in the 1980s seemed an almost knee-jerk reaction to the decade of extensive environmental regulation that preceded it.

One might go so far as to suggest that the 1980s were to the right what the 1960s had been for the left.[27] The political fulcrum shifted, fostering a dramatic cultural and political correction, transforming the relationship between the public and its government. Within this process was an especially violent reconceptualization of what a number of historians have called the "environmental-management state," the manner in which environmental management has been a central tenet of the modern state's purview.[28] In the late 1960s and throughout the 1970s, American environmental policy expanded dramatically, implementing strong controls on how air, soil, and water could be used as sinks for industrial waste.[29] This legislation culminated with the Comprehensive Environmental Response, Compensation, and Liability Act, signed into law in December 1980, at the very end of the Carter presidency. The famous "Superfund" constituted tacit acknowledgment that chemical pollution posed real and present dangers to

Americans and their neighborhoods. In the ensuing decade, however, deregulation limited federal agencies' capacity to measure and define the extent of myriad environmental risks. And the new Reagan administration was not especially invested in taking environmental issues seriously. After nearly two decades of intense environmental engagement and discoveries that pollution was a serious problem, Americans entered the 1980s with a new leadership that was openly dismissive of and cavalier toward the severity of the problem. The radical change of tune was jarring.

Further, as a vehicle for analyzing the deep divisions in risk understandings that manifested themselves at the height of the 1980s chemical anxieties, neoliberalism offers powerful perspective. One underlying inspiration in my analysis of toxic fear—and my attempts to outline both rational and irrational chemical anxieties—comes from the sociologist Ulrich Beck's interventions on the relationship between risk and modernity. Beck described a world in which advanced industrialization produced hazards that undermined its own notions of safety and security. The "risk society" was one where potential dangers—nuclear power, chemical pollution, genetic engineering, nanotechnology—transcended time and place. If any experiment in the risk society went wrong, the consequences would be grave and irreversible. Further, the whole world was the bench in this experimental laboratory. "The more modern a society becomes," went Beck's famous maxim, "the more unintended consequences it produces."[30] Unintended consequences are the drivers of fear, and "in the risk society the unknown and unintended consequences come to be a dominant force in history and society."[31]

* * *

The history of toxic fear in the American 1980s trades heavily on such narratives of unintended consequences, but I am more interested in the uncertainties and anxieties that living with those consequences promulgated. In this respect, *Toxic Fear* differs from many works on the history of chemical pollution. Rather than concentrating on the mechanisms that galvanized toxic proliferation and/or mediated their control, I focus on how Americans responded to the genie out of the bottle. The overwhelming response was one of fear, expressed in myriad ways. This is not untrammeled ground. In his critique of management experts, who seemed to show contempt for public perceptions of risk, Beck stressed the *disparate* reactions to modern hazards.[32] Too frequently, the public responded to risks in ways that experts deemed irrational. Expertise, such "traditional wisdom" dictates, studies risk analysis, which trades in quantified probabilities; in contrast, public perceptions—or, better, public understandings—of risk typically respond to qualified possibilities.[33] Fear manifests itself because, as the sociologist Lee Clarke explains, "organizations, not disparate members of the general population, are the final arbiters of hazard."[34] This is an important and overlooked function of what the historian Evan Hepler-Smith has called the "molecular bureaucracy" of managing chemical contaminants: "the global complex of legal structures, administrative procedures, regulatory lists, information systems, and nomenclature conventions that render toxic environments tractable to regulatory politics on a molecule-by-molecule basis."[35] In a similar vein, the science and technology studies scholar Sheila Jasanoff long ago criticized the unilateral aspect of much risk communication "as a one-way street extending from experts to the public," which underestimated "the extent to which perceptions about risk are socially constructed."[36] Toxic fear surfaces when risk, uncertainty, and disempowerment collide. This book is interested in the dissonance between environmental governance and living with chemicals and the role it played in shaping contemporary American history.

Beck's risk society argues that modern publics are prisoners of their own experience and imagination, but risk and fear function independently of each other. In the 1980s a deregulatory push meant that risk experts and policymakers misread the cogs and gears that drove public anxiety around chemicals. During the 1980s many risk experts concluded that in general these environmental fears over pollution were irrational or grossly inflated: Compared with smoking or driving a car or crossing the street, many stated publicly, chemical pollution caused comparatively few deaths. Chemical pollution—its presence and potential—they argued, produced an inordinate amount of fear. But to write off a widespread public response as irrational or poorly founded is to miss the point. In many cases communities found that government agencies were not equipped for or not interested in helping them. Combined with a deep and long-standing distrust of science and government made many calls for calm difficult to swallow. And, too frequently, toxic threats were all too real and a good deal more dangerous than the "experts" asserted. In many instances, the American public *was* being poisoned by industrial mishap, negligence, and cynicism. The scientific and historical record holds up the claims made by Rachel Carson, Barry Commoner, and others who warned about the dangers of chemicals in the environment in the 1960s. After World War II, much chemical pollution posed palpable threats. Each of us today is a walking, breathing artifact of humanity's toxic trespasses into nature. Unwittingly or not, we are all carrying a chemical cocktail in our blood, our bones, and our tissue. That cocktail likely won't strike us down tomorrow or the next day. But our exposure to the various human-made, toxic chemicals that circulate in our environment is a feature of industrial practices beyond our individual control. And they pose carcinogenic and hormone-disrupting risks. While the low-level exposure to individual chemicals that the majority of Americans experience may constitute only limited risk, very little attention has been given to the myriad mélanges of toxins every human carries inside of them. While we cannot see them, we know they are there, and they have produced a palpable cultural anxiety that warrants investigation and understanding.[37]

In this manner, *Toxic Fear* requires the reader to make a modest leap of logic. It trades on the emotional effects of material consequences. Toxic fear does not manifest itself solely on the presence of contamination in a body or in a landscape; it also features in the potential of that presence. This hypothetical source of anxiety—which all too often shifted from potential consequences of contamination into the real ones after further analysis—requires consideration of the individual and collective American psyche. One explanation for toxic fear draws on what the criminologist Richard V. Ericson has called the "catastrophic imagination." In numerous instances, Ericson found that Americans exhibited an irrational amount of fear based on the potential outcomes associated with dangerous events.[38]

Some of that heightened reaction to stimuli might come from what psychologists call the availability heuristic, which served as a key vehicle for entrenching toxic fear. The concept was developed in the 1970s by Daniel Kahneman and Amos Tversky, and its application was evident in media reporting on chemical pollution throughout the 1980s. In a series of groundbreaking experiments, they showed how people overestimate the probability of a particular scenario if it is easy to draw on similar past experiences.[39] A dramatic event serves as the reference point for subsequent potential occurrences, and magnifies the alarm and perceived risk associated with it. For example, *Jaws* (1975), a vivid film that captured the popular imagination, elicited fears of shark attacks that far outweighed their frequency. In the context of toxic fear, Americans amplified risk because they could relate to other examples of environmental pollution, and that increased its apparent severity. After 1978, Love Canal came to encapsulate contaminated communities across the United States; media stories on chemical disasters throughout the 1980s described "another Love Canal" as a means of framing the new event. Statistics be damned: The capacity to recall events elevated the probability of danger in the mind. The availability heuristic works in two ways to drive home the importance of the 1980s as a critical point of study in the history of environmental fear. First, during the 1960s and 1970s the Age of Ecology mainstreamed environmental awareness and created a culture of concern around pollutants in air, soil, and water. Second, the decade began with the perfect storm of a nuclear meltdown at Three Mile Island in 1979 and the seeping terror of a community at risk from underground contaminants at Love Canal. These two major events were followed by a series of smaller but no less alarming incidents. The events and the media firestorms they inspired provided ample reverberations that captivated the popular imagination and influenced Americans' responses. The probability of widespread chemical devastation seemed very real, and it compelled subsequent fears surrounding chemicals in the environment.[40]

Part of my story seeks to unsettle the availability heuristic: Throughout the 1980s, Love Canal was every town in the United States. That is what the availability heuristic would argue. Love Canal became the cornerstone of the availability heuristic for the popular concern over chemicals in neighborhoods. In 1980 a series of unexplained illnesses and a suspected contamination in Frayser, Tennessee, just outside of Memphis, prompted fears of "another" Love Canal.[41] House Representative Albert Gore held two days of hearings on the community's complaints, while the EPA and state and county health departments were mobilized to test air, soil, and water. In 1984 the *Chicago Tribune* reported that mysterious cancer cases in suburban Denver were provoking fears that the area was "Love Canal West."[42] The skeptic argument highlights the perfect storm of perceived disaster mixed with media attention. As the sociologist Barry Glassner argues, "Atypical tragedies grab our attention while widespread problems go unaddressed."[43] Chemophobia marks a middle ground between abnormal tragedy and widespread problem. As the first instances of community contamination emerged in the 1970s and 1980s, these new troubles appeared to be atypical tragedies until they turned up almost everywhere. Chemical pollution was a widespread problem that had long gone unaddressed. Toxic fear was a social response to that problem that reflected a popular desire to see it resolved. Case upon case drew on earlier examples and amplified a growing fear of chemicals. But case upon case also suggested a pattern. Just as invoking the availability heuristic can downplay popular concerns, it can also run the risk of undermining real hazard. Frayser and suburban Denver were hardly the only "Love Canal" sites in the United States. As the extent of illicit hazardous waste dumping became increasingly apparent, as the chemical industry suffered more and more nocuous spills, as a greater number of consumer materials were found to have carcinogenic properties, concern over the prevalence of chemical pollution was not just a heuristic.

* * *

A word on terms. Along with my historical subjects, I use "fear" and "anxiety" fairly interchangeably in the work that follows. "Fear is a variable social emotion—often contagious, often affecting group behavior, and social policy," asserts the historian Peter N. Stearns.[44] But so is anxiety. Both worry along the interstices between risk and danger, between the hypothetical and the practical, between the physical and the psychological. Fear and anxiety dictate individual as well as social responses. If it is necessary to parse the vocabulary, then expressions of fear and anxiety distinguish between objectivities and subjectivities. Fear is a response to objective threats, whereas anxiety suggests a more anticipatory or subjective reaction, perhaps to something more ethereal. Per Sigmund Freud, who knew a thing or two about the topic: "Anxiety relates to the condition and ignores the object, whereas in the word Fear attention is focussed on the object."[45] This is helpful. But in considering the history of chemical pollution, it is not clear where to draw the line between objective fear and subjective anxiety. In the context of deferred harm, both functioned at the same time—and that is precisely what makes for such a rich avenue of investigation. Joanna Bourke addresses this problem as it pertains to historicizing fear writ large. In general, the distinguishing features of these terms are fluid. "In historical time," she argues, "anxiety is easily converted into fear, and vice versa." Moreover, "in the negotiation between the individual and the social group, the difference between fear and anxiety oscillates wildly."[46]

The fearsome lexicon, however, is only a minor worry. The singular challenge with this project is the process through which Americans diagnosed fear, measured its severity, determined its historical significance, and charted its change and continuity over time through the concatenations of popular uncertainties and insecurities. For all that it describes an immediate or objective threat, fear lacks a quantifiable status, wherein sociologists or behaviorists or historians can assign a worthwhile numerical value to various expressions or responses.[47] If there is an underlying refrain to this work it is that chemical risks in the 1980s were rarely rendered legible in ways that experts, policymakers, and potentially exposed communities could engage on common ground.

* * *

The cultural dimensions of these risks are what give this work its flow. I have adopted something of a fractal organization in each chapter of this book, working back and forth between case studies and contexts. This is an organizational choice, but I think it is also a stylistic one: Toxic fear as a phenomenon—its manifestations, iterations, ramifications, and availability heuristics—works fractally across the 1980s. A fractal approach constitutes a departure from the traditional and linear historical narrative arc in favor of case studies, arguments, and themes that fold over and self-replicate to offer a more comprehensive perspective for getting at toxic fears. A strictly chronological accounting of American fears surrounding pollution in the 1980s would amount to a long list of incidents with little room for discussion of the cultural and thematic contexts that inform this work—or interminable repetition of the same contexts. I am trained as an historian, and I believe in chronology's power to organize a story, but I also want to honor the tangle of the past. I think what coheres this work is the analysis of a longer moment in time more than change and continuity across a decade. While I have attempted to ensure some chronological fidelity to the case studies I present, I am drawn to the organic qualities of the fractal narrative that resist the historian's demand for order, however artificial. This approach further seeks to manage the twin task of communicating and expressing at the same time, mapping a cultural psyche but also a more expansive essence of how the historical and the psychosocial are inextricably linked.[48]

Each chapter resets the fractal patterning, however, to reflect the thematic layers and evolving contexts of toxic fear across the 1980s. In the first three chapters, I start by situating fear in place as a means of positing toxic fear as a prevalent and defining feature of the decade. I work through a number of the more and less prominent locations where popular fear of pollution manifested itself, especially in the late 1970s and early 1980s. Toxic fear, as it was expressed at Three Mile Island, Love Canal, and Times Beach, serves as the basis for chapter 1. Chapter 2 establishes the historical contexts for these three case studies; I examine fear, politics, and environmental consequences as they manifested themselves in the 1980s. Of especial importance in this chapter is consideration of the 1980s as a decade deserving of careful study. Building on the key sites from the first chapter that spurred chemical pollution into the national limelight, chapter 3 considers lesser-known cases of environmental pollution to suggest the ubiquity of the problem. Elizabeth, the Butler Tunnel, and Warren County serve as the backbone of this chapter. On the one hand, they constituted kaleidoscopic echoes of the Love Canal availability heuristic. On the other, they demarcated a much larger and more nuanced pattern of environmental despoliation. Chapter 3 also delves into the politics of hazardous waste disposal, which plagued the 1980s and exacerbated environmental fears.

From case study to underlying expression, I examine a group of activities that point toward implicit expressions of fear and anxiety. Chemical pollution, its proliferation, and the unmitigated failure of environmental policy to impose controls were primary drivers of the anxieties that shaped the 1980s. Chapter 4 considers the political context of trying to stem the tide of leaks, spills, and emissions by examining the ways in which hazardous wastes were and were not managed. Deregulation, especially around waste disposal, during the 1980s exacerbated the spread of pollution and the appearing of incompetence from government agencies and experts. Chapter 5 considers some of the social and cultural drivers of toxic fear. Insurance practices in the 1980s indicated a growing investment in protection against technological disasters. This came in the immediate wake of Three Mile Island and Love Canal, which posed some interesting and new problems for insurers, but also suggested that people were alert to these hazards. This awareness also provoked considerable and measurable psychological distress. While studies showed that the citizens of Love Canal did not seem to suffer from increased rates of cancer when compared with the average American public, indications of mental health upset and suicides were higher.[49] The judicial system also recognized this phenomenon. The 1980s marked an important evolution in toxic tort law. Toxic fear was admitted as grounds for seeking damages from polluters. Finally, perhaps the "easy" metric—from which the language of fear is primarily drawn—is the media's impact. Twenty-four-hour, wall-to-wall news was an invention of the 1980s. In *The Culture of Fear*, Glassner claims that during the final quarter of the twentieth century Americans became increasingly inept at independently evaluating risk, due in large part to the manner in which media and politicians manipulated public dialog. The media, he argues, scaled new heights of sensationalism to generate readers and viewers. This was evident not only in shrill headlines, but also in the confusion fostered by such op-ed pieces as the *Washington Post's* mockery of chemophobia.[50] Dependence on any single metric to make a case for toxic fear is nebulous and borders on the anecdotal. Cumulatively, however, the pattern of tendencies hints at a deep, national malaise and how uncertainties surrounding chemical pollution and public health festered.

The relationship between toxic fear and cancer deserves a chapter of its own. Chapter 6 develops that relationship. During the 1980s, the Centers for Disease Control and Prevention and state health agencies experienced a growing number of phone calls from citizens and physicians reporting cancer incidence in their neighborhoods.[51] Americans feared environmental cancer epidemics and were seeing them everywhere. Much of the information was incomplete or inaccurate, which made ascertaining the statistical improbability of the number of cases difficult. But the message was clear: Americans were convinced that chemical pollution was giving them cancer. Cancer clusters emerged in small towns such as Woburn, Massachusetts, and in industrial corridors. But the epidemiological task of identifying environmentally caused cancer clusters took shape only in conjunction with the 1980s fears of cancer being reported.

Chapter 7 investigates the constant tensions between risk perception/understanding and risk analysis as part of an important debate over the politics of expertise and the politics of fear. Experts and publics struggled with the problem of the contested and social processes involved in knowing contamination, and both competed for authority in terms of what chemical risk meant and how it was understood. Building on examples from the previous chapters, I examine how legislative action required legal and scientific norms and consensuses on chemical threats and exposures, but these frequently conflicted with the felt or lived experience of those who had been exposed to those potential harms.

Expressions of fear, hazardous waste disposal and management, cancer, risk: Sprinkled across these chapters are myriad abbreviated case studies where fear manifested itself in different kinds of ways. In order to concentrate on toxic fear as a cultural phenomenon, much (indeed, almost all) of this work avoids—or, at best, skirts—important questions: Where did these materials come from, and how did they come to contaminate the American landscape? Those questions deserve more comprehensive reflection, but the short answer is that profits and growth were encouraged in the absence of checks, controls, or concerns that their materials and by-products might be creating devastating costs. Because these costs were externalized, they did not appear on a company's ledger. By the time that many of these new environmental hazards were found, they were so ubiquitous that it was nearly impossible to do anything about them or imagine a world in which they did not exist. In effect, this book is about coming to terms with that new world.

Plus ça change. Americans remain tethered to this history. Into the twenty-first century, popular anxieties have increased rather than diminished; there is a widespread and growing mental health crisis afflicting the United States. The 1980s are racing out of sight in the rearview mirror: At the time of this book's publication, the first half of the 1980s is already closer to the end of World War II than it is to the present. Nevertheless, an acute fear of toxins—an "industrial hazard regime"—persists in contemporary society.[52] Inchoate noise from all sides drowns out civilized debate and breeds policy inertia and more cultural paranoia. Americans are—noisily and quietly—afraid. It would be good to talk about that more.

The More Primitive the Fear

The greater the scientific advance, the more primitive the fear.
—Don DeLillo, *White Noise*

On the morning of March 28, 1979, a small amount of radioactive steam escaped from the Three Mile Island nuclear power plant in central Pennsylvania. Equipment failure and human error explained the release, but they also prompted a more serious question: Was the nuclear power plant about to melt down? Less than two weeks prior to the accident, *The China Syndrome*, starring Jane Fonda, Jack Lemmon, and Michael Douglas, was released in cinemas across the country. The movie recounted clandestine cover-ups at the fictional Ventana nuclear power plant outside Los Angeles, but the story highlighted the inherent risks associated with a meltdown, which, one physicist in the film coincidentally warned, would render uninhabitable "an area the size of Pennsylvania." Three Mile Island was fiction brought to life.[1]

After consulting with the Nuclear Regulatory Commission, Pennsylvania Governor Richard Thornburgh issued a precautionary advisory. Pregnant women and preschool-aged children living within a five-mile radius of the plant should move farther afield, he announced, while residents within ten miles should take shelter in their own homes. The advisory, delivered in a calm tone, recommended that some 3,500 people living closest to the reactor relocate for at least the immediate time being and that everyone else stay put. Meanwhile, Thornburgh and the state's Emergency Management Agency prepared evacuation scenarios in the event that the reactor should fail completely. Few waited for that development: 53 percent of the population within twelve miles of the nuclear power plant abandoned their homes, and a smaller percentage of residents living farther than twelve miles away also decided to escape.[2] In total, roughly 150,000 central Pennsylvanians were sufficiently alarmed to get in their cars and leave the area. Evacuation is a managed exodus. The frantic departure from the townships around the nuclear power plant was something quite different. "Traffic was jammed on the streets of Harrisburg," an Associated Press story reported. "Service stations were jammed with cars" as people scurried to leave town. Many businesses in Harrisburg closed early and permitted their employees to flee. Telephone lines were overwhelmed, shutting down communications and exacerbating the panic.[3] Outbound Greyhound buses from Harrisburg experienced 40 percent more ridership through that first weekend.[4]

For the purposes of this study, an objective threat presented itself and people responded in a manner that drastically exaggerated the reported dangers as communicated to them by authorities. In so doing, they betrayed their underlying fear of toxic hazards. On the average, the fugitives retreated a staggering hundred miles away from the nuclear power plant. Kai Erikson observes that this was not the largest mass exodus in human history, "but it seems to have involved the widest imbalance on record between the scale of an advisory and the scale of an actual evacuation, and it involved the longest average flight as well."[5] The average distance of withdrawal might have had something to do with central Pennsylvania's geography. Perhaps for many, family members who could furnish them with emergency accommodations lived in Pittsburgh or Philadelphia, on either side of the state. But none of this explains why Governor Thornburgh's advisory sparked such a disproportionate reaction in the first place. Maybe the response evoked panic more than fear, but the two are distinctly related in this context. Regardless of the exact triggers or explanations for the mass exodus, its very fact speaks volumes about latent anxieties surrounding nuclear power. Perhaps the fictional version of the meltdown portrayed in *The China Syndrome* primed Americans to be afraid and untrusting. Alternatively, the meltdown might simply have been the tipping point for Americans' long-held, tentative relationship with nuclear power.[6] Toxic fear, suspicion of the technology run amok, and distrust of scientific and government authority coalesced to breed a foreboding illustration of how Americans would respond to chemical risk in the decade to come.

Whether *The China Syndrome* provoked fear or whether cultural fears inspired the film's creation is almost immaterial. More interesting was the aftermath. Disaster was averted, but the concerns persisted. To wit, officials at the Shoreham Nuclear Power Station on Long Island (New York) surveyed residents on how they would react to a comparable mishap there.

If an accident occurred, one question read, and everyone living within five miles of the plant were advised to stay indoors, what would you do? More than 40 percent of the residents living within a ten-mile radius of the reactor—together with 25 percent of the entire population of Long Island!—announced they would flee. And if pregnant women and young children were advised to evacuate, then 55 percent of the people within ten miles and more than a third of the total Long Island population would leave. In 1980, the four counties of Long Island had a population of more than 6.5 million people. From a disaster management perspective, Three Mile Island seemed a poor dress rehearsal for a real catastrophe. Even if an accident at the Shoreham plant was equally benign, imagine the logistics of that kind of flight from Long Island, where the only escape would involve infrastructure leading exclusively to and through the most densely populated corridor in the United States.[7]

The takeaway here is that the threat of nuclear harm provoked popular fear. But while nuclear meltdown was certainly a catalyst for the decade of toxic fear that followed, it was not alone. Three Mile Island represents one point on a triangle of high-profile chemical disasters that enlivened the early 1980s, captured the national imagination, and instilled a widespread and deep-seated fear of chemical pollution. If Three Mile Island was the primed tinderbox, Love Canal, outside Buffalo, New York, was the slow-burning fire. Times Beach, south and west of St. Louis, Missouri, where dirt roads had been saturated with dioxin, was confirmation that toxic chemicals could be found everywhere and in quantities that required immediate action. The 1983 evacuation of Times Beach reinforced in the national consciousness that chemical threats were everywhere and Americans were on the run from a threat they could not contain. There were, in fact, more evacuations, though Love Canal and Times Beach captured the national attention. In April 1983, only a month after evacuation notices were posted in Times Beach, eleven families were offered a buyout to leave Imperial, Missouri, some twenty miles to the southeast, where dioxin levels in Romaine Creek prompted action. Just over a week later, the EPA paid residents of fifty-three properties in asbestos-ridden Globe, Arizona, to leave their homes. Fear was no less prevalent in Imperial or Globe, even if it didn't resonate within the national consciousness. Delays, uncertainties, and frayed nerves were commonplace. Through tears Catherine Scott, a Globe resident, told an investigative subcommittee about how she feared for the health of her family in the wake of their asbestos exposure. The first warning signs had been raised three years before the evacuation decision was taken by the EPA. "It seems that the recent EPA leadership won't move until they see dead bodies," Scott lamented.[8]

But even in the midst of evacuations, toxic fear was not produced by some multiheaded sea creature rising from the deep to inflict massive and violent harm. Rather, it came from a failure to definitively diagnose the inherent risks posed by new contaminations. This chapter establishes toxic fear as a feature of the American 1980s. It shows how fear manifested itself locally and nationally within the context of the disasters at Three Mile Island, Love Canal, and Times Beach. Each involved climactic and urgent evacuations, but these three case studies also shared in common a degree of scientific uncertainty surrounding the real threats posed by contamination and a failure to communicate the potential risks to concerned local residents in a functional and vernacular language that might foster public participation and subdue panic.

* * *

If Three Mile Island prompted technological alarm, Love Canal was the sacrificial community that set the stage for toxic fear in every community during the American 1980s. It was the original toxic time bomb, after New York State Health Commissioner Robert Whelan titled his September 1978 special report "Love Canal: Public Health Time Bomb."[9] The story of Love Canal is well known and well told.[10] It is a parable about the incongruities of keeping dangerous chemicals and people in the same place. For several years in the late 1970s and early 1980s, Love Canal was "a neighborhood of fear," so dubbed by New York Governor Hugh Carey in June 1980.[11] What Carey didn't say was that much of that fear stemmed from an intense distrust of the government agencies and officials tasked with addressing the contamination. By 1980 Love Canal residents refused to participate in government studies on chemical pollution in their neighborhood. The research required them as case studies, but few of the findings seemed to be "for" them. Public consternation—much of it expressed as fear—stemmed from the fact that Love Canal's residents saw little action from officials in response to what locals perceived to be a serious health risk.[12]

No one questioned the gravity of the problem or the potential for harm. Between 1947 and 1952, the Hooker Chemical Company dumped

21,800 tons of chemicals at Love Canal in accordance, it insisted, with the environmental regulations of the time. In 1953, when threatened with property condemnation, Hooker sold the dump site to the Niagara School Board for one dollar. The deed was transparent: Chemical waste rested beneath the surface, although for a time at the height of the unrest no record of Hooker's famous disclosure could be found. The contract also absolved Hooker from any responsibility for subsequent injuries at the site; subsequent legal proceedings would question the extent to which Hooker had been sufficiently forthright about the acute toxicity of some of the waste. The school board built a school and sold the remaining land to developers. Houses and roads sprang up. Working-class families moved in, raised their children, and made Love Canal their home.

Signs of trouble appeared not long after construction. Noxious smells wafted through homes. Chemicals found their way into sump pumps and through walls into basements. Black sludge came up through the ground, creating deep, creviced puddles on the school grounds. An abnormal number of Love Canal residents showed signs of illness. Locals also noticed disturbingly high frequencies of cancer, miscarriages, and birth defects. The concerns became widespread. In October 1976, the *Niagara Gazette* began reporting on the "industrial horror story" at Love Canal.[13] By the beginning of November, chemical analyses near the dump site had identified fifteen organic chemicals, including three highly toxic chlorinated hydrocarbons, that were seeping through the ground.[14]

Heavy snowfall during the winter of 1977 exacerbated the problem. As the spring weather melted the snowpack, the excess water seeping into the thawing ground helped to bring further chemicals to the surface. The initial point of concern was the area directly around the 99th Street School. Upon reading the early reporting in the *Niagara Gazette,* Love Canal housewife Lois Gibbs was especially concerned. Her son had begun experiencing seizures after starting at the school. She began researching the situation more carefully. After being rebuffed from trying to transfer her son, she began canvasing the neighborhood. A growing number of concerned homeowners and parents pushed the Department of Health to conduct tests on the school.

The breakdown in trust between residents and officials began in the spring of 1978, when a series of air quality tests demonstrated the incongruity between scientific inquiry and the urgency surrounding local anxieties.

"Scientific professionals are trained to think analytically," the sociologist Adeline Levine points out. "They try to select narrow problems, communicate chiefly with each other and do so in precise, technical terms."[15] In contrast, the Love Canal residents were interested in nontechnical answers to social questions, not scientific ones. Were they safe? Were their children at risk? How dangerous were their homes? They were questions that could be asked of science, but science couldn't pretend to answer them with any authority.[16] So when a public meeting was convened and health officials distributed mimeographed lists of polysyllabic chemicals and number values associated with readings taken from their basements, the residents had questions: "'What do these numbers mean? We have a playroom—a family room—a bedroom—in the basement. Should we stop using it? Is the rest of my house safe?'"[17] To which the scientists maintained an awkward refrain of not knowing the answer. "The scientists were trying to communicate what they had learned, leaving open the question of interpretation," Levine explained. "They could not communicate their own broad context of understanding. The people interpreted their action as incomprehensible and responded with fear and anger."[18]

By July 1978, high levels of lindane were found in backyards and at the school, where children played.[19] Also during the summer, epidemiological studies conducted by the state determined that Love Canal residents experienced higher than normal birth defect and miscarriage rates. Something was definitely wrong. Love Canal residents campaigned for action. Closing the school was a necessary first step, but the community was also at risk. The *Niagara Gazette* captured the tone of the community. In a front-page article titled "Worried Mothers Feel They're Stuck," the newspaper reported on three mothers who "admitted to being frantic and frightened." The mothers feared for their children's health, in the short and long term. But they also felt trapped, unable to escape the unhealthy space: "The real estate agents won't even come out and put a sign on your house," Mrs. Robert Neubauer opined. "There's nothing we can do."[20]

On August 4, 1978, the first exodus began. The announcement of a federal package to support the evacuation of residents adjacent to the canal was met with great relief within the community.[21] Two days earlier, State Health Commissioner Robert Whalen, in Albany, had issued an official emergency declaration for the area immediately surrounding the canal. His official order reported on two findings: that toxic chemical leaches were found in some Love Canal homes and that miscarriage rates among women living adjacent to the old canal were higher than should have been expected.[22] Whalen's "very strong" recommendation moved two pregnant women and twenty families with children under two out of homes on 97th and 99th Streets and along Colvin Boulevard.[23] New York State Health Department officials declared a health emergency for the area and ordered an evacuation of thirty-seven of the most vulnerable families, those with pregnant women or infants. By the end of August two hundred more families followed.

But that wasn't enough for the remaining residents. Gibbs and fellow activist Debbie Cerrillo founded the Love Canal Homeowners' Association to organize the community and to push for a more comprehensive relocation plan for the rest of the neighborhood. State and federal officials didn't know what to do. There was no precedent for an evacuation of this magnitude, especially considering the uncertainties surrounding the hazard. The real dangers remained unclear for the extended community. Meanwhile, state and federal agencies played a sort of jurisdictional hot potato on who was responsible for the growing crisis and who would make the decision (and pay for it). This was a dangerous precedent to set: Absent certainty around the hazards at Love Canal, would this open the door for further evacuations from contaminated sites around the country?

On October 4, a Love Canal resident, seven-year-old John Allen Kenny, died of kidney failure. Media reports were quick to connect toxic chemicals and organ failure. Though he lived outside the evacuation zone, Kenny regularly played behind his home in a creek, a catch basin for part of the canal.[24] A state autopsy was inconclusive. Anxious parents felt trapped. Weeks later, the *Niagara Gazette* reported that James L. Clark was willing to give his house on 101st Street to anyone who would assume the remaining mortgage. "The mental anguish is just not worth it," he claimed, citing a "multitude of health problems" suffered by his family.[25]

By November 10, 1978, local fears intensified further after the discovery that two hundred tons of trichlorophenol had been buried in the canal.[26] Trichlorophenol was notorious for being one of the foundational building blocks for 2,4,5-T, a herbicide better known as Agent Orange, used heavily by the U.S. military as a defoliant in the Vietnam War and causing a litany of health problems for Vietnamese victims and U.S. soldiers alike. News of the admission that trichlorophenol was present at Love Canal prompted further fears that dioxin had likely been buried as well. Connotations of Agent Orange were unsettling. Even before dioxin was discovered, workers digging the trenches expressed concerns about the safety of the work.[27] Journalist Michael Brown, whose *Laying Waste* offered perspective on chemical poisoning across the United States in the immediate wake of Love Canal, described efforts to contain information about the extent of the hazards as a means of suppressing public fears. They downplayed dioxin's risks should it be present. "Some officials," Brown wrote, "ever wary of more emotionalism among the people, argued that because the compound was not soluble in water, there was little chance that it had migrated offsite."[28]

Dioxin has a singular place in the history of toxic fear. It was the "in" chemical at the beginning of the 1980s—"the substance of the moment is dioxin," according to a 1979 *Wall Street Journal* editorial—and widely hailed as "the most toxic chemical made by man."[29] Minute doses were found to be lethal in chickens and guinea pigs.[30] By the 1980s, popular awareness and fear of dioxin—more precisely, 2,3,7,8-tetrachlorodibenzo-para-dioxin (TCDD), one of 210 members of the dioxin family, made up of polychlorinated dibenzo-*p*-dioxins and their close relatives, the polychlorinated dibenzofurans or furans—was as commonplace as its occurrence in the environment. As with many chlorine-based chemicals, dioxins were fat soluble and concentrated in human tissue.[31]

After the state refused to relocate another fifty-four families living near the site, protests outside the remediation site on December 11, 1978, resulted in seven arrests, although the charges were subsequently dropped. The remediation of the Love Canal site provoked concerns after fears of dioxin surfaced. Some experts recommended that dioxin be kept in one place, prompting protesters to block trucks from leaving the contaminated area. "They're tracking dioxin all over the place," Gibbs declared.[32] Further, the locals were not alone in calling for evacuation. At the Roswell Park Memorial Institute in Buffalo, cancer researcher Beverly Paigen also counseled a more extensive evacuation of Love Canal. The original evacuation had concentrated on the immediate surroundings of the dump site. By late January 1979, Paigen's work supported residents' claims that disproportionate rates of kidney and bladder ailments, birth defects, and miscarriages were present among Love Canal families relative to the general population.[33] These could be traced to families living in greater proximity to the creeks and depressions that had been filled in when the neighborhood was originally built. Chemicals were seeping into homes and gardens and sewers and spreading to the various creeks and water systems throughout the Niagara region.[34] Later that spring, it also emerged that the dioxin levels at Love Canal were markedly higher—as much as a hundred times higher—than previous reports had indicated.[35]

In response to Paigen's results, State Health Commissioner David Axelrod recommended temporarily relocating pregnant women and children under two from a broader perimeter around the original relocation. To Gibbs and the Love Canal Homeowners' Association, that precautionary measure sounded like an admission of unacceptable risk. "If pregnant women and children under two were at risk," Gibbs wrote later, "so were the rest of us."[36] DIOXIN KILLS signs became a fixture on Love Canal front lawns. At a subsequent public meeting, one woman—shaking and in tears—interrupted Axelrod's prepared statement, screaming, "You can't play games with my life. You have no right to make me stay here."[37]

Through 1979, tensions mounted. On March 29—coincidentally, the day after the failure at Three Mile Island—ABC News aired "The Killing Ground," an hour-long documentary on toxic waste with a focus on Love Canal. "The Killing Ground" highlighted to the nation the severity of the Love Canal problem and garnered considerable attention. It received two Emmy Awards, first prize at the Monte Carlo Television Festival, and a nomination for Best Documentary Feature from the Academy Awards. That attention turned Love Canal—and toxic waste more broadly—into a topic of national interest and conversation. Footage of distraught mothers at Love Canal beside themselves at public hearings, begging authorities for more information, struck a chord in similarly contaminated communities across the country. "Would you please tell me," one mother asked while fighting to contain her emotions, "do I let my three-year-old stay? She has a birth defect now. What do you expect of us? That is my child," she shouted over panelists trying to restore order to the proceedings. "Where is the difference?" she asked, between the two-year-olds recommended to evacuate and her own child. "How can you discriminate?" In another heated public forum, another mother was more direct: "You're destroying us," she screamed at the panel, which included Axelrod.[38]

Tension and inaction persisted, even after the state paid to move 425 residents into motels between August and November 1979. But these were temporary measures. No solution seemed in sight. An April 1980 open letter to Governor Hugh Carey from Mr. and Mrs. Joseph Dunmuire beseeched the governor to declare a health emergency. It reiterated what was becoming a tired refrain. "Every mother in the Love Canal," they asserted in the letter, printed in the *Niagara Gazette*, "is scared to death."[39]

Part of the fear extant at Love Canal had to do with the waiting and the sense of feeling trapped. While a growing number of houses were boarded up as some residents found ways to get out, others felt stuck. "Being left behind is the most terrible experience, horrifying," Marie Pozniak told *Niagara Gazette* reporter Mike Brown. Those left behind could not shake the persistent fear that they were at risk. "I know a woman who had to take her child for counselling," Pozniak continued. "The kid was afraid of dying."[40] Residents found themselves living, working, and playing in a contaminated community, unable to escape. They were stuck for a variety of socioeconomic reasons. Gibbs told Brown that her husband, Harry, a chemical plant worker, was paid $150 a month. After mortgage payments, groceries, clothing for their two children, and other expenses, there was little to no money left, and certainly not enough to afford a rental apartment in a safer environment.[41] The Gibbs's situation was not uncommon. Pozniak again: "My family is going to pieces, and there are divorces all over this place. My husband is so desperate: There is no way for him to protect his family, and that gets to him."[42]

In addition, the story of Love Canal became international in its scope. The little *Niagara Gazette* wondered at the influx of journalists and television crews from all over the world to report on the story of their contaminated community.[43] The widespread media attention likely forced the government into action, but the story spoke to communities across the country and heightened both awareness and fear of toxic chemicals. Indeed, in the reporting of the dioxin contamination a few short years later at Times Beach, Missouri, parallels with Love Canal were regularly evoked in the media.

* * *

The story of chemical pollution and community evacuation associated with Times Beach begins as part of a more ranging account of an almost statewide dioxin contamination. After Georgia, Missouri ranked as the worst state in the union for protecting its citizens from toxic wastes, according to a 1979 National Wildlife Federation survey.[44] In the early 1970s residents in the small towns surrounding St. Louis paid Russell Bliss, the owner of a waste oil business in nearby Frontenac, to spray oil on dirt roads to control the dust, not an uncommon practice. Bliss was also contracted by farms and horse stables to provide the same service. However, in May 1971, Judy Piatt found hundreds of dead birds in the stables at her Shenandoah Arena in Moscow Mills, east of St. Louis. This was days after Bliss had passed through. Her cats subsequently lost their fur and died. Over the next four years, sixty-two of her horses—appaloosas and quarter horses—died. Piatt and her daughters started suffering chronic headaches, chest pains, and diarrhea. One of her daughters experienced hemorrhaging.

Samples of the stable's soils were sent for analysis to the Centers for Disease Control in Atlanta. The stable soil was clearly contaminated. Arthur Chase, a professor of veterinary science at the University of Missouri, told the *New York Times* the samples were so noxious that it "would knock your hat off, make your nostrils burn and your ears ring."[45] But there was no clear indication of what the contaminant was. It took three years before lab technicians discovered trichlorophenol crystals in the sample and identified 2,3,7,8-tetrachlorodibenzodioxin (TCDD), a dioxin, as the source of Piatt's troubles. The samples showed that her property contained more than 30,000 times the concentration levels at which the CDC recommended cleanup. The culprit was toxic sludge containing trichlorophenol, likely a by-product of herbicide manufacture. Bliss had been contracted to remove the waste from tanks at the defunct Northeastern Pharmaceutical and Chemical Company plant in Verona. In total, Bliss had hauled roughly 18,000 gallons of dioxin-contaminated waste from the Northeastern plant. The sludge was added to oil, and Bliss laid what state Assistant Attorney General Edward F. Downey called "a trail of sickness and death" around swaths of the state.[46]

But for all the fears that dioxin constituted a real environmental hazard, little action followed. Part of the problem was that scientists thought dioxin degraded fairly quickly, that its half-life was only a year. As a result, the emphasis of cleanup efforts concentrated on the Verona plant and not the sites that had been sprayed. Patrick Phillips, a young veterinarian with the Missouri Division of Health who helped Piatt in her initial investigations, was one of the few authorities to continue pursuing the dioxin question. He returned to various sites to collect samples in 1975 and 1976. The samples showed dioxin concentrations similar to those taken the previous year.[47] That should have set off alarm bells, but it didn't. The EPA monitored dioxin in Missouri sporadically but took no action. In 1982, the Environmental Defense Fund leaked an EPA document that listed Missouri sites known to have high dioxin concentrations. The document indicated that the agency would act if levels exceeded one hundred parts per billion. The Centers for Disease Control, however, had established their actionable level for dioxin at one part per billion. On August 19, 1982, the Missouri Division of Health issued its first health advisory on dioxin, some eleven years after Piatt and her daughters showed symptoms of illness.

This spurred the EPA into action. Soil samples were taken from a variety of sites, including Times Beach. But the appearance of incompetence persisted. On November 1, the *St. Louis Post-Dispatch* reported that the EPA had never interviewed Russell Bliss, who had been responsible for distributing the dioxin throughout Missouri, or requested his business records. Their explanation was a meek "because we have more to follow up on than we can follow up on now."[48] Most state agencies had been generally preoccupied with the remaining waste at the Verona site, which they felt constituted the greater environmental threat. However, the EPA bore the brunt for the "leadership vacuum" that many Missourians perceived.[49] At a November 10 meeting in Hillsboro, anxious voices from residents mixed with Missouri officials pointing squarely at Washington's inaction. One Merramec Heights resident demanded a government buyout akin to the evacuation at Love Canal: "Who would want to buy my property?" he asked the panelists. "It's tainted property. It used to be beautiful—but it's a terror living there any more." Fred Lafser, the director of the Missouri Department of Natural Resources, beseeched the EPA for more assistance. "It's incredibly important that the Washington office recognize that this is a bigger problem than the Kansas City office can handle with its own resources," he stressed.[50] The state's Lieutenant-Governor Kenneth Rothman echoed the public call, telling the EPA officials in attendance, "We're in trouble, we need help and you can provide it for us." U.S. Representative Richard Gephardt was more vociferous. "We've got people out here who don't know what to do," he stated. "They're scared to death, and they're being put in limbo for months."[51] Further, rumors of EPA internal memos that considered relaxing its dioxin cleanup standards for Missouri provoked ire, although one EPA official insisted that the site testing for dioxin at higher levels was quicker and cheaper, and had no bearing on the cleanup standards that would be established in January.

The following week, another hearing—this time in Arnold, Missouri—was convened by the State House Energy Committee. Jim Cisco, a Jefferson County resident, told the hearing, "I am scared. My wife's scared. Other residents are scared. I feel that sufficient evidence of the effects of dioxin is known to have a greater sense of urgency about this problem."[52] Dennis Lynch was equally upset: "The emotional strain that we're going through right now—no money can pay for that. It's something where you wake up in the morning, you think about it. It's something you think about when you go to bed." Lynch's two daughters had medical problems that he feared might be attributable to the dioxin. "Notice that our children are not here now," he told the hearing. "We don't want them to know what we know. We are scared."[53] Film footage of the hearing also stressed the anger and distrust locals felt toward the various health agencies charged with keeping them safe. "I don't understand why the safe levels have not already been set," Lynch testified. "It seems to me that you waited to find out the test results . . . before you determined what is safe. It seems a little fishy," he declared to applause from the audience. Cheryl Vickers, whose garden was found to contain nine hundred parts per billion dioxin, listed the various and severe ailments her four children suffered. "I just want to know why somebody didn't tell us," she inquired. This was a recurring theme. The various officials at the front of the room had known about the dioxin for several years, but in order to avoid causing alarm they had refrained from telling residents. In Jefferson County, this was unacceptable. A distraught Elaine Baczynski berated the panel: "Our children have been playing in the woods, picking wildflowers, moving rocks. All this for nine years. The EPA knew about this. The DNR knew about this. How many local officials knew about this? What have you done to our families?"[54]

The hearings prompted—or, more accurately, were a response to—greater mobilization. The sampling in Times Beach was completed in the first week of December, just as the Meramec River jumped its banks and flooded the town.

* * *

The end of 1982 would be remembered by one longtime Times Beach resident as the "time of flood and dioxin."[55] Times Beach was not a "pretty place," according to one memoir.[56] In her own recollections, EPA administrator Anne Gorsuch described the rundown cottages sitting on the floodplain as "gloomy and dull," as though they were from a surrealistic scene "written by Kafka or, perhaps more accurately, painted by Munch, a man who specialized in depicting pain and fear."[57] Seventeen miles southwest of St. Louis, the small town was a bit of a backwater. "Dilapidated houses, mobile homes and old cottages resting atop cement-block foundations shelter a population of 2,500, many of whom call themselves 'river rats'—an affectionate reference to the nearby Meramec River."[58] During the 1920s, the vision for Times Beach was an escape from the hot and crowded St. Louis summer. Small parcels of land along the river invited city dwellers to put up modest cottages and enjoy the fishing. A small, tight-knit community grew. "Cottages on stilts were replaced with modular homes and even a few brick houses . . . four churches and four taverns, a perfect balance."[59] By the 1960s and 1970s, trailer parks became a common sight. Then a 7-Eleven arrived. The retreat idyll was in decline. Times Beach became an affordable suburb of the sprawling St. Louis. Apart from the highway, the roads were unpaved. In the early 1970s, Bliss had sprayed these roads as well.

The Meramec was prone to flooding. Times Beach had voted itself out of the federal flood insurance program, which meant that their homes and possessions were not insured.[60] Many of the first buildings in Times Beach rested on stilts in anticipation of the river streaming over its banks. But the December 1982 floods were especially bad, and they came just as locals were learning more about the risks of dioxin. The EPA tests from sites all over town uniformly returned dangerously high levels of dioxin. The rising waters reignited fears and raised questions about whether the waters would spread the dioxin even farther throughout the town. Echoes of Love Canal loomed large. In both instances, the EPA came under fire for moving slowly and acting with indecision. Government agencies had known about dioxin at a number of sites across Missouri. The Times Beach flood had seemed only to accelerate the timing of action because it coincided with the recent tests and because of the new discoveries pertaining to dioxin. Scientific reports indicated that dioxin remained very stable in the ground. It seemed to bind with soil, which protected it from degrading. Some science suggested that the difficulty in extracting dioxin from soil might signify a reduction in its risk.[61] But its persistence, combined with the flooding, enlivened fears that contamination could spread. Already, the EPA had been vehemently criticized for doing nothing. Compared with Love Canal, the EPA response—to buy out Times Beach—was relatively rapid. On February 22, 1983, less than three months after the flood, EPA administrator Anne Gorsuch announced a $36.3 million package to buy out homeowners. The Centers for Disease Control recommended that residents stay away. Roadblocks prevented access to the town. EPA "moon men"—science teams in masks and white hazmat suits—descended on Times Beach.

* * *

Building on the suggestion that chemical pollution produced new kinds of public anxiety, it warrants asking another, related question: Why did chemicals provoke such fear? I think part of the answer comes from the history I have just outlined. Expanding environmental awareness in the 1960s and 1970s prepared Americans to be concerned about chemical pollution. Popular memory plays a role here, too. During the 1980s, the regular occurrence of new sites of pollution, the contamination of communities, and heightened alarms over new chemical threats increased Americans' likelihood of associating new harms with chemicals—the availability heuristic. In the absence of context, popular probability algorithms swung toward recent past precedents. Which is to say that crises begat crises.

The historical answer is not entirely satisfying on its own, however. Toxic fear also emerged because of four factors distinct to the nature of chemicals and chemical pollution: their invisibility, uncertainty surrounding their risks in the environment, the latency of their threats, and their relative novelty as an environmental danger. Combined, and wrapped in historical context, toxic chemicals bred a very credible model for modern fears.

The trauma of chemical invisibility is an important departure point. Invisible enemies—latent enemies—instill a special kind of fear. Toxic poisons floated sightlessly in the air, swam unseen in waters, and nestled unobserved in soils. They penetrated foods and accumulated in bodies unannounced. In human bodies an accumulation of chemicals stimulated health problems. Miscarriages or birth defects or cancer were by-products of chemical pollution, certainly. Asbestos exposure was unequivocally linked to mesothelioma. But frequently there was no such straight line. Correlation, hypothesis, and guesswork were the real scientific tools. Further, to the public, the toxicologists' tools and measurements were intimidating. As scientists began talking in parts per million and parts per billion, the concept of such minute quantities defied comprehension, but it also created invisible lines in the sand—reference doses—that separated acceptable and unacceptable exposure. That one part dioxin per billion constituted actionable response according to the federal Centers for Disease Control meant nothing to the public. What were visible were contamination suits, gas masks, complicated instruments. These were faceless, technical, and impersonal. And their work was charting the hypothetical.[62]

Invisibility bred uncertainty. The very fact that chemical poisons were unseen but present alarmed. But nobody could definitively determine the real risks and dangers of various chemical substances in the environment. For the nonexpert, distinguishing between "good" and "bad" chemicals is tricky business. If people were terrified by what they couldn't see, they were equally afraid of what they could not understand. Uncertainty provoked fears of toxic poisoning, which manifested themselves in a new kind of hypochondria. In many instances, Americans experienced a degree of confirmation bias in sensing symptoms of chemical poisoning, which they immediately associated with pollution. But uncertainty also divided opinions. Where some people expressed concern, others rejected anxieties out of hand. For example, in caustic response to a 1987 Environmental Protection Agency warning about chloroform—a suspected carcinogen—in water, a *Washington Post* op-ed article mocked, "Anyone with an ounce of foresight would have realized some time ago that showering would eventually be found by researchers from the EPA to be dangerous, and bought a gas mask to be prepared."[63] A chemist, David Mog, fired back in a letter to the editor that such farcical dismissal of chemical risks did untold damage. "Understanding, which reduces fear and guides action," he wrote, "is needed to confront difficult realities and break the paralysis that 'chemophobia' brings on society." Informed journalism, he opined, played an important role in spreading information, not adding to the noise.[64]

Too: it is important to remember that these pollutants were already in the environment. The hypotheticals surrounding chemical risk did not feature the potential harm should PCBs or dioxin escape from factories, but rather determining the real hazards they posed *because* they were already everywhere. Evaluating acceptable exposures did not occur within a controlled environment; it transpired in communities across the country. Citizens facing a knowledge deficit and ongoing uncertainty surrounding the environmental risks in their homes and neighborhoods—those bred fear. Insofar as uncertainty constituted contested ground, the problem of suspense contributed to this new kind of fear. Toxic substances infiltrated bodies silently and without provoking alarms. Then they accumulated. With few exceptions, environmental exposure to chemicals rarely produced immediately lethal or acute symptoms.[65] Acute illness on occasion, but even in the most severe cases in the United States, the fear stemmed primarily from their latency. While Americans in many communities complained of headaches, dizziness, nausea, and other ailments that were ultimately associated with contaminated air, food, or water, it was the long game that ultimately created a new landscape of fear around chemical toxins. Much as paranoia surrounding being buried alive captivated the popular imagination before the rise of modern medicine, chemical exposure implied having one foot in the grave.

Addressing chemical pollution also suffered from an apparent lack of precedents. Spills, emissions, exposures were relatively new, which made it difficult to effectively calculate risk. In his study on how Americans responded to disasters (poorly, he argues), sociologist Robert Wuthnow noted two recurring traits. The first was the need to do something. Anything. Sitting still is not an option. The second trait involved acting based on experience drawn from the last disaster.[66] The problem with this second criterion in the context of chemical pollution is that aside from the occasional train accident and spill or late discovery of toxic emissions into water systems, environmental disasters were rarely categorized as such until the 1970s or 1980s. What turned Love Canal into such an important environmental moment was the popular notion that this had not happened before in the United States. In the absence of context, Americans didn't know how to respond. Of course, Love Canal was nothing new, even if the media scale of the disaster suggested otherwise. Much as the prevalence of chemical fears was unprecedented, the availability heuristic was quick to mark analogies to which the public could adhere. Solutions, however, remained elusive.

CHAPTER TWO

Some Seasonal Perversity of the Earth

This was death made in the laboratory, defined and measurable, but we thought of it at the time in a simple and primitive way, as some seasonal perversity of the earth like a flood or tornado, something not subject to control. Our helplessness did not seem compatible with the idea of a man-made event.
—Don DeLillo, *White Noise*

Storytelling is a critical tool for establishing legitimacy. "The most powerful thing you have is your story," wrote Lois Gibbs at the beginning of her 1982 account of life and activism in Love Canal.[1] What made Love Canal a national story was the manner in which the community's residents were able to communicate their toxic fears. Shari Stone-Mediatore has posited that storytelling is a mode of translation that imbues "fleeting phenomena with lasting form," and "transforming phenomena that are experienced in a plurality of lives into publicly recognized history."[2] This happened quite poignantly in the 1980s through a new kind of environmental writing that Richard Newman has dubbed "toxic autobiography." Gibbs's recounting of Love Canal—putting her story into her own words and communicating the pain, the uncertainty, the fear of living in a contaminated community—has a special place in environmental literature, not least because its inspiration and message reach beyond mainstream environmentalism in a more complex array of social movement literature. Newman contends this was consistent for many such works of toxic autobiography, while also noting the influence of investigative journalism. At Love Canal, that was the work of Michael Brown, who first broke the Love Canal story and helped to usher it into the national mainstream.[3] Reflecting many years later on his experience at Love Canal, Brown told an interviewer with the PBS *American Experience* series that "when you saw what was going on at Love Canal it was very difficult to remain a reporter."[4] Brown was a part of a generation of young journalists practicing the New Journalism, which encouraged journalists to write themselves into their reporting. His book, *Laying Waste: The Poisoning of America by Toxic Chemicals,* which provided coherent narrative to the hundreds of independent Love Canal stories he had written over the previous two years, gave readers unprecedented access to the voices and fears of Love Canal. Narratives of personal fear—lived experience—turned into a potent form of political activism instrumental in putting "hazardous waste issues on the nation's political radar."[5]

It is, nevertheless, important to acknowledge (and reflect upon the fact) that not all stories are received or amplified equally. A similar kind of engagement with toxic autobiography took place in the American Southwest in response to fears over radioactive waste and the prospect of establishing a repository for that waste on Western Shoshone sovereign land in Nevada at Yucca Mountain. While these events and stories received considerable regional traction, they were less able to break onto the national stage, prompting the ecofeminist scholar Valerie Kuletz to ask, "How do we talk about violence when it is neither seen nor acknowledged?"[6]

In 1987, the U.S. government amended the 1982 Nuclear Waste Policy Act to accelerate the establishment of a national disposal site for nuclear waste. The 1987 amendment was colloquially known as the Screw Nevada Act, after its insistence that Yucca Mountain constituted the only viable site.[7] At a 1990 hearing on the Yucca siting, held by the U.S. Nuclear Waste Technical Review Board, Ian Zabarte, a planner for the Western Shoshone National Council, asserted his nation's contention that a nuclear repository was incompatible with the land and Shoshone territory. "The site characterization of Yucca Mountain for a high level nuclear waste repository presents a land use activity in conflict with Western Shoshone use and occupancy," he argued. "Social values, religious values and economic values of land within the borders of the Western Shoshone Nation and the effect of the Yucca Mountain site studies upon these values are being discussed by Western Shoshone people. These discussions reflect every change in the Yucca Mountain project, as do the attitudes of the participants involved. Uncertainty, despair, disbelief, and fear, just to name a few."[8] This was another kind of toxic autobiography. In addition to objecting to continuing or evolving nuclear practices on tribal lands in Nevada as part of the deliberative process, Zabarte's testimony should also be treated as a representation of firsthand experience with nuclear colonialism.[9]

Deep-seated fears of radioactive hazards had turned American nuclear practices during the Cold War into a genie out of the bottle. After a brief period of euphoria at the end of World War II, atomic weaponry and energy quickly became a source of consternation and fear.[10] By the 1980s, that fear, coupled with the stark reality that nuclear waste had to go somewhere, created an intractable problem the historian J. Samuel Walker has called "a perplexing national problem that was too important to ignore, too controversial to compromise easily, and too complicated to settle conclusively."[11] The national problem was more than enough to provoke further local fears, "produced by the 'unthinkable' longevity and lethality of radionuclides."[12]

Zabarte's activism spoke to a legacy of environmental destruction in the American Southwest, perpetrated by the American military-industrial complex and furthering an even older history of conquest and colonization. The Nevada Nuclear Test Site was inside the parameters of Western Shoshone traditional territory, which between 1951 and 1992 had borne witness to 928 nuclear weapons tests by the United States and Great Britain. Speaking at the 1992 Uranium Forum in Salzburg, Austria, Zabarte reminded listeners that "the Western Shoshone Nation is the most bombed nation in the world."[13] Where, for the Western Shoshone, the history of nuclear weapons testing constituted a violation of the 1863 Treaty of Ruby Valley, which did not cede land to the United States, the military perspective of this landscape is one that might best be described as a sacrifice zone that the geographer Donna Houston defines as "places that bear an unequal environmental burden for the greater 'public good' of economic and national development."[14] These sacrifice zones and the "public good" for which they are sacrificed exist largely outside the popular imagination, but they nevertheless pose significant health risks for their inhabitants and neighbors. Kuletz further highlights the persistent connection between sacrifice and destruction; the contaminated nature of the testing site further justified the area and its surrounds for continued hazardous siting, such as the nuclear waste repository at Yucca Mountain.[15]

Toxic storytelling, in whatever form, presented a counter to dominant narratives and to traditional forms of power. In Gibbs's case, *Love Canal: My Story* was a playbook on successful community organizing against toxic hazards while also making space to tell her own story. Brown's offered an intimate outsider's perspective of what those uncertainties and fears looked like and was able to translate them from the local to the general;

"Love Canal, U.S.A." reinforced the premise that toxic fears could happen anywhere. For Zabarte, toxic autobiography merged questions of contamination, sovereignty, and future hazards to make a case that transcended toxic fears. As Donna Houston, drawing on Giovanna Di Chiro and Deborah Bird Rose, argues, "Environmental justice activists are called to witness environmental degradation and its effects on their livelihoods, places and bodies. The tasks of witnessing, storytelling and memory work create a space through which the 'unimaginable' of environmental pollution and unequal environmental protection can be expressed."[16] Newman concurs, suggesting that toxic autobiography reframes popular understandings of toxic waste, and "compels Americans to see the vernacular landscape with new eyes."[17] The sharing of the story is the act of adding to the number of witnesses. I think fear works in similar ways. For the historian, emotions constitute an important way of reading witnessing, organizing, remembering, and storytelling, and vice versa. In so doing, it seems vital to acknowledge and stress the expression of fear—as an authentic and legitimate component within and alongside these environmental politics—as a form of historical agency.

The 1980s possess no monopoly on toxic storytelling, but as the previous chapter showed, the responses to and aftermaths of Three Mile Island, Love Canal, and Times Beach suggest a special place for the relationship between fear and lived experience. This chapter builds on that focused discussion of toxic fear to situate those stories within larger environmental and historical contexts. I make a special case for why the 1980s were so important and why they deserve our continued attention. A fascinating convergence of culture, economics, and politics—from Cold War fears to drug and health crises—propelled a fracturing of American traditions and prompted new expressions of fear.

* * *

Perhaps it is too soon to talk of a "long" 1980s, but it is never too early (or too late) to bemoan the rigid dictatorship of time measured by decades or centuries. The decade of toxic fear in the American 1980s needs a little calendric flexibility. The early reference points for toxic fear (Love Canal and Three Mile Island) occurred in the late 1970s, but these examples share more similarities with subsequent events than with earlier ones. I want to stress that that fear burned especially brightly beneath the fluorescent tube lighting, bad typeface choices, and buoyant material world of the 1980s.[18]

Fear's place in public discourse has ebbed and flowed over time. The historian Joanna Bourke argues that fear is modern society's dominant and ineluctable emotion. It is an explicit feature of modern malaise, even if the motivations for fear are in constant historical flux. In modernity, Bourke explains, degenerative disease outpaced contagion as the primary catalyst for our reflections of personal vulnerability and mortality.[19] The popular discovery that harmful chemicals were omnipresent in American living spaces fed into those concerns. Of course, chemical anxieties were hardly unique to the 1980s. Early twentieth-century public health work might be reread as a protohistory of environmental (avant la lettre) concern, while historians have noted the incipient stages of the modern environmental movement in toxic pollutions worries in the 1940s and 1950s.[20] But the 1980s warrant our careful attention because the decade witnessed the emergence of a new relationship with chemical pollution. Whereas a rising tide of pollution awareness swept American popular culture in the later 1960s and early 1970s, much of the concern and rhetoric revolved around a larger ecology.[21] During the 1970s, the pollution focus shifted to human health. The 1980s mark the coalescence of that process. As human health matured as an environmental issue, it also seemed as though the presence and severity of environmental hazards were increasing. According to a 1974 report prepared for the Environmental Protection Agency, five hundred natural and technological disasters in the United States required some kind of civilian evacuation between 1960 and 1973. The study estimated that on average almost 90,000 people were displaced each year. Of that number, only a quarter were derived from technological disasters.[22] By the 1980s, the landscape of disaster had shifted quite markedly. According to one EPA estimate, the first half of the 1980s witnessed 7,000 toxic chemical accidents of one kind or another, which had claimed 135 lives and injured nearly 1,500 people. Evacuation numbers in response to toxic disasters are difficult to isolate, but they are considerable.[23] At Three Mile Island, at Love Canal, at Times Beach, panic and evacuation in reaction to public understandings of technological harm were commonplace. New forms of harm entered the mainstream environmental lexicon. With respect to air pollution, the general wisdom in 1970 was that only five pollutants—carbon monoxide, particulates, sulfur oxides, hydrocarbons, and nitrogen oxides—were responsible. Thresholds for each were set and enforced. Over the following decade new knowledges emerged. The revised general wisdom of the 1980s dictated that there were lots of sources of air pollution and that the most serious—among them lead, asbestos, benzene, and formaldehyde—were far more dangerous than the original five targets, and more dangerous in much smaller quantities.[24]

* * *

Chemical pollution certainly wasn't the only source of mainstream anxiety in the 1980s. The American novelist E. L. Doctorow wrote about the atomic bomb as a compelling and enduring cultural artifact of the second half of the twentieth century. "We have had the bomb on our minds since 1945," he wrote in 1986. "It was first our weaponry and then our diplomacy, and now it's our economy. How can we suppose that something so monstrously powerful would not, after forty years, compose our identity? The great golem we have made against our enemies is our culture, our bomb culture—its logic, its faith, its vision."[25]

Cold War normalcy and the stalemate insanity of mutually assured destruction (MAD) were dealt an uncertain blow in the early 1980s with regime changes in both superpowers. In the United States, the Reagan administration seemed determined to confront communism at every turn. The Reagan Doctrine doubled down on providing aid to anticommunist military forces all over the world. Worse, Reagan seemed to think a nuclear war could be won. He opposed the very premise of MAD, and plunged massive amounts of money into national defense spending, to counter a Soviet nuclear offensive. The cornerstone of these expenditures was a new strategic defense initiative, announced in March 1983 and designed to shoot down enemy missiles from space. Reagan's logic was based on the notion that an effective defense system could discourage growing nuclear arsenals and could, in the long run, lead to disarmament. At the same time, his fiery rhetoric—referring to communism as a "sad, bizarre chapter in history whose last pages are even now being written," and to the Soviet Union as an evil empire—upped the ante over the potential for conflict.[26] But where the Reagan presidency was not altogether unpredictable, a great deal of instability followed the end of the Brezhnev era in the Soviet Union. After Brezhnev's death in November 1982, Yuri Andropov was elected general secretary. Andropov was an "enigma" to the American media. He was, at once, a reform-minded liberal and a "former KGB thug" who, as ambassador to Hungary in the 1950s, had been instrumental in ruthlessly quashing the 1956 rebellion.[27] More than either of these, Andropov was desperately ill and dying. That did not stop him from fighting Reagan's incendiary rhetoric with some of his own. He castigated the Reagan administration for its "imperial ambitions" and the "outrageous military psychosis" that was driving American defense spending. The détente of the 1970s appeared to be on its last legs. The prospect of nuclear conflict seemed temporarily more imminent than it had for some time.[28]

The backlash against the 1960s sexual revolution precipitated another strain of cultural fear in the American 1980s. In the late 1970s genital herpes attracted media attention that crescendoed in the early 1980s. *Time* devoted an entire issue to herpes in August 1982; herpes, it declared, "threatens to undo the sexual revolution." Moreover, "the old fears and doubts are edging back. So is the fire and brimstone rhetoric of the Age of Guilt." *Ebony* called herpes "the scourge of the 80s."[29] The table was laid for a mystery disease that was poorly understood during the 1980s but whose effects left a ravaging legacy. Acquired immunodeficiency syndrome (AIDS) was first noticed in 1981, but the speed at which it spread forced its way into the mainstream consciousness in very little time. Fears that AIDS could spread from toilet seats, from kissing, or through the air prompted widespread hysteria and produced an "epidemic of fear," according to a June 1983 front-page story in the *Washington Post*. Where Reagan stoked the fires of Cold War conflict, his indifference toward AIDS entrenched a culture and language of homophobia around "Gay Related Immune Deficiency" and the "gay plague" that stunted health research, public education, and understanding.[30]

American racial tensions also experienced change and continuity during the 1980s. On the one hand, surveys hinted at a decline in racial prejudice across American society through the seventies and into the eighties, but racial discrimination remained widely evident. As the sociologist Benjamin P. Bowser noted in 1985, "At the beginning of the 1980s, blacks within the central city, as well as within newer suburban enclaves, are as tightly confined as ever in segregated communities."[31] Racially motivated restrictions were evident in segregated communities, in socioeconomic opportunities, and in incarceration. Incarceration rates jumped as the Reagan administration invested heavily in the war on drugs. According to a 2000 Human Rights

Watch report, "Between 1979 and 1990, the number of blacks as a percentage of all persons admitted to state and federal prisons increased from 39 to 53 percent."[32] Where herpes and AIDS provoked new sex-related fears in the 1980s, highly addictive crack cocaine inspired new fears. In addition to disproportionately rising incarceration rates, foster care placings of African American children doubled during the 1980s; the number of children exposed to cocaine rose from 17 to 55 percent between 1986 and 1991.[33]

Vaguer fears around crime and safety afflicted the American middle classes during the 1980s. The rise of American suburbia after World War II—referred to in some corners as "white flight" from urban centers—appealed as a kind of edenic safety for middle-class Americans, removed from crime and crowds and surrounded by safer streets, quiet, privacy, and parks. The rapidly growing suburbs of every American city presented a white vision of affluent living that exacerbated the kind of racial segregation that Bowser described. Cracks in the idyllic veneer were almost immediately apparent. Keeping up with the Joneses through frenetic consumerism put paid to the peaceful mirage. Fears over burglars and kidnappers—both fears greatly influenced by the availability heuristic—established a kind of suburban siege mentality for the middle class. When some of these same suburban communities—sold as safe places to raise families—started seeping chemicals from under houses, they found groups of people whose anxieties were primed for panic.[34]

The story of popular toxic fears in the American 1980s, then, is one dominated by anxieties expressed through an unmistakably white lens. As the examples that describe toxic fear through this book show, fear of pollution was by no means the exclusive preserve of white communities—quite the contrary, in fact—but it is worth stressing how a white and middle-class "mainstreamism" became the dominant lens through which it was experienced most vociferously. That privileged position elevated the feeling of horror that encapsulated the unspoken belief of the living spaces in which pollutions did and did not belong. As Love Canal and Times Beach were being evacuated, contaminated African American communities in Warren County, North Carolina, were being told to stay put and studies were finding an unmistakable corollary between the siting of polluting industries and poorer communities of color across the United States.

The white fear of environmental hazards was particularly frightful because of its supposed improbability. Don DeLillo's 1985 novel *White*

Noise went to lengths to say out loud the parts of American discourse that were usually kept quiet. Confronted by an industrial explosion that gives rise to the book's climactic "airborne toxic event," DeLillo's protagonist, Jack Gladney, an English professor in Small-College-Town-U.S.A., captures the essence of this toxic fear from the white middle-class perspective. This disaster shouldn't happen here: "Society is set up in such a way that it's the poor and the uneducated who suffer the main impact of natural and man-made disasters," Jack reasons. "I'm a college professor. Did you ever see a college professor rowing a boat down his own street in one of those TV floods?"[35] He repeats this deeply held faith, perhaps a sign that he is already lacking conviction. "I don't see myself fleeing an airborne toxic event," he tells his son. "That's for people who live in mobile homes out in the scrubby parts of the county, where the fish hatcheries are." DeLillo's tone is satirical, but this is environmental history's enduring and deadly serious constant: Disasters are rarely shared equally.[36]

* * *

Toxic fear intermingled with these other forms of popular fear. None predicated another, but they were mutually constitutive. Collectively, they gave shape to the landscape of fear in the 1980s. But toxic fear in the American 1980s also strikes at a much deeper cultural fragmentation that emerged during the final quarter of the twentieth century. If the long 1960s constituted an "age of contradiction"—the historian Howard Brick contends this was a decade confounded by knowledge and ideology, authenticity and artifice, community and mass society, systems and the distrust of order, peace and violence—what emerged by the 1980s was a rejection of such binaries and what the historian Daniel T. Rodgers has called "a great age of fracture."[37] The last quarter of the twentieth century "was an era of disaggregation," Rodgers argues. "Strong metaphors of society were supplanted by weaker ones. Imagined collectivities shrank; notions of structure and power thinned out."[38] The social, moral, and economic boundaries that defined previous American generations lost concrete definition. That mainstream culture had run adrift was perhaps nowhere illustrated more incisively than in DeLillo's *White Noise*, a troubling paean to the postmodern world of indefinite connections and meanings. DeLillo's world—much like the United States in which it was written—is caught in the terrible paradox of rapid technological progress producing a primitive and all-consuming fear. Fracture contributes to fear becoming the dominant cultural undercurrent of the decade. DeLillo's characters articulate an uncontrolled and uncontrollable—paralyzing—fear of dying, fear of uncertainty, fear of existence.

Fracture was also a consistent theme in the environmental context. Whereas concerns about nuclear fallout and pesticides during the early 1960s ushered in a popular environmental consciousness, its 1980s offspring appeared less defined or contiguous. At the first Earth Day in April 1970, Americans thought they were confronting a singular "environmental crisis." A decade later that vocabulary had ebbed. Where images of the earth from space crystallized the environmental mission around the notion that we lived on a fragile ball with finite resources—where pollution episodes appeared representative of a systemic misuse of these concepts—that discourse had shifted by the 1980s. Fractured. Love Canal and Three Mile Island and Times Beach were, of course, still symbolic of countless other environmental trespasses, but they were first and foremost local issues.[39] A singular environmental crisis had devolved into a series of punctuated and local environmental *crises*. And these crises were independently terrifying. Less prominent in the 1980s, surveys showed, were widespread apocalyptic fears associated with Cold War annihilation. In their place were more latent, chronic, and individualized concerns about exposure to environmental carcinogens.

* * *

This issue was the sense of insecurity and uncertainty that any community, anywhere could discover a new contamination crisis. Stories in magazines and newspapers across the country warned of ticking toxic time bombs in incinerator ash, at Love Canal, in the San Joaquin Valley, in the perils of PCBs, and in hazardous waste disposal sites. A widely circulated report to Governor Carey was titled "Love Canal: Public Health Time Bomb." In a 1982 *New York Times* piece that treated environmental contamination, the science writer Maya Pines deliberated on how toxins, more broadly, constituted the potential for a series of "psychological time bombs." In the face of environmental dangers, her byline read, "fears multiply." The Ideas and Trends article deliberated on the profound psychological impact of environmental catastrophe. In the face of toxic hazard, Pines wrote, "people face the danger of severe illness in themselves or their offspring, now or in the future. But they also face the dangers of stress and anxiety, which can generate physical and emotional illnesses that are often impossible to distinguish from purely physiological diseases."[40]

One line of argument suggests that such fears generated as profound and enduring an impact on the residents of Love Canal as the chemicals that prompted action. With the benefit of further hindsight, subsequent data indicated that Love Canal residents suffered more stress-related deaths—heart attacks, motor vehicle accidents, and suicides.[41] This is no exoneration of chemical pollution or denial of its very real impact in many situations. But all evidence says the psychological impact of evacuation and the waiting and uncertainty that preceded it were overwhelming. And it persisted, prompting a culture of flight, but also fight, both of which were stimulated by environmental fears. Flight was motivated by health fears and by the economic insecurity of plummeting property values. Its delay and its actuation increased levels of psychological stress for homeowners, parents, and children. Fight, however, had the curious effect of strengthening community ties as neighbors rallied together to effect change, even if that change was a dissolution of community.

Government action on toxic contamination was frequently slow enough that local residents had to engage in fight so that flight became possible. In October 1979, the state legislature approved the state purchase of Love Canal homes from residents wanting to leave. But the process stalled. Six months later, not a single house had been purchased, even though dozens of residents had indicated they were ready—indeed anxious—to move. While some reports compared the psychological distress of Love Canal residents to the stress that followed a natural disaster, one Red Cross worker retorted, "Give us a fire or a tornado or a flood any day."[42] Across the country in Washington State, the volcanic activity at Mount Saint Helens crescendoed on May 18, 1980, just as the Love Canal controversy erupted into climax. In spite of the death and mayhem at the initial volcanic outburst, the disaster response was tidy, efficient, and brief. This was in stark contrast to the protracted chaos at Love Canal. The nature of a technological disaster is counted in months and years rather than days and weeks.

The tipping point at Love Canal came with a botched chromosome study, which provoked intense emotional reaction and captured in a microcosm the ways local residents felt that government, science, and policy had let them down. According to Lois Gibbs, the EPA report "was one more frightening, scary thing and we couldn't take it anymore."[43] In January 1980, the EPA tested thirty-six adult Love Canal residents—seventeen adult men and nineteen women—for chromosomal aberrations. The thirty-six were handpicked because they showed symptoms of chronic illness that might have resulted from chemical exposure. In May, the EPA shared with the media and the community that eleven of the samples returned signs of chromosome breakdown. The *New York Times* reported that such changes were believed to be "linked to cancer and should be taken seriously as a harbinger of the disease and that in adults they could lead to genetic damage of offspring."[44] Patricia Sandonato, one of the eleven with chromosome damage, recounted her meeting with the EPA: "They just said my chromosomes were abnormal and handed me a letter. . . . I asked if it affected my kids, and they said they didn't know. I fear that my kids might be dying. I'd be afraid to bring another child into the world."[45] The letter itself was a form letter, indicating only a positive result for chromosomal abnormalities.[46] Another positive test subject, Phyllis Whitenight, had previously recovered from breast cancer. "Now," she said, "the fear comes back."[47] The study was limited in scope—only thirty-six subjects were tested—which left many other residents concerned that they, too, might be affected. Beyond informing individuals about their results, the EPA remained tight-lipped about the long-term implications of the results and the health risks they faced, in large part because they did not have answers.

In very short order, however, it transpired that the whole study was a mess. Robin Bannerman, a geneticist at the State University of Buffalo Medical School, told the *Buffalo Evening News* that he doubted the significance of the results. "There certainly aren't any reasons for these people to go into a panic," he declared.[48] "The study that triggered the latest evacuation scare," the *New York Times* reported, "turns out to be not just flawed but a dud."[49] Analyzing chromosome damage was a tricky exercise, "as much an art as a science," and the final report wasn't much of either.[50] The EPA had contracted the research to Houston's Biogenics Corporation, which put the project in the hands of Dante Picciano, who had acquired a controversial reputation in chromosome analysis through some previous research on Dow Chemical workers. According to a review of the study conducted by a panel of experts for the Department of Health and Human Services, the chromosome analysis was rife with "technical deficiencies," which the report outlined in eight bullet points, approved unanimously by the entire panel.[51] The cytogeneticists on the panel pointed to the absence of a control group as the work's major flaw. In the absence of controls, the data were next to useless. Chromosome damage is a fact of life, spurred by illness, infections, x-rays, or exposure to chemicals, sunlight, and some medications. Without a clear sense of how the test subjects' chromosome damage compared with a control population, blaming the pollution at Love Canal seemed a problematic leap of logic. The Department of Health and Human Services concluded that the study held almost no scientific significance—it was basically worthless—and questioned why the EPA had even bothered to engage the study in the first place. For their part, the EPA dodged the criticism by stating that the study was conducted at the behest of the Justice Department, which was exploring a suit against Hooker Chemical. Said the EPA's assistant administrator for research and development, Stephen Gage, "This [study] was a small fishing expedition. The Justice Department asked us to undertake it in connection with our suit against Hooker."[52]

In retrospect, the real error was in sharing the results with local residents, especially before the study had been scrutinized. It was "like shouting 'fire' in a crowded theater," remarked a bitter David Axelrod at the time.[53] A July 1980 piece in the *Lancet* concurred: The handling of crisis, information, and public could not have gone worse, opined the short editorial titled "How Not to Cope with a Pollution Crisis."[54] Tensions at Love Canal were so fraught that one mental health worker admitted, "We thought [the residents] were going to torch the neighborhood."[55] That assessment might not have been far off. On May 19, in the immediate wake of the chromosome study's initial release, a group homeowners locked two EPA officials in the Love Canal Homeowners' Association offices for five hours until the FBI arrived and ordered their release. Residents remained defiant. From inside the house, twenty-nine-year-old Barbara Quimby, whose chromosome analysis indicated abnormalities, told one reporter, "I'm more afraid of the chemicals and what has happened to my kids, and what may happen to their kids, than I am of the police if they storm this house."[56] The "hostage situation" coincided with a demonstration where homeowners burned their mortgage papers and demanded immediate evacuation of the neighborhood. Lois Gibbs insisted that the EPA officials were not captives. "We're protecting them," she explained, "because the crowd outside will tear them apart."[57] On May 21, at the EPA's insistence, President Jimmy

Carter signed an emergency order whereby the federal government would underwrite the cost of relocating an additional 710 Love Canal families, roughly 2,500 residents. In a prepared statement on the relocation, EPA Deputy Administrator Barbara Blum noted that none of the health studies "examined in isolation, would warrant the action I am announcing today. But in the aggregate . . . they are sufficiently suggestive of a threat to public health that prudence dictates relocation while further definitive studies are being carried out." Love Canal, she continued, "presents special circumstances demanding extraordinary action."[58]

* * *

Evacuation was also a touchstone for emotional distress at Times Beach. Where Love Canal homeowners and their families demonstrated and posted signs begging that they be evacuated, the Times Beach story is somewhat different. People left of their own accord. Nonresidents avoided the town. By March 1983, after the government's $36.3 million buyout, the *Wall Street Journal* could call it a "modern-day ghost town, desolate and all but deserted."[59] Of course, Times Beach was originally desirable because of its low real estate costs. Moving put a financial strain on many families, even with government assistance. And small businesses, which relied on building community, customer familiarity, and goodwill, suffered. Setting aside the trauma of upheaval, displaced Times Beachers also discovered that they continued to struggle with the social stigma of dioxin and the fear it provoked in others. "If you're in a store, and you mention you're from Times Beach, people edge away from you," Carolyn O'Leary described. "They treat you like you've got a disease." Another longtime resident, Paul Benson, recounted the troubles his children experienced on the schoolyard at nearby Eureka. "Oooh, you're a dioxin person," classmates would jeer. "We won't play with you."[60]

The cost of flight required a more complex algorithm than was possible simply by measuring economic loss or the impact of social stigma. Even in the absence of any physical chemical injury or illness, Americans exposed to toxic fear suffered concrete health problems. Several years after Three Mile Island, psychologists Andrew Baum and India Fleming showed that higher blood pressure and higher epinephrine levels remained common among the central Pennsylvania evacuees. And lest we separate the psychological from the physical altogether, elevated levels of stress exacerbate heart, respiratory, and immune problems.[61] Later studies of former Love Canal residents returned similar results.[62] Mental health was a long-term casualty of toxic fear. While assessing the "uncanny fear" elicited by toxins, sociologist Kai Erikson also described the trauma suffered after the threat of chemical harm. On the whole, he found depression, helplessness, restlessness, and agitation to be commonplace among individuals, but also throughout whole communities that had been affected.[63]

Such stresses existed even in less dramatic toxic cases. Indeed, similar emotions persist. Sociologists J. Timmons Roberts and Melissa Toffolon-Weiss relate the stresses of living with constant fear. In dealing with the risks and uncertainties of living next to a toxic waste dump or a chemical factory or a nuclear power plant, an anonymous interviewee from 2000 discussed the importance of being perpetually prepared for the worst: "like making sure before you go to bed that there is a half tank of gas so that if there is an evacuation in the middle of the night you will be able to get your family out."[64] Such a mindset highlights the daily stresses of living with chronic fear. But it also discreetly says something about its severity. Even at the most conservative fuel efficiency estimates, a half tank of gas suggests capacity for a fairly radical flight—or a lot of idling in the gridlocked chaos of a mass exodus. More often than not, though, many of the psychological stresses imposed by toxic fear came less from flight instincts than from inertia born from uncertainty. Even if flight—moving elsewhere—was an option, was it necessary? What were the real risks? Concentration on the potential for physical harm invariably relegated the more serious psychological hazards to the background. A recurring theme in environmental justice literature is the perpetual anxiety of living with uncertainty.[65]

Another recurring theme in environmental justice is the inconsistent treatment of communities based on color. The sociologist Dorceta E. Taylor notes that the EPA bought out and relocated seven white communities between 1978 and 1994 and that the manner in which Black communities were approached regarding relocation was noticeably distinct. She highlights the example of the Carver Terrace subdivision in Texarkana, Texas, which was built on a former wood treatment facility. In 1984, the site was added to the Superfund National Priorities List because wood preservative chemicals—pentachlorophenol (PCP), arsenic, and creosote—were detected in the groundwater. The narrative at this stage is somewhat familiar: EPA technicians in hazmat ("moon") suits came and collected samples and went away. Their tests indicated that contamination levels were not high enough to warrant a relocation, and the EPA explored alternatives to buying out the community. The residents felt trapped. Their neighborhood was on the Superfund site, but the EPA did not think the hazards warranted relocation. Faced with growing resistance from the EPA and the discovery that the all-white community of Conroe, Texas, was receiving a federal buyout under much the same conditions, they mobilized and cited a lack of clear answers from the EPA and racial discrimination as grounds for pushing to be moved. In 1990, Congress allocated $5 million for the purchase of homes on the Superfund site and for relocation assistance for the residents. In 1992, the eighty-five Black homeowners brought a discrimination suit against the EPA. They alleged that they were coerced into selling their homes at below-market value and that the relocation compensation was insufficient. The suit contended that the appraisal letters from the U.S. Corps of Engineers contained threatening language that demanded that homeowners accept the valuation or risk having their property condemned. No such ultimatum was present in letters to the seven white communities. The Carver Terrace residents did not win their suit, but their testimony pointed toward discrepancies between the EPA's and Corps of Engineers' communication with white communities and Black communities facing buyout and relocation.[66]

Environmental racism—the systemic exposure to environmental contaminants and deprivation from clean air, soil, and water experienced by communities of color across the United States—was not a product of the 1980s. Nor was community organizing to combat environmental racism. However, the 1980s constitute a critically important chapter in the struggle for environmental justice. Communities of color frequently suffered a greater neglect from protection agencies than did white neighborhoods. They also received less attention from media and mainstream environmental organizations that might have helped to amplify their worries. As the data on environmental contaminations expanded through the 1980s and into the 1990s, it began to show distinct patterns and proximities between the siting of hazardous facilities and minority communities. That the data pointed toward a deliberate practice of environmental discrimination was corroborated by the infamous Cerrell Report, commissioned in 1984 by the California Waste Management Board, which recommended targeting poor and disenfranchised communities when siting waste incinerators.

The report reasoned that more conservative, rural communities with lower income and education rates were much less likely to put up resistance against the construction of a polluting facility. Predominantly Catholic communities were also less likely. Without saying race, the checklist unequivocally preferred Latinx communities in California.[67] A similar playbook targeted Black communities in the South. Attempts to dump hazardous waste on Native American reservations were another consistent feature of the same strategy. The takeaway was the growing and accurate sense that polluting industries targeted poor and marginalized communities, and had been for some time, because they typically lacked the political power to mount effective opposition.

If an absence of information could provoke fear, the number of grassroots organizations that emerged to confront polluters and government and health agencies—and membership and local participation within them—marked a collective activism designed to address that neglect. In the United States there remains a deeply entwined relationship between race, poverty, and pollution. But the emergence of environmental justice groups makes a strong counter to the notion that a fear of pollution that threatened health was a passive emotion.[68]

The sociologist Ulrich Beck boldly stated, "Poverty is hierarchic, smog is democratic."[69] He was only half right. There is no question that toxic exposure had (and has) a political geography. Air- and water-borne pollutions are not discerning on *who* they contaminate, but their point of origin does influence *where*—and by extension, then, *who*—they contaminate most. Downwind and downstream geographies are infrequently democratic. One of the interesting aspects of following American environmental policy since World War II is that its record has been most effective against hazards that do not discriminate by race or class—that "make boundaries [of sacrifice zones] obsolete."[70] Radioactive fallout from aboveground nuclear weapons testing and mercury were ubiquitous in American land- and bodyscapes, and their threat was rapidly curtailed. But when an environmental problem was more geographically situated, or when it did not pose a universal threat, the record is less good, especially when less privileged sectors of society were the most threatened. Solutions have typically been hard-won results of local organizing.[71] To reflect on the topics and themes of this chapter, those more disenfranchised (politically, economically, racially) were much more susceptible to poisoning from chemical production through waste disposal. And, it should be noted, the siting of toxic facilities and industries in disenfranchised communities rarely provided much in the way of economic benefit for those neighbors. Minority communities suffered a disproportionate amount of chemical trespasses; they found themselves living with noxious smells and experienced continued economic disadvantages since polluting industries invariably curtailed the value of their homes. And to hearken back to the beginning of this chapter, discrimination also involved a kind of narrative violence that silenced or neglected their toxic stories.[72] As Samuel Broder, director of the National Cancer Institute, declared in 1990, "Poverty is a carcinogen."[73]

* * *

If this chapter and the previous one sought to establish toxic fear as an important feature of the 1980s, the next chapter examines chemophobia through the lens of toxic waste. Where dioxins and radiation were invisible poisons that provoked fear at Three Mile Island, Love Canal, and Times Beach, the problem of hazardous waste introduced a visible quality to toxic fear. Not always, but abandoned barrels, smoke plumes, and toxic sludge were common features of the threats implied and imposed by the problem of poor hazardous waste disposal practices and the reminder that misplaced matter constituted a social and environmental source of fear.

CHAPTER THREE

Wear the Same Disguise

How strange it is. We have these deep terrible lingering fears about ourselves and the people we love. Yet we walk around, talk to people, eat and drink. We manage to function. The feelings are deep and real. Shouldn't they paralyze us? How is it we can survive them, at least for a while? We drive a car, we teach a class. How is it that no one sees how deeply afraid we were, last night, this morning? Is it something we all hide from each other, by mutual consent? Or do we share the same secret without knowing it? Wear the same disguise.
—Don DeLillo, *White Noise*

In the run-up to the first Earth Day (April 22, 1970), the February 2, 1970, *Time* cover represented the stark choice confronting Americans. Depicted was a portrait of the scientist and environmentalist Barry Commoner, whom *Time* dubbed "the Paul Revere of Ecology." Behind his trademark horn-rimmed glasses, Commoner's face was split down the middle. On the left, in color, he was set in front of an idyllic landscape, drenched in color and sunlight. On the right, an ominous black-and-white scene of industrial mayhem and destruction foreshadowed the dystopian future confronting Americans at the dawn of the new decade. The choice and its implications were unmistakable. A decade later, *Time*'s cover suggested that the dystopian future had arrived. For its September 22, 1980, cover, *Time* offered a similarly bifurcated portrait, which echoed the Commoner cover from a decade earlier. This time, though, the division was horizontal. Blue sky and green parks contrasted with skeletal fish swimming in a murky, toxic pond. In the foreground: a man, a face, leering out at the reader. The bridge of the nose to the top of the head rested above the waterline. The lower half of the face—jawbone exposed: macerated, excarnated—implied latent death lurking beneath the waters. The message was just as emphatic. Americans were drowning in toxic pollution even if they didn't know it.[1]

During the 1970s, that transition from choice to submersion happened with more a whimper than a bang, driven more likely by insufficient knowledge than by poor actions or inaction. It is important to acknowledge that there was a lot of action. While the 1960s are typically regarded as the dawn of the Age of Ecology—born from challenges to the Cold War's aboveground nuclear weapons testing and the spread of radioactive fallout and from the critical lessons and warnings brought home in Rachel Carson's *Silent Spring*—the policies introduced in the 1970s provided substance to a much larger environmental awakening. Indeed, the 1970s were unquestionably the environmental decade. The birth of the Environmental Protection Agency, the first Earth Day, and federal policies mobilizing to clean air, soil, and water and to control chemicals constitute one of the most rapid, radical, and progressive turns in environmental policy in history. But it wasn't enough.[2]

* * *

On the eve of Earth Day's tenth anniversary, an explosion at the 3.4-acre Chemical Control Corp. facility in Elizabeth, New Jersey, shook the community around it. Leaking chemicals from poorly kept and corroding drums mixed and ignited. Fifty-five-gallon barrels of hazardous chemical waste "thudded like bombs" as they were thrown two hundred feet into the air, "and burst into cascades of flashing light."[3] One local referred to the explosion as a thunderclap; its plume looked like an atomic mushroom cloud. "I heard the noise, and it just scared me to death," said Roxie West, another neighbor, who lived across an open parking lot from the facility. "I looked out and saw these big barrels flying in the air like they were soda cans."[4] A thick and black plume of smoke and ash spread over a fifteen-square-mile area, provoking fears of chemical contamination. The four-alarm fire ripped through the dilapidated warehouse and storage yard. It took ten hours for firefighters to bring it under control. Police and fire officials rapidly coordinated an evacuation plan for surrounding residents. Dark clouds loomed ominously over Staten Island, dropping ash. By morning, favorable winds helped to dissipate the plume before the evacuation plan was set in motion.[5]

Where the previous chapters identified moments where toxic fear was likened to a psychological time bomb, the Elizabeth explosion was the toxic time bomb that actually detonated. Thousands of New York and New Jersey residents could hear, see, and smell the fire. The explosion "sounded like someone beating on a drum," said one Staten Island resident. Many complained of dry throats and irritated eyes. Some left their homes to stay with relatives farther afield. "I didn't want my three-month old daughter breathing in this stuff," said another Staten Island resident. "I sent my wife and kids to stay with her mother on the other side of the island."[6] The next morning, public schools in Elizabeth and neighboring Linden were closed, along with those across the Arthur Kill on Staten Island. State authorities issued an environmental advisory urging residents to stay indoors. Barring mass exodus, it looked like Three Mile Island all over again. A week later Patrick and Mary Ann McCloskey filed a $510 million suit against Chemical Control Corp. They and their two children experienced "serious and severe illness and untold mental anguish" brought about by the "highly toxic smoke, debris and acid rain" from the fire.[7] Most authorities downplayed the air pollution risks from the fire—and the McCloskeys lived on the far side of Staten Island—but their suit received national media attention. The McCloskey case might have been opportunistic, but the toxic cloud had challenged the sense of security to which most Americans believed they were entitled. The explosion had shock value, but air quality and pollution had frayed nerves around the Elizabeth waterfront for quite some time. Mary Duffy of Staten Island told the *New York Times* that "I have to keep my kids inside at least once a month because of the smell." Two of her four children were asthmatic. "Even when there is no explosion, we get plenty of pollution from New Jersey."[8]

Even before the explosion, the chemical drums on the Elizabeth waterfront had gained notoriety as an example of the nation's toxic waste problem. The site was regularly listed in the popular media alongside Love Canal, Hopewell's Kepone contamination, and Kentucky's Valley of the Drums as one of the most polluted spots in the United States. William Carracino, president of Chemical Control Corp., was one of the more colorful—if all too typical—characters who profited from illegally storing and dumping hazardous waste. By the time of the explosion, Carracino had already been fined and sentenced on various counts of illegal dumping. His facility at Elizabeth was little more than a rundown warehouse and storage yard. The plant's small incinerator was unable to keep up with the quantities of hazardous waste that Chemical Control Corp. brought in. Thousands of old drums full of unmarked chemical hazards were simply stockpiled on-site.[9] In 1979 the *Philadelphia Inquirer* printed photographs of Chemical Control Corp. pouring chemical wastes onto a bulldozed plot of land that did not belong to Carracino. After pouring close to five thousand gallons of waste, Carracino's employees mixed in household waste to absorb the dangerous chemicals before delivering the toxic stew to a municipal landfill.[10] In other instances, Carracino was responsible for pouring liquid chemical wastes straight into municipal sewers. Carracino claimed—alternately—that he had been framed by environmental authorities and that organized crime had stolen Chemical Control Corp. from him by gunpoint in 1977. Later, he resisted testifying before a New Jersey grand jury investigating alleged organized crime involvement in toxic waste disposal. He insisted that "the mob" wanted to kill him. In 1981, after being arrested for failing to appear before the grand jury, Carracino suffered a seizure at the police station, though an electrocardiogram failed to show any evidence of a heart attack.[11]

In 1979, before the Elizabeth explosion, state inspectors had visited the waterfront facility and expressed horror at what they saw. Corroded, leaking drums were everywhere: seventy thousand of them. Officials worried about the safety of the site during any kind of cleanup: They were unsure how to proceed since they did not even know what the drums contained. They ultimately removed many of the worst drums in order to avoid what they called a "chemical time bomb." But the Chemical Control Corp. site still constituted what one authority called "the Three Mile Island of hazardous waste sites."[12] Among the drums that environmental officials removed were five hundred pounds of such explosives as TNT and picric acid. Military nerve gas, nitroglycerine, cyanide, benzene, PCBs, and propane tanks had also been recently removed from the site. But for fortuitous timing, the explosion could have been much worse.[13] After the explosion, Chemical Control Corp. went into receivership, leaving nobody to inventory and clean up the hazardous and still potentially volatile mess that had been left behind.

* * *

The Elizabeth explosion was no isolated event. Only three days later, state and federal officials ordered another evacuation after a cloud of toxic fumes escaped from the ICI Americas factory in Bayonne, New Jersey.[14] A mile away and less than two weeks later a series of explosions at the Kenrich

Petrochemicals plant injured two workers.[15] Similarly, in July 1980 a dramatic fire at a Duane Marine Salvage Corporation chemical waste dump—this time in Perth Amboy, New Jersey—prompted evacuation and provoked fears of repetition of the Elizabeth fire.[16]

One of the dirty secrets of the American chemical industry was the exorbitant amount of waste it created as the by-product of the materials it sent to market. Growing amounts of hazardous waste put strains on a limited toxic disposal infrastructure. When New Jersey closed the massively overloaded Kin-Buc landfill in Edison Township in 1976, for example, the state found itself without a single licensed hazardous waste dump.[17] In the absence of the Kin-Buc repository, that somewhere became just about everywhere. Clandestine dumping became commonplace as unscrupulous waste disposal operators charged high fees and looked for cheap ways to "disappear" the waste they collected. The creators of the waste were typically all too happy to look the other way. Or, at least, not ask any questions. By 1979 Pennsylvania's chemical industry generated ten times more waste than the state could safely accommodate in its infrastructure of hazardous waste disposal sites.[18] Further, states were only slowly coming to terms with how best to regulate safe disposal. The 1976 Resource Conservation and Recovery Act had tried to address these problems, by defining for the first time what hazardous waste was and by requiring "cradle-to-grave" manifests to monitor any registered toxins that left the factory from manufacture to disposal. At each step, the toxic waste needed to be accounted for and it needed to be handled by a licensed operator. Stiffer penalties for careless disposal were implemented. Policy historian Richard N. L. Andrews argues that improvements in waste management during this period constitute "one of the most impressive yet least noted successes of American environmental policy."[19] True. The predominance of toxic waste fears in the very early 1980s was a product of greater awareness shining a light on past transgressions. But for an American public fearful of contaminants leaching into their drinking water, the damage had likely been done. Even the chemical industry recognized this as it sought to improve its environmental image. Hazardous waste was, according to a Chemical Manufacturers Association spokesman, "a motherhood issue."[20] Furthermore, the price of hauling hazardous waste escalated dramatically because of these new laws. For example, in New Jersey, the state with the highest concentration of chemical manufacturing plants, the cost quadrupled.[21] In the immediate short term, the increasing costs for disposing of waste likely inspired novel methods of clandestine waste disposal.

* * *

In February 1980, the Environmental Protection Agency was alert to the mountain it was climbing. In a report titled "Attack on Hazardous Waste," it lamented that the most highly industrialized society in history was woefully ill-equipped to manage, monitor, or resolve its own pollution problems. Some 750,000 businesses generated hazardous waste; 10,000 transporters shipped it from point of production to disposal site; 30,000 sites treated, disposed, or stored hazardous materials; and "more effort has heretofore gone into the regulation of restaurants or taxicabs than into establishing a safe network for waste disposal."[22] Only 10 to 20 percent of the hazardous waste was legally disposed of under the newly created guidelines of the 1976 Resource Conservation and Recovery Act. *Time* reported similar numbers in 1980: 77 billion pounds of hazardous chemical waste. Only 10 percent was being handled safely. According to EPA official Gary Dietrich, at least half the wastes were "just being dumped indiscriminately."[23] A 1981 report found that the nation's waste disposal sites were in distress and disrepair. Of the 10,000 toxic dumps strewn across the country, at least 2,000 posed real or potential threats to public health.[24] Problems were myriad. Among the most significant was the lack of a coordinated waste disposal infrastructure. Industry was producing ever more hazardous waste; regulations, enforcement, and facilities for its proper disposal lagged behind the demand. By the 1980s cavalier practices turned into awareness of the threats they posed. Midnight dumping was not uncommon in the late 1970s and 1980s. Even regions distant from the source of wastes or their "legitimate" final resting points found themselves contaminated by illicit dumping in the nascent stages of more rigorous policy to control toxic waste disposal. In some cases, organized crime was behind dumping practices that skirted or flaunted state and federal regulations.[25] But not always.[26] Edwin Stier, New Jersey's Division of Criminal Justice director, lamented in 1980 that after spending considerable efforts over the previous two years to prosecute illegal dumpers, progress remained slow. "We felt that, if we prosecuted illegal dumpers, a legitimate waste disposal industry would develop and the problem would go away," he reasoned. "But we found that was not the case." Stier's surveillance found that legitimate waste disposal companies were just as prone to illegal dumping.[27]

* * *

In the immediate aftermath of the Elizabeth explosion, New Jersey Governor Brendan Byrne told reporters, "If there is one message that comes out of a day like today it is that government . . . cannot trust private industry to dispose correctly of its toxic wastes."[28] Carracino was a microcosm of the toxic waste disposal industry; his case certainly supported Byrne's bitter claim. In his trial, Carracino insisted that he had entered into the waste hauling industry because "I really care about the environment."[29] Elsewhere, however, he articulated the financial benefits of hazardous materials disposal: "There are millions to be made in this business," he told *Philadelphia Inquirer* reporters in 1979 as he appealed his conviction. "The overhead is nothing. You find a place—don't buy it, don't buy anything, just rent it—and dump. When they catch up to you, just declare bankruptcy and get out."[30]

Absent stiff regulation and enforcement, there was money to be made. Wastes threatened to inundate chemical production if they weren't disposed of. Unscrupulous businessmen could dump the waste out of sight, out of mind, and off the company ledger. Illegal dumping circumvented the hefty fees associated with using sophisticated facilities equipped to handle hazardous wastes, which netted truck companies sizeable profits. In addition to poorly kept warehouses such as Carracino's, toxic waste drums were unceremoniously stacked and left in fields, in vacant lots, on abandoned waterfront piers. Chemicals were poured into residential streets, creeks, and sewers. Waste was deposited in dilapidated tenements due for demolition.

Too frequently, accidents happened. On September 1, 1978, a drum on Edward Cherkowski's trailer broke loose and split open as he waited to dump it (illegally) into the Old Forge Landfill, between Wilkes-Barre and Scranton, Pennsylvania. A white fog that "would take your breath away" poured out of the broken drum. "I was afraid to get out of the truck," Cherkowski claimed a year later. "It looked like death to me." The cloud drifted toward the town of Old Forge, where several residents "suffered odor and skin irritation so bad that at least a dozen left their homes." Cherkowski's account came after he was recruited to testify against his employer, Peter Iacavazzi, the president of Lackawanna Refuse Removal Inc., which illegally dumped an estimated 100,000 drums of toxic waste at the Old Forge Landfill between September 1978 and March 1979. The trial revealed some of the contents, which included phenols, toluene, chromium, cadmium, cyanide, arsenic, tetrachloroethylene, and mercury.[31]

In 1979 Pennsylvania and New Jersey were arguably the epicenter of the toxic dumping problem. "The chemical time bomb ticks loudest here," reported one story.[32] In 1977 officials discovered a clandestine dump site for hazardous chemicals under the Commodore Barry Bridge in Chester, Pennsylvania, a predominantly Black city on the western bank of the Delaware River, southwest of Philadelphia. Thousands of barrels and many six-thousand-gallon tankers had been abandoned. More waste had been poured on the ground and in the adjacent lagoon, which fed into the Delaware River. Two major fires at the site in 1978 destroyed many of the drums, but left the remaining waste at even greater risk of causing harm. One of those fires had incapacitated "45 firemen who inhaled the chemical fumes." A reporter describing a similar fire at the same site in 1979 observed that the firefighters seemed appropriately tentative about getting too close.[33]

In July and August 1979 one hundred thousand gallons of oily waste leaked out of the Butler Tunnel in Pittston, Pennsylvania. The source of the contaminated oil (it was mixed with numerous hazardous chemicals) was an abandoned mineshaft. The region, previously known for its anthracite coalfields, had acquired a dubious reputation as a toxic waste dumping ground. Abandoned mines became popular (and discrete) places for illegally depositing contaminated waste. Further, the common regional practice of using bore holes—vented holes from the old mines—for residential waste exacerbated the problem. In addition to toxins in the water, which escaped through a tunnel built forty years earlier to help drain the mine of water, dangerously high concentrations of dichlorobenzene vapor emanated from the tunnel.[34] Fear and uncertainty prevailed. Nobody could be sure how much waste had been dumped in the mine, though estimates in September 1979 ranged from one million to twenty-seven million gallons.[35] One of the enduring challenges of coping with illegal dumping was that nobody had reliable information regarding the chemical composition of the waste. This made determining the hazards for workers tasked with the cleanup difficult, never mind communicating risks to residents downstream. By October warnings that cyanide gas had been dumped at the site caught everyone by surprise. "This is much worse than Three Mile Island,"

Republican Senator John Heinz stated during a press conference in October. He echoed the Red Cross worker who preferred the certainty of Mount Saint Helens's eruption to Love Canal: "At Three Mile Island we knew what we were dealing with. Here, we don't know what we're dealing with."[36]

* * *

During the 1970s, New Jersey deserved its dubious distinction of being "Cancer-State, U.S.A." The state had the highest concentration of chemical manufacturing in the country, and for years health officials wrestled with disturbingly high cancer fatality levels, among the highest in the nation. Researchers at Rutgers University pointed to "air and water pollution caused by improper disposal of hazardous waste" as a contributing factor.[37] The 1980s also revealed that New Jersey had been turned into one massive toxic dumping ground, from the Meadowlands to the Pine Barrens. The numbers of toxic waste drums uncovered, the millions of gallons of waste pumped into water systems, and the amount of dangerous materials spread in lands across the state defied the imagination. By 1980, the state was engaged in a more proactive method of addressing chemical waste. State officials practiced a two-pronged approach of remediating dangerous sites and enforcing more stringent waste disposal practices. Companies found to be contravening disposal regulations were handed hefty and regular fines along with prison sentences for company management.

But the problem seemed insurmountable. "We've got toxic time bombs all over the state where illegal dumpers have been at night," one state official told the *New York Times*.[38] In addition to the Elizabeth site, Chemical Control Corp. had stored six thousand more drums at Duane Marine Salvage Corporation. Meanwhile, a couple of months before the Elizabeth explosion—and only a few blocks removed from it—a state and federal strike force raided a plant operated by Iron Oxide, a recycling firm. Toxic waste haulers had been watched entering and exiting the facility, and officials had reason to worry about illegal dumping. After the raid, the Army Corps of Engineers found an underground pipe that delivered pumped liquid waste from the structure into the Arthur Kill, separating New Jersey from Staten Island. Officials estimated that more than sixty thousand gallons of waste had been disposed of in this manner.[39] Less than a week after the Elizabeth fire, a *New York Times* story reported that the state of New Jersey had identified sixteen hazardous waste dumps that required a remedial "crash program" that spring and summer. The Chemical Control site was one of these. So, too, was the A-Z Resource Recovery dump in New Brunswick, whose owners had abandoned it, along with almost ten thousand drums of various toxic substances. Some were believed to have been received from Chemical Control prior to the explosion. But a part of the problem that remedial efforts faced was the mystery of what they were up against. A three-month cleanup costing $750,000 was planned for the A-Z site, but the cost and time frame risked doubling if workers had to test each barrel to determine its contents (and risk).[40]

In other instances, fear stemmed from how to act. Where the most egregious cases required immediate response and locals worried about the health impact of having been exposed to contaminants, many old dumps lay benign. Between 1953 and 1970 chemical waste drums were dumped in pits and trenches on land outside New Egypt, New Jersey. In the wake of the Elizabeth explosion, renewed sensitivities to toxic waste galvanized local worries. Township and state officials tried to determine whether removing the drums was the correct course of action, or whether that risked making more of a mess than leaving them undisturbed. This was no less a toxic time bomb: to many residents, it just hadn't yet detonated. Leslie Rader, an antiques store owner, had helped to bury much of the waste many years earlier. "I was younger then and didn't think about what it might be doing to the environment," he said. "There were no laws against it and nobody tried to stop us, so I thought it must have been all right. Now I can see that we have to worry about the future." Trying to calm nerves in communities throughout the state, officials pledged to test wells for contamination. But much of this work was delayed by the resources that needed to be devoted to cleaning up the Elizabeth explosion. Latent threats provoked further anxieties.[41]

However, the simple fact remained that there was money to be made in waste disposal and one didn't need to be a shyster like William Carracino to profit. As Americans generated more trash after World War II, industrious towns and companies discovered that receiving that waste was an effective method of generating much-needed revenue. In 1972, Jackson Township officials opened a landfill south and west of the township's residential center. In short order, the small rural community in southern New Jersey's Pine Barrens began accepting waste from all over the state. At its peak, the landfill received 300,000 gallons a day. Charging six dollars per thousand gallons, the business was lucrative. On November 8, 1978, the Jackson Township Board of Health closed wells in its Legler neighborhood after toxic and carcinogenic chemical pollution was found in the drinking water supply. Their findings included benzene, chloroform, trichlorethylene (all known carcinogens). Dr. Dhun Patel of the State Department of Health also noted that other chemicals in the water had "acute toxic properties" that might have accounted for the widespread cases of kidney, nervous system, blood, bone marrow, respiratory tract, and digestive problems among residents.[42] "We drank the bad water for four years," said Mrs. Benesch, who started suffering from kidney stones in 1977. "Some health problem may not show up for years from now. We moved here because it was nice for the children to live in the country with woods all around. Now we have to worry about whether they will get cancer." She echoed many residents' sentiments when she told the *New York Times*, "I'm very fearful of the future."[43] A month after the EPA hostage situation at Love Canal, Legler resident James McCarthy, whose nine-month-old daughter Karen died from a rare form of kidney cancer in 1975, expressed a certain kinship with the angry residents there. "Our hearts and prayers went out to them," he told the *New York Times*. "We know what they are going through." More than two years after being told not to drink their tap water, residents near the landfill were still waiting for clean water to run through their taps. Information about their health also stagnated. McCarthy, who had also lost a kidney, spoke for many residents in Legler—but also Love Canal and elsewhere: "We were told that no health tests could be done and not to worry about it. They don't give a damn about us."[44] In the eight houses surrounding McCarthy's seven people suffered some kind of kidney disease.[45] As seemed too frequently the case to residents, perceived inertia within township, county, state, and federal agencies produced only more fear and anger. "The Environmental Protection Agency, the [New Jersey] Department of Environmental Protection and the Department of Health kept passing the buck," McCarthy fumed, "using us as guinea pigs."[46]

As Legler residents hung white flags made of diapers, towels, and T-shirts from their mailboxes—a sign that they required bottled water from the township's roving tank truck—ninety-six families filed a $50 million lawsuit against the township for mismanaging the landfill. On September 8, 1980, they also filed a $822.5 million federal suit against SCM Corporation. SCM's subsidiary, Glidden-Durkee, was a Cleveland-based paint manufacturer that had mined ilmenite in Jackson Township until 1972, when it sold to the township their open-pit mine and surrounding lands. These 135 acres became the site of the township's landfill. The suit accused Glidden of failing to warn the township that the land was unsuited for a landfill. Glidden's pit had dug into the Cohansey Aquifer, which fed the township. Glidden had also been delinquent in dumping various wastes and contaminants on the property. Two months later, EPA officials discovered that 20,000 gallons of aviation fuel had been dumped into the ground at the Naval Engineering Center in nearby Lakehurst. High levels of trichloroethylene were found at the site. Legler residents hired a private detective to determine whether there might be cause to file suit against the Navy.[47] It seemed anyone could be responsible, and yet Legler residents still waited for clean water and clarity on their exposure to harmful chemicals. White flags of surrender continued to hang from their mailboxes.[48]

* * *

What was true for Pennsylvania and New Jersey was equally true for California, Colorado, Michigan, Alabama, Louisiana, and all points in between. And if toxic waste sites prompted worry, so too did the transportation of toxic materials. On July 26, 1980, for example, fifteen Illinois Central Gulf train cars carrying toxic chemicals derailed outside of Muldraugh, Kentucky. Over the next two days three of the tanks ignited, emitting clouds of poisonous smoke. Four thousand residents in a four-mile radius were evacuated.[49] In 1984, the ignition of methanol from two derailed train cars at Marshville, North Carolina—outside of Charlotte—resulted in the evacuation of 2,100 nearby residents and the closure U.S. Highway 74, the main thoroughfare through town.[50] Fire from a derailment southwest of Pine Bluff, Arkansas, in June 1985 prompted another evacuation—this time 2,800 people—because of unspecified "regulated hazardous or toxic chemical commodities" in the inferno.[51] Those damage and evacuation numbers paled in comparison with a crash on July 8, 1986, near Miamisburg, Ohio, when a derailed train car carrying several hundred gallons of yellow phosphorus broke apart and ignited. The toxic cloud forced the evacuation of roughly 30,000 people over the next forty-eight hours.[52] Not all such accidents were so explosive. On New Year's Eve 1984, a switchman in North Little Rock, Arkansas, discovered a tank car leaking ethylene oxide in the

Missouri Pacific Railroad Company's train yard. As experts were called in to transfer the highly flammable spill, 2,500 people within a one-mile radius were evacuated for precautionary reasons due to "concern about the tank car rocketing should ignition occur."[53] While much of the fear surrounding toxic chemicals stemmed from slow infiltrations of groundwater and concerns about latent disease from low-level exposure, such evacuations—and many more like them—were an ominous reminder that chemicals were regularly on the move.

In train wrecks, however, manifests and waybills helped to quickly identify the materials involved and determine potential risks of ignition and to health in the surrounding area. In many illegal waste sites, this was not the case. No paperwork or signs were left with abandoned drums to help cleanup teams assess the hazards confronting them. There was no paper trail. Even though the 1976 Resource Conservation and Recovery Act sought to correct this problem by requiring that all licensed carriers of hazardous waste materials maintain careful records of the products they handled, countless tons of toxic chemicals continued to disappear as midnight dumpers fudged numbers, made up landfill site names in other states, and found other ways to cut corners. Unaccounted for chemical wastes corroborate the hypothesis that illicit dumping was rampant. And while different—and still nascent—state laws on hazardous waste disposal made the matter of tracking dumping difficult across states, the enduring problem for waste haulers was the simple fact that some materials were especially hard to dump anywhere. Few facilities were licensed to receive the most hazardous of substances. Waste frequently mysteriously disappeared into a labyrinth of manufacturers, waste haulers, paperwork, and illegal sites. Keith Welks, an attorney at Pennsylvania's Department of Environmental Resources, outlined the special problems associated with wastes crossing state lines: "[The manifest data provided by New Jersey] many times contain a substantial number of entries of places we've never heard of and cannot locate or identify and which we believe do not exist. . . . I think that New Jersey's conclusion is that the waste went to Pennsylvania. I don't know that that's true." Confronted with the difficulties associated with dumping such toxic materials as asbestos or cyanide residues or hexavalent chromium waste—which many disposal facilities were unequipped to receive—many haulers elected to leave their loads roadside or in some well-hidden field. In these cases, many shipments did not travel far from their point of origin. Welks again: "We have found that waste haulers do not drive ten miles to dump illegally when they can drive five miles."[54]

* * *

One of the irrefutable laws of environmental history is that disasters are not shared equally. There is nothing new about the poorer and politically disenfranchised segments of society bearing the brunt of a civilization's environmental hazards; I raised the specter of environmental racism at the end of the previous chapter. However, the movement for environmental justice is a product of the 1980s. Seven years after Russell Bliss sprayed the dirt roads around Times Beach, Missouri, with dioxin-laced oils, Robert Burns and his sons drove their own waste-hauling tanker along the state roads of rural North Carolina. Bliss had been unaware of the dioxin in the oil. Burns was party to a more surreptitious dispersal of environmental contaminants in direct contravention of the Toxic Substances Control Act. Burns was paid $75,000 by the Ward Transformer Company in Raleigh, North Carolina, to dispose of 33,000 gallons of PCB-contaminated liquids. The original contract involved hauling the PCBs to a warehouse in Youngsville, Pennsylvania. Distance and cost prompted Burns and Ward to investigate local midnight dumping. In June 1978, Burns dumped two truckloads of PCB wastes at the Fort Bragg Military Reservation just outside of Fayetteville. He then procured a contract from the state to oil the dirt shoulders of country roads in fifteen eastern counties.[55] The PCBs were spread through an open valve in the bottom of his tanker in July and August as he rumbled through the state.[56] Discolored grass and soils at Fort Bragg first alerted officials to the spill. Subsequent discoveries of similar stains along roadsides galvanized a more thorough search and analysis. The lab reports returned exceptionally high levels of PCBs.[57]

Like dioxin, PCBs were good at provoking public concern in the 1970s and 1980s. Some share toxicological properties with dioxins, which meant they were often a part of the same environmental conversations. Polychlorinated biphenyls are a family of synthetic, aromatic compounds, made up of more than 209 variants, or congeners. PCBs were used as dielectric and coolant fluids to prevent fires in capacitors and transformers. Starting in 1929 PCBs were manufactured in the United States almost exclusively by Monsanto. As with so many of the ingenious products of the chemical industry, what made PCBs such a valuable substance constituted its threat to the environment. PCBs are stable compounds that are not water soluble. They don't break down in nature, which means they persist. This is good in industry, but not good in the environment. Or in human bodies, where they are just as likely to persist. According to the biologist Joe Thornton, "In very low doses, PCBs affect brain chemistry and produce long-lasting behavioral changes and deficits in the ability to think and learn, particularly when exposure occurs before birth or early in life."[58] The EPA also lists PCBs as probable human carcinogens. During the 1970s, the EPA discovered that a General Electric plant along the Hudson River had dumped massive quantities of PCBs into the river. Monsanto voluntarily stopped making PCBs in 1977; the EPA banned their use in 1979.

Action in North Carolina was swift. The state moved quickly to store contaminated soils in a covered landfill. By December 1978, North Carolina applied for approval to develop the landfill site in rural Warren County, between Warrenton and Afton. State officials had considered ninety sites in twenty different counties. Not all the sites fulfilled the EPA's requirements that the landfill rest more than fifty feet above the water table, but neither did the Warren County site. The groundwater level at the proposed landfill site was only seven feet below the surface. At a January 1979 public hearing in Warrenton, the EPA was asked to waive three of its landfill siting requirements, including the groundwater depth. After further tests, the EPA acquiesced. The landfill was approved on June 4, 1979.[59] That's when the fight began.

* * *

The modern landfill is an engineering solution to a social problem. It is designed to hold in perpetuity the invisible detritus of modern living: the stuff of unspecific origin that cycles into and out of modern homes and is subsequently forgotten when rendered to the curb. The mysteries of invisibility are not lost in the story of toxic fear because the most harmful components are rarely meant to be seen at all. They are, rather, the secret manufacturing by-products of the materials of everyday use; the unwanted; the worker elves of better living (through chemistry), shunted into waste pools and landfills, forgotten until they remind us of their labor by leaching back to the surface, infiltrating our groundwater, our bodies, and our imaginations. Chemophobia reflects the *dietrologia*—the truth behind the mask or the motivation—of the culture of disposability. There is more to the landfill than the substance of the surface. According to Barry Commoner's Second Law of Ecology, everything must go somewhere. But there is a persistent dynamism in most contaminants that ensures they rarely stay still after they have gone somewhere. So the landfill as engineering solution is only ever a temporary solution. Even the best seals and storage tanks crack, leak, seep, overflow, and degrade before the chemicals have been rendered benign. This was more or less public knowledge. One 1980 poll revealed that most Americans didn't want a hazardous waste landfill within a hundred miles of their homes.[60]

This last point suggests that the modern landfill is also a social problem to an engineering solution. Warren was one of the poorest counties in North Carolina, ranking 92nd out of 100 in median family income in 1980. It also had the highest concentration of African American inhabitants. Where African Americans made up 24.2 percent of North Carolina's population, Warren County's population was 63.7 percent Black. Afton was more than 84 percent Black.[61] The proposed landfill project incited not just environmentally concerned citizens, but also civil rights activists who petitioned, marched, and protested against its construction. The Atlanta-based Southern Christian Leadership Conference helped garner national attention for Warren County, drawing on their well-established media savvy to keep the protest in the national spotlight.[62] Dr. Charles E. Cobb, director of the United Church of Christ's Commission for Racial Justice, urged the local African American community to "move in a swift and determined manner to stop yet another breach of civil rights." Siting the PCB landfill in a Black community was "no less than attempted genocide."[63] The explicit connection between environmental health fears and civil rights was stark. The unequal distribution of environmental risks was not new—nor the fact that they skewed along racial and socioeconomic lines. But the public discourse that explicitly articulated environmental injustice and environmental racism resonated across the country. Further, photographs of African American protesters lying face down on a road to block dump trucks from depositing PCB-laced dirt in their community captured the national imagination. It enlivened numerous local environmental struggles and complicated the nature of toxic fear. At Love Canal, the national narrative followed a white community reckoning with the discovery of a chemical hazard beneath them; in Warren County, the chemical hazard was being brought—deliberately—to them.

Warren County wasn't alone. In 1983, the U.S. Government Accounting Office reported that three out of the four toxic waste landfills in the American South (the EPA's Region IV) were located in majority-Black communities. All four communities were poor: at least 26 percent of the population in each lived below the poverty line.[64] Between 1986 and 1996, the Pennsylvania Department of Environmental Protection approved five commercial waste disposal facilities in Chester. The economically depressed town, with a large African American population, compared with the rest of Delaware County, became the dumping grounds for the rest of the county.[65] Hazardous waste disposal was not the lone issue for environmental justice, either. Just as old factories leaked, emitted, spilled, and exploded toxic substances into neighboring communities, more of that seemed to happen in poor communities and communities of color, such as Triana's DDT contamination. And new facilities seemed to gravitate toward similar towns and counties across the country. Chemical corridors—"Cancer Alleys"—in northeastern New Jersey and in Louisiana produced conglomerations of race, petrochemical manufacturing, poverty, and health worries. The Union Carbide plant in Institute, West Virginia, was built next door to the West Virginia State College, an historically Black school. St. Louis. Detroit. Tucson. South Central Los Angeles. Chemical plants and hazardous waste facilities lodged themselves adjacent to poor, Black, Hispanic communities and Native American reservations across the country.[66]

With apologies to Beck, one might conclude that "smog is hierarchic, *fear* is democratic." Even then, in spite of the extensive disparity of the burden of chemical contamination imposed upon Americans of color and of lower household and per capita income, the predominant voices of chemophobia from the American 1980s were white. "Racism has forced African Americans to live apart from the larger society," the sociologist Robert Bullard observed in his important work, *Dumping in Dixie*, published in 1990.[67] The African American experience with toxic fear is one that is likely lived quite apart from (certainly in the shadow of) the white and mainstream American narrative of toxicscapes. Part of what makes the movement for environmental justice so interesting and important is that it worked to create connections and networks of shared experiences across the country among disenfranchised communities. While outlining systemic racism's environmental footprint, in many respects, this constituted establishing alternative reference points—new markers for the same availability heuristic—for contamination. It also encouraged greater citizen participation as playing a critical role in re-creating a stronger sense of personal and social security. One of the lessons derived from crisis is that people feel compelled to act. The movement for environmental justice mobilized that need to act into productive forms of citizen activism that valued information, community, and public health. In many respects, then, the continuing role and legacy of the environmental justice movement has been to break down the racial apartheid of American environmental politics by highlighting common interest in healthy places in which to live, work, and play.

* * *

Inasmuch as landfills are an engineering solution to a social problem, there's another side to this story. It is important to stress that landfilling, which provoked so many fears, was common only because it was less expensive than on-site neutralization and incineration. As the EPA's own chief of its hazardous waste implementation branch, William Sanjour, told a rally in Warrenton, landfilling appealed because it was cheaper than the alternative. "Basically, hazardous waste landfills don't work, and the decision to build them is purely political and not based on technology," he said. "It's hope, not engineering. Not science. Hope." Landfills are also easily forgotten. Once the landfill is completed, Sanjour told Warrenton activists, little maintenance to prevent leaks would happen. "I think they'll just forget about it."[68] When they do their job, landfills preserve the invisibility of the hazards they hold. But, the chorus of concerned activists and citizens around the country intoned, "it will only be a matter of time before the PCBs end up in these people's wells."[69] Which is not to say that there was a simple solution to this apparently intractable problem. Opponents of landfilling advocated incineration as a solution to the leaching and land use problems, but incineration came with its own problems.[70] Burning hazardous waste did not magically disappear toxic pollutants any more than did burying them in a landfill. Rather, an alchemical practice of transforming one kind of hazard into another simply introduced a new series of problems. Burned waste left sludge residues that still required disposal. Further, during the 1980s and 1990s, one of the greatest concerns surrounding waste incineration was the creation and release of dioxin. Just as Americans were adamant about not wanting to live near landfills, they were no more keen on living next to incineration stacks.[71]

There are two ways to think about the kinds of chemical waste disasters and their relationship to environmental policy that populate this chapter. The first is to chronicle a series of punctuated moments in disparate places. The resonant tone of most sites of chemical fear is that they occurred in isolation. The urgency with which fear manifested and expressed itself at Elizabeth or Pittston or Hopewell or Institute or Afton demanded immediate action, not reflection on its relations to other disasters. Indeed, the immediacy of fear on the ground drew attention away from making more careful and explicit connections. As previously noted, toxic discourse is a low priority when individual and public health are under assault.[72] But the fact that the number and severity of chemical disasters seemed to crescendo in the United States around the 1980s encourages the consideration of disaster through a wider lens. Disasters—and not least chemical disasters—might be profitably examined collectively rather than as a series of individual incidents. To pull back and look at the hazardous waste crisis of the early 1980s is to acknowledge a consistent series of trends pertaining to patterns of risk assessment and risk perception, political and technological dysfunction, an economic system that favored growth over human health, and a power hierarchy organized by race and socioeconomic standing. "Disasters have a history," asserted an abstract at the American Historical Association's 2015 conference in New York City. "Reactions to disaster often re-inscribe historically traceable patterns of social vulnerability."[73] When chemical disasters are viewed in unison, they reveal a more holistic and cohesive perspective of the serial events that fostered such toxic fear during the 1980s.

This satellite view helps to visualize chemophobia as a singular, slow disaster. The idea of a slow disaster invites us to contemplate not just the eruption of mishap but also the systems that permitted it to happen in the first place as well as its aftermath. Barrels vaulting into the air at the Elizabeth explosion suggest a traditional understanding of disaster as sudden and violent. But an historical perspective insists that we consider the events and policies that gave rise to that explosive night. In many instances, the availability heuristic, a breakdown in trust and technical communication, meant that toxic fear preceded and followed the key moment of discovery of a chemical disaster. In others, disasters lacked a specific flashpoint. Rather, hazardous materials slowly infiltrated a community over many years. Even at Love Canal, it would be problematic to start an analysis of the contamination there with the local protests. Indeed, one recent study of Love Canal saw value in taking a much longer view of the disaster.[74] More to the point, however, slow disasters insist that deeper connections between disparate events are recognized. Chemophobia as it manifested itself in the American 1980s constitutes a single disaster, not a series of individual moments. That fear did not emerge simply from the discovery of accidents, spills, emissions, and contaminations, although the echoes of the availability heuristic reverberated throughout the decade. Rather, the uncertainties and insecurities that prompted Americans to fear chemical pollution were born out of a popular sense that government had reneged on its responsibility to keep the public safe from harm.

This perspective also lends credence to what Rob Nixon has called "slow violence."[75] In much the same way that a slow disaster is one that festers, slow violence is a more gradual—and frequently invisible—form of social and cultural oppression. It is incremental and persistent. Slow violence freely acknowledges that some people are much more vulnerable to environmental hazards than others. And it relies on the latency of its threats to mask and render apparently benign its real harm. Exposure to dangerous chemicals, for example, can take years to manifest itself as illness. Slow violence is also well-hidden in plain sight. The spectacles of an Elizabeth explosion or toxic sludge flowing down the Susquehanna River or acres of corroding barrel drums piled on a field in rural Kentucky belie the interconnectivity of these events and mask the slow violence of their origins as a formulaic practice of economic and technological decisions that calculated private short-term profits over public and long-term interests. By way of an example of the continuation of slow violence: Between 1988 and 1992, more than 34,000 chemical release events occurred in the United States.[76] Culprits and victims might have differed in each instance, but the systems that permitted them remained constant.

From slow disaster to slow violence to fear as slow boil. In combining the legislative and experienced histories of toxic waste disposal and their accidents in the 1980s, this chapter has explored the politics of involuntary risk in American environmental history. A big part of the toxic fear story is a product of such cowboy dumping and local communities' sobering realization that Barry Commoner's Second Law of Ecology—that everything must go somewhere—was a constant that certainly applied to waste. Commoner's First Law of Ecology—that everything is connected to everything else—provided the template for human exposure to any number of harmful chemicals escaping from the places they were dumped or abandoned.[77] The next chapter picks up this story by examining the neoliberal politics that frustrated a more careful administration of hazardous waste production and management.

CHAPTER FOUR

The Queer Part We Play

I feel sad for people and the queer part we play in our own disasters.
—Don DeLillo, *White Noise*

This chapter discusses the evolution of environmental legislation introduced in the late 1970s and early 1980s to address American pollution concerns, but I think it is important to underline the results of the Reagan administration's chemical legacy first. "In sharp contrast to the Environmental Decade" of the 1970s, writes the environmental policy scholar Michael E. Kraft, "the 1980s stand out as an era of challenge and conflict over the goals and values of environmentalism and the specific public policies and programs adopted to help achieve them."[1] The new government was intent on doing less rather than more—or its energies were concentrated on an ardent desire to cut red tape for industry. The 1980s U-turn on pollution control, prevention, and enforcement produced two outcomes. The first was that the Reagan administration's adherence to deregulation and pollution inaction provoked a surprising amount of opposition across the United States. Indeed, environmental deregulation appeared to exacerbate toxic fear in the public. Related to this popular opposition was that rollbacks of existing laws and a lack of enforcement made it easier and more profitable for waste disposal companies to continue practices of illicit dumping. Incidences of widespread contamination increased and reinforced the notion that industry needed more government oversight.

The shorthand summary of this chapter is that it is difficult to correct environmental wrongs if it is impossible to ascertain the extent of the hazard. The new toxic waste policies engaged in two different missions. The first was to maintain careful records of a growing list of dangerous chemicals: the who, what, when, wheres of their manufacture, transportation, use, and disposal. The second involved developing budgets and protocols—legal and logistical—for rectifying intransigent contaminations. The new toxic waste policies also engaged with two different pollution philosophies from the White House. During the 1970s, Republican and Democratic administrations introduced and passed groundbreaking legislation that they hoped would curtail the spread of toxic pollution across the country. During the 1980s, the White House embraced a neoliberal approach to economic management that had no room and less appetite for the kinds of oversight and correction that chemical hazards still required. Put another way, the new pollution laws of the 1970s marked an important step toward acknowledging the extent of an environmental nightmare, but the Reagan administration moved in the opposite direction, when evidence kept revealing that those landmark 1970s laws hadn't actually gone far enough.

If the social and cultural politics of fracture loomed large in many of the instances of toxic fear, this chapter also confronts head-on neoliberalism's influence on the decade and its history of toxic fear. Neoliberalism was not simply an event whose ascendency happened to coincide with or prompt toxic fear. Rather, fear was a desired outcome. Neoliberalism trades on uncertainty and ignorance and, by extension, fear. Social confusion and unrest undermine the sanity of the polis, but that is a feature—not a bug—of neoliberalism's design. Ignorance was a virtue, according to Friedrich Hayek, one of neoliberalism's key architects; the market was the real and only arbiter of knowledge. This is also the line where economic theory trips into social theory, bringing with it the tools for monopolizing not just markets but ideas and politics. Turning authority over to the dictates of the unfettered market and individual pursuits of self-interest have deep implications for how society should be administered.[2]

Deregulation permitted the production of more hazardous chemicals, broadened their application, cared little for their hazards, and less for where and how they were disposed of. Moreover, smaller government resulted in more lapses in enforcing the safe handling of chemical hazards from laboratory to landfill, and fewer resources for remediating damage with the care and speed some disasters required. These were the drivers—explicit components of the neoliberal playbook—that spurred American fears of chemical pollution in the 1980s. In many instances, though, chemicals and the fear they provoked forced the Reagan administration to intervene against free markets in order to stem popular worries. That they did so reluctantly and retroactively is ingrained in the historical record. Nevertheless, American toxic fear as an expression of cultural angst was sufficiently significant that it constitutes a fissure in what seems like the impregnable bulwark of American neoliberalism.

* * *

By the beginning of the 1980s, safe disposal of toxic waste had become an American priority. Popular demand for stricter controls was rampant. It was not a priority, however, for the new government that had campaigned vociferously on a probusiness and antienvironmental platform. As the nation seemed to be swimming in ever more toxic waste—per the September 22, 1980, *Time* cover—the Reagan administration settled into office by trying to relax controls over hazardous chemicals. The order of the day was deregulation, which under the Reagan administration was part of a tripartite plan that also involved tax cuts and reductions in social spending. Combined, they involved paring back existing regulation and reducing enforcement. Deregulation was designed to grease the wheels of industry, to get government off big business's back and thereby stimulate economic growth. In business circles, government regulation—as opposed to fluctuations in the global economy—was responsible for the economic stagflation of the 1970s.[3] Deregulation was the pillar of Ronald Reagan's 1980 presidential campaign. On the campaign trail, Reagan had reassured business audiences that he wanted to roll back the taxes and bureaucratic red tape—to "turn you loose again to do the things that I know you can do so well."[4] In terms of environmental policy, deregulation meant relaxing the strict laws created in the previous decade to control air and water pollution and how to manage toxic waste. Some pollution was the price of progress. As one elected official opined, "It would be a hollow victory to have crystal clear waters and no jobs."[5]

The Reagan administration ushered in a unique political climate that had a transformative effect on public affairs and on American culture writ large. This was the first explicitly antienvironmental administration. Deregulation and declining access to information, while simultaneously shifting the burden of responsibility from industry and government to the individual, had the unsettling effect of "sharply [curtailing] citizen participation" in American environmental politics.[6] In effect, Reagan-era policies promoted public uncertainty and insecurity. Those bred fear. But as dismissive as it might have been about environmental pollution, the Reagan administration did not create the chemophobia of the 1980s. It inherited the mechanisms that created the tempest and handled them poorly. Moreover, it also inherited the legislative tools to combat the sources of chemophobia. In this respect, Reagan's health and environmental agencies at best blundered, at worst practiced a curious combination of inept understanding and deliberate neglect. Reagan's preference for the probusiness neoliberal model that was also emerging in Margaret Thatcher's Great Britain at the same time was counterintuitive to the slow worries provoked by toxic pollution.

Reagan's pushback against the Carter administration's environmental efforts consisted—in theory—of an attempt to render environmental policies more efficient and more effective. One of his first actions upon entering the White House was to issue an executive order for all government agencies to audit the costs, benefits, and efficiencies on all regulations. "Regulatory action shall not be undertaken," the order stated, "unless the potential benefits to society from the regulation outweigh the potential costs to society."[7] How those costs and benefits to society were to be measured was not stated. It was, rather, the responsibility of the Office of Management and Budget to make that determination.[8] But it was clear that Reagan was intent on giving industry a break at the expense of the environment. Less than a fortnight after the November election, Reagan received a memo authored by David Stockman, a young Republican House representative from Michigan. The twenty-three-page memo—which was subsequently leaked and widely circulated—was titled "Avoiding a GOP Economic Dunkirk," and pressed for rapid and radical economic reform. "President Reagan should declare a national economic emergency soon after inauguration," it asserted.[9] Among other cuts, Stockman warned the president-elect that the EPA was a "ticking time bomb."[10] Its regulations severely threatened the new administration's economic recovery program. In effect, the memo was Stockman's job interview for the directorship of the Office of Management and Budget. Within two months, Stockman would settle into his role, managing the government's purse strings, including the EPA's budget. The memo made no secret of his plans.[11]

Indeed, to critics the Reagan administration appeared to be in an all-out war against the environment and denied the nature of the crisis. The Reagan administration's rollback of many Carter policies gutted recent investments in personnel and resources for the Occupational Safety and Health

Administration, the Food and Drug Administration, the National Cancer Institute, and the Environmental Protection Agency, as well as at the Bureau of Land Management and the Department of the Interior. Many of these rollbacks—a part of Reagan's Regulatory Relief program—were downright cynical. Reagan's appointments to various federal agencies that engaged with health and the environment provided a clear indication of how the next four years would go. At the head of OSHA, for example, the public health activist Donald Kennedy was replaced with Thorne G. Auchter, whose Florida construction business had regularly been cited by OSHA for health and safety violations.[12] Just as Auchter had run afoul of OSHA directives before being appointed to manage that agency, the new director of the Bureau of Land Management was Robert Burford, a Colorado rancher who had regularly been charged for grazing violations. Burford had been a prominent leader in the Sagebrush Rebellion's fight to destroy the Bureau of Land Management and its control over public lands in the western United States. At the Department of the Interior, James Watt was another Sagebrush Rebellion leader and president of the Mountain States Legal Foundation, created to block federal agencies from enforcing environmental legislation. Watt was convinced that the end of times was near and applied the most radical "wise use" approaches to public lands. Watt, the historian Sean Wilentz asserts, "vowed to follow what he called the scriptural injunction 'to occupy the land until He returns,' by which he meant more mining, more cutting of timber, and more drilling for oil."[13] To head the Environmental Protection Agency, Reagan appointed Anne Gorsuch (later Burford). All three became known as Reagan's "Colorado Mafia."[14] They were beholden to staunch conservative and antienvironmentalist Joseph Coors, the beer magnate, who had been centrally responsible for Reagan's landslide victory in Colorado.

Gorsuch was neither the first nor the most prominent choice for EPA chief within the administration. Nevertheless, she had a record of being driven, independent, and exacting. She seemed the ideal deputy to administer the kinds of changes to environmental governance Reagan sought. After an early meeting with economists at the probusiness American Enterprise Institute, who briefed her on market-based incentives to reduce pollution, Gorsuch came away claiming she didn't want better regulation: Her mandate was scaling back the red tape and reducing costs. This was consistent with the Reagan mission of sweeping regulatory reform. As a means of cutting the fat out of the federal budget, the new administration sought to outsource environmental cleanup and authority to the states from the very start.[15] Such measures were met with stern resistance, but Gorsuch hewed to the administration line, reducing the agency's profile, portfolio, and personnel. Even Russell Train, the Republican former EPA head under Nixon and Ford, acknowledged that Gorsuch's leadership seemed intent on destroying the agency.[16]

For Gorsuch, the EPA was an important contributor to the Reagan administration's efforts to promote economic development. It was not an activist watchdog agency. Among critics, Gorsuch was cut from the same ideological cloth as Watt: eager to exploit resources and dismissive of environmental hazards. Her single-mindedness rubbed many in Washington the wrong way. "She came in like a whirlwind, itching to shake up the agency," one disgruntled former EPA official told the *Wall Street Journal*. "Now she's out there trying to test the political winds to see what's possible." Her young staff, equally idealistic in their capacity to bring about rapid change, were described by one agency press officer as seeming "to be in way over their heads."[17] Exploratory efforts occasionally turned into blunders that required backtracking. One of Gorsuch's first attempts at preparing new environmental legislation consisted of rewriting (and crippling) the Clean Air Act. By all accounts her attempts to weaken the act went too far. Testifying before the House Subcommittee on Health and the Environment exploring Gorsuch's revisions, the pollster Louis Harris warned against gutting the act's authority. "Clean air happens to be one of the sacred cows of the American people," he reported on public attitudes.[18] Indeed, that applied to environmental pollution writ large. After attempting to reverse a ban on dumping drums of toxic liquids into landfills in 1982, the Reagan administration confessed surprise at the vociferous backlash.[19] Their ninety-day trial was curtailed after twenty-seven days. Americans wanted stricter controls over dumping, not regulatory relief. A Roper survey from September 1982 found that only 21 percent of those polled thought "environmental protection laws and regulations have gone too far." In contrast, 69 percent approved of the existing laws or thought they didn't go far enough. Surveys also showed Americans willing to sacrifice some economic growth for waste controls. A 1983 ABC-*Washington Post* poll, for example, found that 75 percent of Americans acknowledged that while compliance with antipollution laws cost business firms a considerable amount of money, those laws were worth the cost. The tide was swelling against deregulation. In September 1981, 45 percent of Americans agreed with the statement that "protecting the environment is so important that requirements and standards cannot be too high." In April 1983—little over a month after the Times Beach evacuation was announced and Gorsuch resigned as EPA head—58 percent of Americans shared this view.[20]

By 1983, the Reagan administration's environmental agenda was unraveling. Four different deregulatory initiatives were overturned in federal court because the EPA lacked either the authority or the scientific foundation to see them through. Disorder reigned: Gorsuch's agency personnel and priorities were reshuffled more frequently than a casino deck of cards. Her management style struggled to come to grips with the delicate balancing act of getting the agency to function in response to a still-growing pollution crisis while simultaneously gutting its budget. Career environmental experts were removed. Young conservative idealists were brought in. Few had any environmental experience. Even the business world rebelled. "What was once a robust, dynamic entity has shrivelled to a gray shadow of its former self, wracked by internal dissension, run by people with little expertise in environmental issues, and dogged by a paranoia that has virtually brought it to a standstill," intoned the probusiness *Automotive News*.[21] The chemical industry was also up in arms. Where Reagan's deregulation had afforded them some business-friendly freedoms, the federal outsourcing of environmental regulation to the states posed a whole new series of problems. Instead of one regulatory agency, the chemical industry would have to adhere to as many as fifty different requirements on how to manufacture, sell, and transport their products. Worrying about how to satisfy different states with waste disposal was a whole different headache. New municipal and state "right to know" laws required the industry to account for all their hazardous wastes. Every drum, tanker, and pipeline required explicit disclosure statements and manifests. In the absence of EPA oversight, there was no guarantee that there would be any consistency. David F. Zoll, general counsel for the American Chemical Manufacturers Association, lamented that "some states require container labelling while others require posting of a hazardous substance list or safety data sheets."[22] Moving hazardous chemicals and waste between states would become laborious and expensive.

Amid ever louder charges of Gorsuch's incompetence from all corners, new investigations revealed gross mismanagement of Superfund budgets. Over its first two years, Superfund had cleaned up only two sites. Alleged sweetheart deals, politically motivated slowdowns, and destroyed documents galvanized at least six congressional panels to investigate. Rita Lavelle, Gorsuch's assistant administrator in charge of solid waste and emergency response, was fired and under investigation for gross misuse of Superfund money pertaining to what the media called Sewergate. The moniker, coined by James Howard, a New Jersey Democrat in the House of Representatives, referred to the improper shredding of documents that indicated sweetheart deals between environmental polluters friendly to the White House and Superfund cleanups. This was in special reference to the Stringfellow Acid Pits, the "Love Canal of the West," outside Riverside, California. Further allegations charged that the EPA was ordered to delay their action so that Democratic Governor Jerry Brown could not take any credit for the remediation.[23] Gorsuch was held in contempt of Congress in December 1982 for refusing to turn over subpoenaed Superfund documents. Ostracized and deemed a liability by the White House, she resigned in early 1983.[24]

* * *

Throughout the 1970s, legislative approaches to environmental regulation oscillated between the proactive and the reactive. Discussing environmental policymaking in the 1960s and 1970s, the historian Samuel P. Hays describes "an intense debate between those who argued that regulatory action should proceed once tendencies in evidence indicated 'reasonable anticipation of harm' and those who argued that it should wait until 'conclusive proof of harm' had been established."[25] If hazards were present, waiting for certainty guaranteed greater health risks. Further, waiting for certainty would exacerbate local fears, as they would at Love Canal. But as the American economy faltered in the middle 1970s, the industrial sector begged Washington for a freer hand. New and aggressive environmental laws limited their growth and frustrated the economy, they argued. As the economy continued to stumble, the Republican challenge to the Carter administration was one that argued for a more reactive response to environmental hazards: It was preferable to unshackle business from expensive and unnecessary restrictions. Reagan's unflappable calm and charisma appealed to

Americans. His intonation—that in the absence of conclusive harm, why worry?—made ample sense as the country stagflated in the throes of recession. His probusiness approach to the environment—his appointment of Gorsuch, Watt, and others—was consistent with his campaign promises, and consistent with the viewpoint that the environmental policies of the 1970s had gone too far and had overworried Americans. But in order to see those campaign promises through, Reagan needed to cut budgets and red tape. And in this, the Reagan administration went too far, too quickly. In June 1981, Gorsuch suspended a series of EPA regulations, including the requirement that hazardous waste facilities carry liability insurance.[26] The real source of toxic fear in the 1980s came with the discovery that the federal environmental safety net was in jeopardy. The paradox of American environmental politics is that Americans dislike regulatory oversight until it isn't there. Waiting for conclusive proof of harm frayed nerves.

This lesson echoed loud and clear in the growing fears surrounding what appeared to be an epidemic of midnight dumping through the 1970s. As stricter environmental controls were introduced and enforced by the fledgling EPA, it remained unclear whether the wave of new environmental regulations was equipped to effectively address the mounting worries—public and political—over toxic waste disposal, both controlled and illegal. In 1979, when public concern about illegal dumping was mounting, cartoonist Dana Fradon's *New Yorker* illustration of a toxic chemical waste truck captured the essence of how environmental policy seemed to address the hazardous waste problem. The truck drivers reassured a woman walking her dog that "We're not dumping it anywhere, Ma'am. We're just going to keep driving it around." To many, it seemed as though the midnight dumping was the order of the day because environmental laws were lax or nonexistent. While Fradon's cartoon captured the essence of popular imagination, there was more to the policy response than haplessly moving toxic waste from one place to another.

According to the 1976 Resource Conservation and Recovery Act (RCRA), it should have been possible to trace the biography of the chemicals being carted around in Fradon's cartoon, from their creation to their final resting place. As a means of confronting midnight dumping, the EPA was charged with developing manifests to identify, list, and track hazardous wastes throughout their lifespan. RCRA also sought to establish more stringent regulations for landfills, and created the Office of Solid Waste

Management Programs within the EPA. The EPA was also authorized to litigate against sites that they deemed to be "imminent hazards" and to compel industry to pay for their remediation.[27] RCRA's implementation was painfully slow. And its interest in chemicals was decidedly unimaginative. It seemed more intent on addressing known hazards than trying to develop new waste control measures. The manifests were designed to ensure that haulers delivered all their wastes to appropriate dump sites. While disposal costs remained high, the manifests sought to discourage roadside dumping as a means of saving money. Further, landfills needed to be lined with clay and monitored for leachate.[28] At the same time, RCRA made no accommodations for closed or inactive dump sites. Those left unmonitored typically constituted the higher risk.

If RCRA was designed to respond to existing problems, the Toxic Substances Control Act (TSCA) was explicitly preventive. The 1976 act, signed into law by Gerald Ford on October 11, ten days before RCRA, acknowledged that prevention of toxic disasters was preferable to cleaning up after them. It provided the EPA with a mandate to administer new and existing chemicals. There was little information on many of the chemicals already in production. Indeed, EPA administrator Russell E. Train outlined the need for TSCA precisely within the context of American toxic fears. "Most Americans," he told an audience at the National Press Club in February 1976, "had no idea that, without their knowledge or consent, they were often engaging in a grim game of chemical roulette whose result they would not know until many years later. It is time we put chemicals to the test, not people. It is time we gave the people of this country some reason to believe that, every time they breathe or eat or drink or touch they are not taking their life into their own hands."[29] Here was the state—chastened—responding to a growing sense that Americans were not safe.

TSCA was a sensible measure, designed with good intent. Chemicals should be treated with care and their hazards be understood before the public was exposed to them. However, pragmatics and logistics limited its ability to protect Americans. Where the EPA had hoped to conduct comprehensive screening of new chemicals before they were marketed, the chemical industry balked and pushed Congress toward a less strenuous process of "premarket notification." Manufacturers were still required to notify the EPA that they intended to introduce a new chemical. But the burden of proof rested with the agency, not with industry. The burden was also really more of a mountain. In 1976, more than sixty thousand chemicals were already in production in the United States. Under TSCA, they were grandfathered into safe status unless new risks were identified.[30] Testing each in the wake of TSCA was an impossibility. Which is to say that no studies were conducted to determine the safety of these products. But the rapid expansion of the chemical industry meant that even many new chemicals did not receive sufficient scrutiny.

Neither RCRA or TSCA relieved the mounting pollution crisis that gripped American fears. A series of high-profile cases involving accidental spills and illegal disposal sites rattled the nation in the late 1970s and early 1980s. The Velsicol Company's wastes in Hardeman County, Love Canal outside Buffalo, the Valley of the Drums, just south of Louisville, Kentucky, California's Stringfellow Acid Pits all inspired further, more stringent legislation. After the ubiquity of midnight dumping and countless other pollution crises with lower national profiles, the country was primed for more and better environmental regulation. In the immediate aftermath of the Love Canal evacuation and the Elizabeth explosion, an ABC News–Harris poll reported that almost 93.6 percent of Americans wanted much stricter federal standards on toxic waste dumping.[31] Five years later, a September 1985 poll found that 79 percent of Americans still believed that "not enough" had been done to remediate toxic waste sites. Of respondents, 64 percent also indicated that they would be "willing to pay higher state and local taxes to fund [local] cleanup programs."[32] Americans wanted clean and safe neighborhoods.

* * *

Gorsuch's departure from the EPA marked a major shift in environmental activity in the Reagan administration. Returning to the head of the EPA was William Ruckelshaus, who had served as the agency's first administrator after its creation in 1970, resigning in 1973 after refusing to follow Richard Nixon's order to fire the independent special prosecutor tasked with investigating the president's role in the Watergate scandal. Ruckelshaus faced two parallel rebuilding challenges during his second tenure at the head of the EPA. The first was to rebuild the gutted agency: rearticulating its mission and hiring responsible managers to oversee its activities. The second rebuilding project involved regaining public confidence. In a relatively short period, Ruckelshaus revived the Superfund program and set the

EPA's agenda in moving toward mitigating hazards posed by acid rain. In an oral history conducted in 1993, Ruckelshaus related the mood swing at the EPA "from despair to jubilation" after his return: "The people felt their long nightmare was over, and it *was* a nightmare."[33]

But back to business was easier said than done. Public and media scrutiny and distrust of anything associated with the environment and the Reagan administration had cut deep. Nevertheless, during his brief tenure—he retired in January 1985, at the beginning of Reagan's second term in office—Ruckelshaus oversaw the further implementation of risk assessment principles as a key pillar of the EPA's practice. Ruckelshaus embraced this technocratic turn as a pathway toward a less fearful environmental future. He wrote in 1991, "We are now in a troubled and emotional period for pollution control; many communities are gripped by something approaching panic, and the public discussion is dominated by personalities rather than substance. . . . I believe that part of the solution to our distress lies with the idea that disciplined minds can grapple with ignorance and sometimes win: the idea of science."[34]

In spite of a return to relative normalcy in the EPA's operations—albeit with a greatly diminished budget—the damage was largely already done during Gorsuch's time in charge. Part of the neoliberal playbook is to let the market dictate prices; there is a political corollary to this kind of art of the deal, whereby liberal spending and conservative cuts overreach and are corrected in response to legal interventions and/or public outcry and/or elections. But the precedents are set in these overreaches, especially in the context of cuts to personnel and the operating budget. It is easier to cut red tape than it is to stick it back together again. The radical cuts that took place during the first years of the Reagan administration caused irreparable changes to the EPA's operation and mission.

* * *

If Americans were actually drowning in chemical contamination, as *Time* magazine averred, the desire for clean communities was hardly enough. Along with the control legislation, the end of the 1970s witnessed a deliberate effort to rehabilitate polluted places. The Comprehensive Environmental Response, Compensation, and Liability Act—CERCLA or Superfund—was enacted on December 11, 1980. It was one of the last laws introduced by the outgoing Carter administration, and it marked a sea change in American environmental policy. Throughout his presidency, Carter's focus had been on energy conservation. Until Superfund, toxic legislation had taken a backseat. Where TSCA and RCRA were the best legislation possible at the time, but beholden to limited funds, authority, and industrial influences, CERCLA recognized the severity of the pollution crisis and meant to address it. Whereas RCRA seemed intent on responding only to existing problems, CERCLA joined TSCA in acknowledging a greater fluidity and uncertainty surrounding the pollution crisis. The act provided the EPA's Office of Emergency and Remedial Response the authority to intervene and arrest the spread of pollutants or contaminants that pose a threat to human health or the environment. The act also constituted a trust fund of $1.6 billion for five years to assist in the repair of damaged substances when it was impossible to find a responsible party. This constituted emergency relief in the short term, but there was a catch. The 1980 legislation required that states contribute 10 percent of the costs for cleaning up private property, and 50 percent of the costs for public lands. In 1983, only eight states had special budgets assigned to such environmental remediation. In the absence of discretionary funds for severe disasters, the other forty-two were hard-pressed to qualify for federal cleanup money and support.[35] Its budget was designed to clean up contaminated sites first and impose fines on polluters later. The EPA was given the license to sue responsible parties for up to three times the cleanup cost.

Superfund was the right bill, probably at the wrong time. The benefit of hindsight says that the right time for a comprehensive environmental remediation bill was back when *Time*'s Commoner cover offered Americans a choice. By 1980, environmental officials were out of their depth, and that did little to ease public anxieties. "We are producing many more chemicals than we were 10 or 20 or 30 years ago and the population is larger now so there is more exposure," a Council on Environmental Quality official admitted to the *Los Angeles Times* in 1979. "We don't know a lot about most of these chemicals. What is worse, sometimes it takes years for the effect of a chemical to show up in humans so we are just starting to reap the horrors of things that happened 20 or 30 years ago."[36] As a more proactive tool, Superfund might have enjoyed even more federal and popular support. As a result, it was clearly a reaction to a problem that had spiraled out of control. Where the 1970s witnessed a significant amount of impressive environmental legislation, each new act was met with an almost Sisyphean discovery of new depths to the environmental crisis. In this respect, Superfund was unquestionably reactionary as a piece of legislation. As House and Senate committees deliberated on how to respond to the dangers posed by toxic waste, journalists referred to Love Canal as inspiration for the legislation. Bipartisan support for the bill appreciated the necessity to act in cases of acute environmental contamination where no one would claim responsibility for the pollution.

This had been the case in Kentucky, in the euphemistically named Valley of the Drums. Beginning in the 1960s, A. L. Taylor ran a small-scale waste disposal operation with his dump truck. He collected liquid waste, no questions asked, from companies all over Kentucky. He piled the barrels all over his seventeen-acre field in Bullitt County, about thirty miles south of Louisville. Unmarked barrels, "rusted, dented, buckled, or riddled with gunshot holes," sprawled across the property. Thousands of them. It was a graveyard of toxic chemical waste, and a curious spin on William Carracino's cheap solution to an expensive problem: here, at least, Taylor was maybe less cynical in depositing the drums on his own land. State authorities charged Taylor with a number of pollution violations in the middle 1970s. But when he died in 1978, the drums were left unattended. Fines and violations and court orders meant little. Wilson Creek flowed through the property on its way to the Ohio River. It was so contaminated that a water quality engineer refused to test the creek since the samples hardly contained any water.[37] A cleanup was necessary, but in the absence of a culpable party, who was responsible? Prior to 1980, the EPA could distribute discretionary funds to support state initiatives, but there was never enough money to go around. Superfund was the solution. Indeed, the Valley of the Drums marked the first success of the new legislation. In 1981, the site was cleared of some four thousand barrels of the most toxic waste.

But timing. By the time that the Carter administration pushed Superfund through Congress, the act was inherited by a country submerged in chemical hazards that was inheriting a new administration that was overtly hostile to environmental issues. A further problem with Superfund stemmed from the popular assumption that environmental remediation was an unproblematic matter: A site was dirty, experts in hazmat suits were sent in, and they cleaned it. The same generalizations that made the availability heuristic such a powerful vehicle in dispersing fear limited Superfund's capacity to treat priority sites. The challenges posed by the Atlas

Asbestos Mine cleanup in Fresno County, California, for example, were different than those confronting the EPA at the Seymour Recycling Corp. waste site in Seymour, Indiana. Combined with administrators reluctant to publicly acknowledge the severity of the pollution problem, the escalating costs and complexities that contaminated sites represented turned into an economic, political, and cultural nightmare. In 1986, in tacit acknowledgment of the scale of environmental pollution, CERCLA was amended by the Superfund Amendments and Reauthorization Act (SARA), which provided a further five years of funding, this time to the tune of $8.5 billion.[38] The General Accounting Office anticipated that more expenditures were likely necessary. "We've learned that these sites are more complicated than anticipated," Superfund Deputy Director Walter Kovalick Jr. told the *Chicago Tribune* in October 1986. "Seventy-five percent of them have some kind of ground-water contamination problems."[39]

* * *

To residents of contaminated communities, this was not a revelation. The difficulties associated with determining hazard had delayed action and frayed nerves in numerous instances. Removing toxic substances was no simple engineering feat, akin to running a vacuum cleaner through an empty room, or dusting the corners. Chemical contaminants rarely sat on the surface. They infiltrated ground, water, and bodies: hard-to-reach places. But the admission that solving the pollution crisis was nearly impossible, especially against the weight of new disasters manifesting themselves faster than old ones could be addressed, was disheartening. The original CERCLA directives tasked the EPA with keeping a National Priorities List of sites across the country in need of remedial action due to the presence of hazardous substances. This inventory of hazardous sites was a matter of public record, based on a scoring system to determine the level of risk at various sites. The preliminary Interim Priorities List, published on October 23, 1981, provided 115 sites as candidates for Superfund action. The following year, an additional 45 sites were included on an Expanded Eligibility List. Much as the Gorsuch EPA had been slow to move on remediation, her office had also been reluctant to add new sites to the list. At a hearing of the Senate Environment and Public Works Committee shortly after Gorsuch's resignation, surviving senior EPA officials indicated that this was consistent with Gorsuch's "implicit policy to curtail" Superfund progress. "There were policies to slow down the expenditure of money" and deny approval for new candidate sites to be added to the priority list in the absence of a discernible "body count."[40] At the time of Gorsuch's resignation, there were 419 sites on the National Priorities List. Only six sites had been deleted from the list.

Conspiracies aside, though, another challenge to remedial action was the exorbitant cost. If venting, dumping, and discharging chemical waste did not inhibit industrial profit margins, the cost of cleaning up all of America's despoiled environments was immeasurable. Even after Superfund was created, its budget could not hope to stay on top of all the sites that required cleanups, not to mention the continuing discovery of new sources of contamination.

And one of these "remediated" sites wasn't even cleaned up. In September 1985 heavy rains from Hurricane Gloria precipitated another toxic waste spill from the Butler Tunnel into the Susquehanna River near Pittston, Pennsylvania. A hundred thousand gallons of "extremely toxic waste" sludged out of the tunnel and into the river. Before the spill, the Butler Tunnel enjoyed the distinction of being one of a very few Superfund success stories. After the EPA claimed the site cleaned in 1982, it was deleted from the 1984 National Priorities List. Monitors were removed from the tunnel's mouth, leaving the 1985 spill to be detected not by environmental officials but by citizens living downstream who noticed the odor. In the aftermath of the spill Representative James J. Florio (D-N.J.) felt compelled to open subcommittee proceedings with the frustrated question, "How clean is clean?" Florio noted that no Superfund remedial work had ever been conducted on the Butler Tunnel to account for its being removed from the National Priorities List.[41]

The story behind the removal is instructive in highlighting the challenges associated with cleaning contaminated sites. In a February 1982 letter to Walter Lee, who oversaw Superfund compliance at the EPA, Michael Steiner of the Pennsylvania Department of Environmental Resources claimed that after the emergency actions in the immediate wake of the 1979 spill, "no remedial action is warranted *at present*." By December the Butler Tunnel was removed from the National Priorities List and labeled as a site whose problem had been resolved. The letter concluded, however, that "due to the complex and dynamic nature of the contaminated substrate and ground waters, it is not impossible that future discharges may occur at this site which may require appropriate emergency/remedial responses on the part of EPA/DER." It remained, however, another "ticking time bomb." While the Department of Environmental Resources acknowledged that the risk of pollution persisted—and it took a hurricane to initiate the spill—one needed to read between the lines a little to understand the state's motivations. The letter's final sentence stated that "it would not be prudent to take any action at this time *which would preclude future responses or make them more difficult to initiate/implement.*"[42] While the subcommittee hearing—and the public—seemed to think that the EPA's remediation of the Butler Tunnel was tasked with removing the toxic waste in the mine, the Department of Environmental Resources seemed to realize that no such work would likely happen. Any limited work conducted in 1982 would hardly resolve the problem.

This was small consolation to government authorities and residents living downstream in 1985. Testifying on behalf of the Danville Water Department, Tom Graham described the spill's impact in Danville, roughly sixty miles downriver. Because of advance warning that the sludge was working its way toward them, the Danville Water Department shut its intakes from the Susquehanna River. In so doing, they reduced their risk of exposure from the water-borne toxic waste, but narrowly avoided catastrophic water shortages to medical centers, industries, and businesses. "The most immediate and long-term effect of the spill can be defined in the word 'apprehension,'" Graham asserted. "The people of Danville are once again reminded that their drinking water comes from the suspect north branch of the Susquehanna. Butler mine serves to reinforce their belief or their misbelief that the Susquehanna is not a viable source for drinking water."[43] Joseph Cosgrove, an attorney representing Pittston in the hearing, added further rhetorical flourish. "Our people are sincere and trusting," he told the committee. "They take their patriotism seriously. If Washington said it, we were at least cordial enough to accept it and would demand strict proof to the contrary." Proof to the contrary, he continued, was the sludge that Hurricane Gloria had released from the Butler Tunnel. "Now . . . that trust has turned to anger and to fear, a fear for the safety and conditions of our families, our friends, our children, and the very existence of our community." Cosgrove, likely speaking for many communities that had faced similar toxic disasters, noted the changed tenor in town: "For the past few weeks, the usual small talk of passersby has turned from sports and the like to the deep-seated questions about 'that stinking hole.' The questions are quite solemn: Who lied to us? Will they clean it this time? Are we another Love Canal? How safe is it for our children?"[44]

This second spill at Butler Tunnel came during a particularly tense showdown over the future of the Superfund Act and budget. House Representative Bob Edgar, a Democrat from Pennsylvania, articulated a disparity between the concerns and intentions of EPA staff on the ground—and in regional offices—and their managers in the Washington office. "[They] are uneasy about the decisions being made in Washington," he told the subcommittee hearing. "They are uncomfortable that the administration fought to avoid reauthorizing Superfund when the House passed a tough Superfund bill last year. They are not happy that [EPA Administrator] Lee Thomas has declared a slowdown in EPA cleanup actions until the bill is passed this year." More tellingly, Edgar continued, "[The EPA regional staff's] reaction is the same as so many citizens I talk to who are afraid of the toxic wastes in their water, air and their soil."[45] Slowing down EPA cleanup operations worked on a curious rationale of reducing annual expenses even if it intensified the sense of urgency felt at many sites. Further, reports in 1984 suggested that the Butler Tunnel wasn't the only site whose cleanup was left wanting. Thousands of tons of contaminated soil from the Velsicol plant on the Pine River in Michigan were simply dumped at another Velsicol site, also on the National Priorities List. Indeed, three of the original six remediation projects were deemed inadequate, and two of the sites that were cleaned up probably shouldn't have been on the priority list in the first place, according to a National Campaign Against Toxic Hazards study.[46]

* * *

There were other instances, too, that struck at the pivot between government negligence and the nature of wicked problems posed by chemical pollution. Even if rehabilitating the Butler Tunnel was unfeasible, and calling it repaired posed dubious semantic questions, the EPA readily acknowledged that sometimes a thorough remediation project wasn't possible. One such instance came from Superfund analyses of how to remove Kepone from the James River.[47] Kepone was the brand name for chlordecone, a carcinogenic insecticide patented by the Allied Chemical Company in the 1950s that proved effective in killing roaches and fire ants. The Life Science Products factory in Hopewell, Virginia—the self-proclaimed "Chemical Capital of the South"—was the sole Kepone producer when it attracted nationwide media attention in the mid-1970s after many of its workers and their family members showed signs of poisoning. Subsequent reports and court proceedings indicated that OSHA regulations were blatantly ignored. Working conditions "might have shocked Charles Dickens." Employees, without safety equipment, were "virtually swimming in the stuff."[48] Some workers dismissed the early warning signs of involuntary twitches and tremors. But after a suite of hospitalizations due to more serious symptoms, including liver damage and slurring speech, the factory shut down at the end of July 1975.[49] After operations had ceased, more in-depth investigations discovered Kepone in the James River, which ran adjacent to the plant. Kepone was subsequently found in the riverbed sediment from Hopewell all the way down to Chesapeake Bay. Governor Miles Godwin imposed fishing bans along the river. Popular seafood restaurants in town closed their doors. To allay consumer worries, local grocery stores advertised that their fish came from out of state.

Ten years later, in 1985, the James River remained highly contaminated. Fishing bans remained in place. Cleanup costs were estimated at a colossal $2 billion, and the techniques available could not ensure a safe and tidy resolution. Letting the Kepone sit in the river sediment appeared the safer and more viable option to many experts. Whereas Kepone was fat soluble, it remained insoluble in water, meaning it was relatively benign at the bottom of the river, even if it wasn't breaking down. Agitating the riverbed in a cleanup risked exacerbating Kepone's threat. To some, however, the more passive option was another ticking time bomb, "a sleeping monster."[50] A storm like Hurricane Gloria—which had disturbed the waste in Pennsylvania's Butler Tunnel the month before—or flooding as occurred on the Merrimac River—which precipitated the 1983 evacuation of Times Beach—could stir up the river sediment, unsettling the Kepone and reviving the hazard. Tropical Storm Agnes had blown through the region in 1972. So while it was fiscally prudent—even necessary—to let sleeping dogs lie, local residents worried about an angry dog's potential—inevitable—waking.

Not every case of chemical exposure involved the irresponsible dumping of waste, of course. In some instances, plant failures emitted various toxins into surrounding air-, water-, and landscapes. The most famous of these occurred outside the United States: the Chernobyl nuclear power plant meltdown in April 1986 and the methyl isocyanate release from Union Carbide's plant in Bhopal, India, in December 1984. But if the most devastating disasters happened elsewhere, luck was certainly involved. Just over two weeks before Bhopal, a near miss occurred in the United States, when on November 15 thirty gallons of methyl isocyanate were spilled at the FMC Corp. pesticide plant in Middleport, New York. Nine children and a teacher at a nearby elementary school complained of eye irritation. Another Union Carbide toxic gas leak—this time in Institute, West Virginia, an unincorporated, African American community—in August 1985 reinforced the growing sentiment that the company was not a good neighbor.

For Union Carbide, the Institute leak was additional bad press that magnified its trespasses at Bhopal: The availability heuristic loomed large in the media reports. "Last Sunday's leak raised echoes of Bhopal in our minds," one local asserted a week later.[51] Bhopal had been on the minds of many members of the community since the spill several months before; concerns about the plant's safety and the surrounding population's health had been a regular source of worry since the tragedy in India.[52] Union Carbide was producing the same methyl isocyanate in Institute—it had also been the point of origin for the materials spilled in Middleport the previous November—and the chemical cloud that escaped the factory came from that production. Though the company insisted that the vented gas was not methyl isocyanate but rather the less toxic aldicarb, the fact that aldicarb was a derivative of the chemical that had sickened and killed two thousand people in India just nine months earlier did little to assuage public worries. To make matters worse, the plant had closed for five months after the Bhopal disaster. The company spent $5 million to upgrade the plant and its safety mechanisms to avoid an American repeat of Bhopal. But when a gasket on a five-hundred-gallon tank failed on August 11 nearby residents smelled the chemical fumes long before the plant's siren gave warning.[53] Some residents got into their cars and left town. Twenty-eight people were admitted to the hospital. Iris Bell, who lived outside Institute, worried that the area was no longer safe: "This stuff makes my head ache and my skin itch. . . . It also makes me really scared about how they let these things out. I guess it means we all have to move out of here if we want to be safe."[54] Bell wasn't alone. The following weekend four hundred residents gathered in the historically Black West Virginia State College auditorium, in the shadow of the Union Carbide plant, to demand more information about the leak and the company's practices. An emotional Cheryl Whiteside told several company officials in attendance, "I'm two months pregnant. . . . I don't want to find out seven months from now that my baby is going to be deformed."[55]

Residents weren't the only ones wanting answers from Union Carbide. West Virginia Senator Robert C. Byrd and EPA Administrator Lee Thomas led a group of top federal health and environmental officials to Institute to tour the Union Carbide plant. As Byrd promised congressional "scrutiny of this whole situation that will be more intense than before," Thomas talked candidly about the company's "credibility gap."[56] That the leak should have happened at all was foremost among the officials' concerns, especially after the new safety measures had so recently been incorporated; they also pointed to the emergency response failure, where local authorities were not notified of the leak until twenty minutes after it had started. The public warning siren was not sounded for another fifteen minutes after that.

* * *

Answers and chemical information: both were in short supply. Lessons were learned through the first half of the decade, though. If the RCRA, TSCA, and CERCLA constituted the generation of toxic legislation in the 1980s, by mid-decade new developments were responding to the growth of concerns over chemical pollution. Amendments to Superfund, upping its budget and expanding its National Priorities List, marked tacit acknowledgment that environmental problems were not going away. Similarly, prompted by the Union Carbide accident in Institute and further public demand, Congress established the Toxics Release Inventory under the Emergency Planning and Community Right-to-Know Act of 1986. The inventory was authored by New Jersey Senator Frank Lautenberg and inspired by the Bhopal disaster and based on a state register in New Jersey, which tried to muddle through the morass of hazardous materials in chemical plants and waste sites across the state. In the immediate aftermath of a disaster, the Toxics Release Inventory was designed to help emergency relief squads ascertain what dangers they were facing, as well as their quantity. The terror of the Elizabeth explosion, for example, came from the uncertainty of the hazards on-site.

The EPA was already drawing up an "acute hazards list" as part of a much more ambitious emergency and evacuation preparedness plan for chemical disasters, but the Toxics Release Inventory provided important public oversight that worked far better than anyone anticipated. In October 1985, David J. Sarokin and Warren R. Muir of INFORM, a Brooklyn-based environmental research organization, had proposed a national register for toxic waste in the *New York Times*. "Despite two decades of environmental regulation of toxic substances," Sarokin and Muir asserted, "government agencies still cannot answer basic questions about even the most common toxic chemicals used at industrial plants throughout the United States." They reasoned that "the public deserves to know the risks it faces from chemicals."[57] In some respects, it was another feature of environmental right-to-know measures that stretched back to the 1960s. More information accessible to the public was good. Especially since the public was intent on using the information. Indeed, the Toxics Inventory Release became a critically important tool in grassroots organizing that did arguably more for controlling and reducing environmental pollution than most other policy initiatives. It served as a vital education tool and mobilized community groups in collaborating with and opposing local industries. It enabled and encouraged local pressure on polluting industries and fostered a new brand of environmental activism. Environmental organizations large and small, from all over the country, drew on inventory data for one reason or another and used it to powerful effect in media campaigns and legal battles. It also let local organizers hold the EPA's feet to the fire if government was slow to act. Because of this, it fostered more voluntary pollution reductions from companies. The inventory was subsequently expanded in 1990 in the Pollution Prevention Act. In 1987, the inventory counted three hundred chemicals on its list. That number had more than doubled by the beginning of the twenty-first century.[58]

* * *

While its primary purpose was to collect and share data on specific hazards, the Toxics Release Inventory is also an archive—an artifact—of the relationship between exposure and shared histories of living in a chemical world. It comes at the history of unmitigated industrial growth along a different but parallel track to toxic fear, but both acknowledge a chastened interpretation of the consequences derived from an unquestioning confidence in technological development. The cultural theorist Paul Virilio has asserted that every new technology also introduces the accident of that technology. "To invent the sailing ship or steamer is to invent the shipwreck."[59]

The chemical industry was the steamship. It emerged in the nineteenth century, expanded during the first half of the twentieth, and grew exponentially into a juggernaut during and after World War II; its products were the engine of a new economy and a new environmental catastrophe. As Kai Erikson observed in a *New York Times* editorial in 1980, its products were "the best-built products of our shoddy age, tough chains of molecules that will not easily degrade or break down."[60] Their durability also constituted their accident: (1) because they were cheaper to produce and consume, American society became dependent on their manufacture and widespread use; and (2) because they resisted bacterial decay, these synthetic materials—which didn't exist before they were created in laboratories—persisted. They became environmental pollutants, present in landscapes all over the world. Their persistence was only a part of the accident; a growing feature of the post–World War II environmental history has been the growing understanding of the extent to which these same chemicals and their proliferation caused harm to human health. The public health scholar Ken Geiser summarized the dilemma effectively: "We rely on a host of chemicals that are central to our economy but could be dangerous to our health."[61] There is a third step to Virilio's history of technology. "The gradual spread of catastrophic events," Virilio noted, "not only affects the reality of the moment but causes anxiety and anguish for generations to come."[62] Chemical exposure, the new accident, introduced the fear of potential harm and a host of symptoms. That third step is not unique to the American 1980s, nor was it invented there, but it reached a new crescendo as new discoveries of chemical exposure and concomitant harm captured the frightened attention of mainstream media consumers.

CHAPTER FIVE

Self-Awareness Raised to a Higher Level

Fear is self-awareness raised to a higher level.
—Don DeLillo, *White Noise*

That pollution produced widespread psychosocial effects was a discovery of the 1980s. Indeed, the scientific investigation of pollution as a stimulus for fear was, the physician Henry Vyner asserted, "more or less forced upon us by several major accidents involving invisible environmental contaminants."[1] The uncertainties various environmental pollutions produced shaped the American cultural landscape more vociferously than I think environmental history has appreciated. Indeed, where the preceding chapters and their case studies assert that toxic fear constituted an important part of the 1980s, the enduring significance of this phenomenon was grounded in the ways misplaced matter altered the social landscape. Chemophobia was not simply a product of lived experience and the aftershocks of the availability heuristic. Rather, fear was further mediated and cultivated through social institutions: politics, law, economics, and media, for example.[2] Changing insurance practices, legal precedents, and media reporting during the decade serve as clues or metrics through which tracking toxic fear historically becomes possible. Put another way, this chapter considers the ripple effect of social changes, spurred by an increasingly harrowing availability heuristic that painted the entire nation as one big toxic wasteland or ticking time bomb.

From the case studies that populated the previous chapters, some consistencies emerge. Poor dissemination of information and swirling contradictory facts were common features of the toxic fear landscape. As a result, a growing distrust of authorities contributed to individual and community feelings of insecurity and anxiety. Given the considerable media attention devoted to Three Mile Island, Love Canal, Times Beach, and other sites of contamination distress, distrust and anxiety from local residents became default responses to many of the smaller catastrophes over the course of the ensuing decade. One method of measuring toxic fear involves following the money. Insurance trends point to what Americans valued and feared and what protections and securities they sought for themselves and what they possessed. It is, perhaps, an unapologetically middle-class marker for fear, but chemical contamination in the 1980s altered the insurance landscape. Changes in insurance coverage prompted actuarial responses of the industry to consumers' desires. But in the case of pollution, insurers balked.

In 1980 the insurance industry defined a catastrophe as an event that caused $1 million in insured losses. The previous year, there had been fifty-four catastrophes in the United States, which resulted in more than $1.68 billion in insured losses. This was the highest amount claimed in a single year to that point, but 1980 was worse. In Washington State, Mount Saint Helens erupted; floods washed out parts of California and the Southwest; and an increased number of tornadoes ripped across the country. "It's like living in a disaster movie," a member of the Insurance Information Institute told the *New York Times*. Another trend, noted by insurance experts, was that "people seem more concerned about man-made disasters."[3] Indeed, the market for insurance surrounding gradual and sudden pollution events experienced a great deal of uncertainty throughout the 1980s as the insurance industry scrambled to respond to this growing demand for coverage. Few companies were even in the business of offering gradual pollution insurance. Fewer still wanted to provide it. Pollution damage to body and property constituted new ground for the insurance industry. It was reluctant to include this harm under its existing policies and sought to explicitly exclude pollution from new policies. Pollution insurance costs were prohibitive and becoming more restrictive. A National Association of Insurance Commissioners' industry report on environmental liabilities from 1986 reflected on the "severe market restrictions in pollution insurance availability. When it is available, it is very expensive and coverage and policy limits are often less than those available in the past." Much as demand for pollution coverage was growing, it remained a losing investment to the industry. "Insurance depends on the ability to spread risk," the report continued. "For pollution liability to be insurable, it must be both fortuitous and predictable. The existing environmental liability schemes combined with the present state of hazardous waste disposal technology leave serious doubts in insurers' minds about whether these conditions are met."[4] The underlying message was that the insurance industry saw no basis for trusting in sufficient environmental salubrity to counter the occasional contamination disaster; there were few greater condemnations of the state of the environment in the American 1980s. Local governments—counties, municipalities—also struggled to renew or acquire insurance protection for environmental exposures. In addition to their prohibitive cost, policies in many instances required expensive environmental assessments before they could be drafted. "Insurers believe the expectations of government, and consequently buyers, far exceeds the insurance industry's capacity to respond, even if it were so inclined," an insurance industry report concluded.[5] Pollution was too unpredictable for insurers.

Changes in environmental insurance corresponded neatly with the evolution of environmental consciousness in relation to disasters. Prior to the 1970s pollution disasters were listed under regular insurance plans as "accidents." They were uncommon occurrences that hardly registered in industry literature. Two oil spills changed that. The 1967 Torrey Canyon spill off the coast of England and the Santa Barbara spill in 1969 resulted in multiple massive claims that forced the insurance industry to rethink its approach to pollution disasters. Removed from the comprehensive general liability coverages, pollution became a niche policy offered by specialty insurers to protect against what they called gradual pollution incidents. But even these failed to keep pace with the chemical disasters that began in the 1970s and became a deluge in the 1980s. Love Canal and Times Beach (and Imperial, Missouri, and Globe, Arizona) warned that every sleepy township across the country could be vulnerable to past transgressions buried under its soils or leached into its waters. Indeed, the Times Beach buyout was still underway when newswires broke the story that in 1980 a 371-page federal report had listed hundreds of industrial sites across thirty-three states where dioxin could be present. Nobody, however, went looking for dioxin. Some states—Alabama, Colorado, Illinois, Indiana, Michigan, Minnesota, Mississippi, and West Virginia—claimed that their state laboratories were not equipped to test for dioxin. Others blamed tight budgets and/or competing priorities. John Mitchell, a Kansas state environmental scientist, explained that in 1980 "there wasn't a dioxin scare—they thought dioxin broke down in the soil."[6] But by 1983, there most certainly was a dioxin scare. Knowledge that dioxin was widespread and had been so for quite some time elicited further fears.

* * *

If insurance trends suggested an anticipatory kind of worry, evolving legal precedents pointed toward the growing impacts of toxic fear. During the 1980s, fear and psychological stress derived from exposure to toxic pollution also emerged as a part of the legal landscape in numerous tort cases and class action lawsuits. Compared with the flight elements in the mass evacuations at Love Canal and Times Beach, the law offered a rather explicit fight response to the fear that chemicals elicited. In many cases of toxic exposure, the first signs of contamination came from people exhibiting symptoms of illness; the cause or source remained a mystery. In others, such as at Three Mile Island, for example, the source of exposure was clear. The long-term implications, however, were less so. In a growing number of instances, that uncertainty provoked fear and stress. And the courts were listening.

In 1982, after the near-disaster at Three Mile Island, the U.S. Court of Appeals for the District of Columbia, which handled federal agencies, ruled that the Nuclear Regulatory Committee would need to carry out a new kind of environmental assessment on subsequent construction projects. The new assessment was designed to review the "psychological stress" felt by residents neighboring nuclear sites. "We cannot believe that the psychological aftermath of the March 1979 accident falls outside the broad scope of the National Environmental Protection Act," the majority opinion argued.[7] It was an unprecedented ruling, but it marked the spirit of the era. Into the 1980s, the most commonly observed negative health effect of the Three Mile Island accident was what physicians and public health experts referred to as "mental stress."[8]

In July 1980, as local residents sought damages in a class action suit, evidence of that psychological time bomb became ever more apparent. Citing psychological trauma as a major outcome of the reactor's malfunction became a key legal strategy. As one pamphlet from the Three Mile Island Alert group argued in 1980, "The accident is not over. Our lives are still in great danger. We face another spring knowing that our children may be irradiated when they go out to play. We do not know whether our air will be safe to breathe, our water safe to drink, our land safe to farm."[9] Further, as historian Natasha Zaretsky has pointed out, state health department researchers believed that "the accident's psychological reverberations were more measurable than its physical ones."[10] In court, Joyce Bourinski related that she had spent the first two days of the disaster living in the shadow of the plant. She also returned home a few times after the voluntary evacuation. Bourinski testified that she subsequently discovered—in April 1979—that she was pregnant. Assuming that she must have been in a very early stage of pregnancy during the scare, she and her husband Leonard (a devout Catholic) feared for the health of her fetus. She claimed they ultimately made the difficult decision to terminate the pregnancy. Bourinski told the court that the abortion spurred chronic gynecological difficulties. In addition to "anguish over the termination," Bourinski also worried about the long-term health effects on her existing children. Another plaintiff—Beverly Ann Gorman—also feared for her future health and that of her children. She testified that these concerns were a prevailing issue with her friends and neighbors. Tellingly, the class ruling found that the diversity of the psychological injuries made by claimants required individual defenses. There was no singular toxic fear, the court decided. But it also acknowledged that toxic fear could be a legitimate cause for damages.[11]

Subsequently, numerous cases recognized the merits of fear of toxins as a legitimate cause for seeking damages. Frequently the biggest challenge involved proving the source of the contaminant and demonstrating negligence on the part of the company that had made or disposed of it. But in other instances, the source was more easily identified. In the hands of tort prosecutors, the Occupational Safety and Health Act of 1970 was a powerful weapon that could be wielded to ensure worker well-being. During the 1970s, crusading lawyers, Ralph Nader and Victor Yannacone prominent among them, investigated and pushed the limits of the legislation. In 1980, the U.S. District Court for the Eastern District of New York certified Vietnam veterans, their families, and their survivors as potential plaintiffs in a class action suit against the manufacturers of Agent Orange. By 1981, twenty-five thousand asbestos-related suits had been filed in the United States. The total amount of the claims exceeded $100 billion. At the same time, more than one thousand suits were filed by the daughters of women treated with diethylstilbestrol (DES) in the 1950s because of their increased risk of cancer.[12]

An article in the *American Bar Association Journal* conveyed the potential stress the revolution in toxic tort law would impose on the insurance industry. "The goose that lays the golden egg may be killed because there is just not enough money to go around," complained William Bailey, a senior vice president at Commercial Union Insurance Co. Bailey was also the chairman of a new Task Force on Cumulative Trauma and Latent Injury and was unequivocal in his concern: "The [tort] system could well grind to a halt by 1984," he warned. "We had better start thinking about alternatives."[13] In a September 1982 article titled "Toxic Time Bombs" in *Newsweek*'s Business section, environmental lawyer Victor Yannacone intimated that the mortgaging of worker health in the interest of industrial gain was a debt that had come due. "Diseases arising from public and worker exposure to toxins like dioxin—and the ensuing litigation—have the disastrous potential of bankrupting many of America's major industries," he noted in the wake of Manville, a prominent asbestos company, filing for bankruptcy.[14] More was to come. Asbestos was only the "tip of the iceberg," according to Bailey.[15] "There are already claims for toxics like benzene and dichlorides. OSHA has a list of 200 toxic chemicals that could be problems to industrial workers."[16]

During the 1980s, toxic tort law evolved into a potent tool not just for industrial workers but also for individuals and communities exposed to chemical threats in their homes and neighborhoods. Above and beyond damages for devalued property or direct physical injury, a series of suits claimed damages for emotional distress and the cost of future medical surveillance. In 1983, a New Jersey jury awarded ninety-seven families in Jackson Township $17 million after deciding that the township had created a "dangerous condition" in their operation of a toxic waste landfill, which had contaminated the plaintiffs' water. Of the damages, $2 million were earmarked for emotional distress, and another $8 million for annual medical screenings to protect against future illness.[17]

The first breakthroughs for claiming a fear of cancer as a legitimate claim for damages, however, came in smaller civil actions. Between 1963 and 1980, the Firestone Tire & Rubber Company illegally disposed of a whole host of hazardous chemicals at the Crazy Horse dump, a Class II landfill located outside Salinas, California. Class II landfills prohibit toxic substances, but the company rationalized the dumping because of growing costs in manufacturing and the disposal of its hazardous waste. This was a corner-cutting strategy to improve dwindling profits. In the refuse from their tire manufacturing, Firestone unloaded considerable quantities of benzene, trichloroethene, and vinyl chloride, all known carcinogens. Toluene and chloroform were also found at the site and traced back to Firestone. In 1984, families neighboring the landfill—Frank and Shirley Potter and their neighbors Joe and Linda Plescia—detected these chemicals in their domestic water wells. The plaintiffs argued that even though they could show no direct signs of illness from the contamination, the prolonged nature of exposure had unquestionably enhanced their risk of developing cancer and other maladies. Because of cancer's long latency and complex origins, it was difficult to prove a causal link between a specific exposure and a subsequent cancer (many years after the fact). Fear of cancer, however, was more immediate and also a key sign of the times. The court found in favor of the plaintiffs. While it averred that it would be impossible to show sufficient certainty in causal connections between maladies and water contamination, it also noted that "plaintiffs will always fear, and reasonably so, that physical impairments they experience are the result of the well water and are the precursers [*sic*] of life-threatening disease. Their fears are not merely subjective but are corroborated by substantial medical and scientific opinion." Firestone appealed, arguing that such damages could be permitted only if the plaintiff could demonstrate a high probability of developing cancer, but the court disagreed. "The fear of cancer damages were awarded for respondents' fear that they will develop the disease, not for the chance that they will contract cancer at some subsequent time; *respondents fear cancer now. Their fear is certain, definite, and real.*"[18] Each of the four plaintiffs received $200,000.[19]

Potter v. Firestone Tire & Rubber Co. was a landmark decision. In effect, it acknowledged that a fear of cancer—in the absence of physical evidence of harm—constituted a legitimate claim where negligent behavior was present.[20] Whereas insurance trends and psychological impact studies suggested a degree of public anxiety over toxic pollutants in the 1980s, *Potter v. Firestone* established a legal precedent for as much. Toxic fear had a legal standing. And fear of cancer became a touchstone for further civil and class action proceedings against various chemical companies. *Sterling v. Velsicol* went to trial in the immediate aftermath of *Potter v. Firestone*. In many respects, the class action suit echoed many of the themes seen in the former case.[21] Beginning in 1964, the Velsicol Chemical Corporation had dumped waste from its Memphis pesticide plant in shallow pits south of Medon, Tennessee, in Hardeman County. Heptachlor, endrin, and dieldrin—chlorinated hydrocarbons, each of which would ultimately be banned as a carcinogen—were buried in barrels—hundreds of thousands in number—in clay and sand resting just above the local aquifer. In 1972, the state health commissioner stopped Velsicol from dumping in the area, for fear of creating undue health risks for the few local residents. By 1977, Steve Sterling, one of the residents adjacent to the dump site, noticed that his tap water smelled and tasted funny and had it tested. Around the same time, an uncanny number of local residents fell ill: kidney problems, respiratory ailments, chest pains. Nausea. Bathwater burned the skin. Sterling's well water contained chloroform, benzene, heptachlor, and chlordane in striking quantities. The carbon tetrachloride levels registered at 2,400 times the maximum daily exposure recommended by the National Institute for Occupational Safety and Health. Velsicol didn't challenge the assertion that their chemicals had entered into the wells. Its defense accepted responsibility in causing a public nuisance, but tried to divide the class by offering compensation to two of the five plaintiffs. The U.S. District Court for the Western District of Tennessee found in favor of the plaintiffs, to a total of $7.5 million.[22]

Under the weight of countless tort cases being brought forward and in the aftermath of the success in *Potter v. Firestone*, rules for reasonable fear of cancer started appearing state by state. In a 1986 Maine asbestos case, plaintiffs sought damages for their fear of contracting cancer in the future, which they described as real and present injuries. This fear, the court heard, "derives from the fact that asbestos is a known carcinogen, that they have had prolonged exposure to asbestos, and that their co-workers are dying at a higher than normal rate from asbestos-related cancer."[23] *In re Moorenovich* established the precedent in Maine law that fear of cancer was a recoverable damage.[24] Also in 1986, the Court of Appeals for the Fifth Circuit, applying Mississippi law, determined that former shipyard workers exposed to asbestos could recover damages due to their increased probability of getting cancer as well as the anxiety derived from that probability. In *Jackson v. Johns-Manville Sales Corp., et al.*, a Mississippi court effectively normalized fear of cancer as an expression of mental distress, which had long been grounds for seeking damages. In the absence of physical injury, the ruling awarded damages because the plaintiff had demonstrated that the defendant's misconduct had been "wanton, reckless."[25]

The evolution of toxic tort history over the course of the 1980s is more complicated than a small number of handpicked examples. Decisions, appeals, and analyses went back and forth and debated various aspects of how best to proceed with damages for fear of cancer, while trying to balance the ominous expansion of chemophobia and cancerphobia across society. Evaluating the *Potter v. Firestone* decision, one commentator wryly observed, "It would be a regrettable irony if in the rush to compensate the psychically injured we make it impossible to compensate those suffering of permanent and serious physical injuries."[26] This was, admittedly, new legal ground, but from *Potter v. Firestone* forward, there was a tacit recognition that toxic fear deserved attention. In that groundbreaking case, the court attempted to establish guidelines for acknowledging fear in the absence of physical injury. The court ruling stated that it required proof that "(1) the plaintiff was exposed to a toxic substance which threatens cancer, (2) the plaintiff's fear stems from a knowledge, corroborated by reliable medical or scientific opinion, that (3) it is more likely than not that the plaintiff will develop cancer in the future due to toxic exposure."[27]

There were limits, of course. As the Potter court admonished, "Nearly everybody is exposed to carcinogens which appear naturally in all types of foods. Yet ordinary consumption for such foods is not substantially likely to result in cancer. Nor is the knowledge of such consumption likely to result in a reasonable fear of cancer."[28] But this cut both ways. While the court was trying to establish parameters for fear of cancer, it also conceded that exposure to chemical hazards (especially those that had been illegally dumped) was grounds for complaint.

* * *

Was this a limited window? In 1993, *Daubert v. Merrell Dow Pharmaceuticals* paved the way for judges to exercise their authority and exclude expert evidence from toxic tort cases. The rationale involved curtailing the gratuitous overuse of expert witnesses, but this "gatekeeping" had a profound impact on plaintiffs presenting their case to a jury. After 1993, judges in civil toxic tort cases were much more likely to prevent scientific experts from presenting evidence to a jury. Fear of cancer claims frequently required medical and psychological testimony, and while expert evidence was still a central part of toxic torts, plaintiffs had to make a strong case for their experts' relevance in order to include their contributions. Over the course of the 1990s, the inclusion of expert witnesses in toxic tort cases decreased. So, too, did plaintiffs' success rates. *Daubert* removed a critical component from the plaintiffs' armory. The absence of expert witnesses on the record also crippled plaintiffs' cases in federal appellate courts. Just as emotional distress and a fear of future ailment had transformed the toxic legal landscape in the mid-1980s, *Daubert* appeared to shutter that strategy.[29]

The insurance industry had had to reckon with the cultural and political significance of toxic fear. Legal institutions followed suit. They were quick to find a scapegoat. Reflecting on the rising toxic fear in American society, the legal scholar E. Donald Elliott argued, "While I have no firm evidence to back up this speculation, I believe that one factor stimulating our collective chemophobia is press coverage of toxic tort cases and precautionary government regulatory actions." This was 1988. He continued, "Hardly a day goes by without headlines reporting either some new government action against a substance that supposedly causes cancer, or a multi-million dollar jury verdict in a toxic tort case. Is it any wonder, then, that much of our population is convinced that 'everything causes cancer'?" Toxic fear, he contended, was a product of the recent history of toxic torts, government policy, and the manner in which the media reported these.[30] He may have had a point. In sociological circles, the Thomas theorem has impressed the importance of perception for almost a century. "If men define situations as real," W. I. Thomas and D. S. Thomas wrote in 1928, "they are real in their consequences."[31] Truth is simply a matter of popular opinion? Well, not quite. Frequency and hyperbole in toxic reporting magnified the perceived dangers surrounding chemical pollution. And they crystallized the manner in which the availability heuristic contributed to Americans' dealings with hazards. Because chemical pollution appeared regularly in news stories on television and in print, the apparent risks seemed heightened to American viewers and readers. It didn't help that health and environmental agencies struggled to cope with these new hazards: This made for dramatic media stories. Media hyperbole mixed with growing familiarity to increase national fears. After the Environmental Defense Fund announced the multiple dioxin sites in Missouri in 1982, for example, the *St. Louis Post-Dispatch* ran a front-page story that began, "Dioxin, believed to be the most potent cancer-causing agent made by man, is more prevalent in Missouri's soil and roads 'than probably anywhere else in the world,' a federal health official says."[32] This, in the wake of Three Mile Island and Love Canal, served as a provocative reminder of the chemical risk.

Further, media storytelling invariably honed in on some stories at the expense of others. Love Canal, for example, was a catastrophe because the media made it so. "It wasn't the worst catastrophe in the country, or even in New York State, or even in Niagara County," declared former EPA official Hugh Kaufman. But it was a compelling story: "It was Love Canal, Hooker Chemical, and Niagara Falls, honeymoon capital of the world. Editors all over the country had orgasms. So Love Canal became catastrophic, not any of the other 10,000 hazardous dumps across America."[33] But thanks to the media—spurred by "The Killing Ground," and the compact and compelling narrative that evolved subsequently—Love Canal became a stand-in for other stories. Other chemical disasters—those in poorer and minority communities, especially—received less attention.[34]

But even national stories failed to connect the dots and acknowledge the translocal context and relevance of environmental crises. The media's role in the production of toxic fear was episodic rather than systematic.[35] The 1980 *Time* cover story, "The Poisoning of America," seemed content to simply declare that toxic waste was a national and widespread issue. The article pointed to tired 1970s tropes of "man's interventions in the natural order" through chemical compounds. Examples from more than a dozen states were invoked, but hardly connected. "The society that created the plethora of new chemicals that so enhanced human life must now use its scientific genius to make sure that those creations work safely for mankind," it concluded.[36]

Such media dialog came with its own risks. In 1979, the *Wall Street Journal* acknowledged the increase in journalistic interest in toxic chemicals. "The stories range from the tragic to the far-fetched," it observed, "but their number leaves little doubt that we're entering a time of stepped-up attacks of this sort on the products of our technological society." But, the editorial warned, it was easy to get caught up in hyperbole. The proliferation of stories constituted "a good preview of how easy it will be for public concern over these health issues to go wrong."[37] This was certainly the case in the ABC news special, "The Killing Ground," which portrayed the entire Niagara Falls region as "the scene of rampant miscarriages, nervous disorders, suicides and a host of other physical and mental ailments."[38] Thanks to their wide reach, the media and its coverage of chemical pollution played a critical role in raising public alarm and galvanizing fear.

Cable television and the advent of wall-to-wall news were also products of the 1980s media storm that exacerbated toxic fear. The Cable News Network (CNN) hit the airwaves on June 1, 1980, and ushered in a new way of consuming current events. The twenty-four-hour format made CNN a hub for "breaking news," but it also created a need for ever more dramatic storytelling to keep viewers' attention. The competition over eyeballs between cable networks like CNN and the existing "Big Three" (ABC, CBS, and NBC) helped transform the news from information to something more like entertainment.[39]

In many respects, the media was a prime mover in setting the agenda for the public consumption of news relating to toxic fears. As the sociologist Robert Stallings argues, "By selecting events to report, by interviewing and quoting experts who interpret those events, and by assembling and distributing news products, news organizations create an important component of public discourse."[40] Further, the fact that national stories—on the cable news networks, across the traditional channels, and in newspapers—tended to strive for some universal quality meant the new media culture concocted its own reading of the mainstream American experience. Mainstream America tended toward white stories, as evidenced by the disproportionate national attention to Love Canal and Times Beach when compared with illicit dumping in Chester, Pennsylvania, or with Emelle, Alabama, and its worries about the commercial landfill illegally sited in their community. This uneven attention had the deleterious effect of erasing the nonwhite experience. This control of the story is important and telling. As the sociologist Allan Mazur has outlined, increased media attention of a hazard "not only makes the risk salient, but also turns public opinion in a negative direction, causing increased opposition to risky technologies and heightened fear of technical hazards."[41] In effect, quantity of reporting can supersede quality of reporting as "the primary driver of audience negativism."[42] Which is to say, journalists, editors, and news and talk programs on television and radio were actors in shaping the culture of toxic fear in the 1980s.

* * *

The power of media to drive public concern was evident in the daminozide story in the later 1980s, where a slick media campaign followed by news reporting galvanized toxic fear. The popular story goes like this: In 1989, the

Natural Resources Defense Council published a damning report that raised alarm bells about the use of daminozide on apples. Daminozide, known commercially as Alar and sold by the Uniroyal Chemical Company, was a chemical growth regulator that helped to keep apples from falling before they were ripe. Earlier in the 1980s, the discovery of daminozide in apple juice and applesauce raised concerns about its effects on humans. In the 1989 report, the NRDC urged the EPA to ban daminozide and provided scientific evidence—using the EPA's own data—suggesting that the chemical was 240 times more carcinogenic than EPA standards allowed. The NRDC hired a publicity firm to help coordinate their efforts. The report was released at the end of February in conjunction with a mainstream media campaign highlighted by a prime segment on CBS's *60 Minutes*.[43] Actress Meryl Streep appeared in support of the ban on the *Today Show* and the *Phil Donahue Show*. Growing nationwide awareness and alarm ensued. The EPA was deluged with calls from frightened mothers.[44] According to one account, state troopers chased a school bus after a desperate call from a mother hoping to intercept and confiscate the apple in her child's lunch. School administrators in many districts removed and destroyed apples and apple products from children's lunch boxes. As one retrospective put it, "Apple markets rotted overnight."[45]

By June, the EPA decided to act, banning daminozide outright on the basis that "long-term exposure" posed "unacceptable risks to public health." After the ban, apple growers in Washington State filed a libel suit against the NRDC and CBS, claiming that the public outrage against daminozide was spurred by media propaganda capitalizing on toxic fears. Their $100 million lawsuit criticized the faulty science upon which the ban was based. Berkeley biochemist Bruce Ames castigated the NRDC's estimates, which he argued consisted of "worst case piled on worst case, and none of it is true."[46]

The story is muddier than this. The science and the publicity campaign do provoke some questions about their credibility, but it would be wrong to exonerate daminozide completely. Alar had already been on the EPA's radar as a possible carcinogen, and it had been moving slowly toward a ban since the mid-1980s after the discovery of daminozide in apple products raised concerns about its impact on humans. Nevertheless, it is clear that the public reaction forced the EPA into quicker action, not a more objective evaluation of the research. Passionate rather than dispassionate rhetoric sealed daminozide's fate. In many respects, the accuracy of claims on either side of the debate—and there is a worthwhile debate—is less interesting here than the fear that the campaign provoked. As effective as the anti-daminozide campaign was, it warrants noting that the American public was well primed to respond negatively to any polysyllabic chemical name based on the litany of historical events in which chemicals from strontium-90 in nuclear fallout to DDT had poisoned people and landscapes. Growing fears over the latency of carcinogens and the emerging understanding of hormone-disrupting chemicals exacerbated hyperbole on both sides of the daminozide debate and others like it across the United States.[47]

The Alar case is also an important example of how fear can be manipulated, stoked, and mongered. The sociologist Barry Glassner attributed a marked shift in American fear culture to media reporting. Mainstream media craved sensationalism in order to sell newspapers and advertising slots on television. "Television news programs survive on scares," Glassner wrote in his far-reaching work, *The Culture of Fear: Why Americans are Afraid of the Wrong Things* (1999). Disasters make for good copy. "No danger is too small to magnify into a national nightmare."[48] Chemophobia was not, however, manufactured out of thin air. The ingredients were already present. While media concerns may have exaggerated and exacerbated public fears over daminozide and apples, the cultural climate was already in place for such a reaction and reception. But no matter how slick the media campaign or how shrill the television news stories, daminozide would not have instigated such alarm in the absence of the historical context—that availability heuristic—that had prepared an American public to think the worst of all things chemical. Recall, too, the historian Robert Darnton's warning that "newspaper stories must fit the cultural preconceptions of news." Which is to say, news stories that resonated did so because the public was already primed for them.[49]

Considering the media's influence risks being thrown headlong into a heated and ideological debate over the wisdom or the idiocy of the crowd, which invites reflection on the relationship between the new media and the new economic liberalism. That the two should emerge at roughly the same time was no accident. Neoliberalism is really "a specific vision of the role of knowledge in human affairs," according to historian Philip Mirowski.[50] On the one hand, the argument that toxic fear emanated from informed local communities to the media gives agency to the residents of contaminated spaces. However, if toxic fear was a media fabrication, it implies that "the public" were passive recipients of information. It relegates "the people" to abstract, agentless status, lacking the shrewdness to properly evaluate or interpret risks as they perceive them. According to many scholars, this is a central feature of the neoliberal project, which puts little stock in people.[51] Creating public ignorance or confusion through media spin is a key strategy in distracting public discourse away from threatening its emerging status quo.[52] Put another way, in the marketplace of ideas, people are irrelevant. "The truth is validated as what sells."[53]

Obviously, the truth likely varied from case to case, and invariably inhabited the interstices between these two positions, but the media's primary role in the promulgation of toxic fear comes in the form of contributing to the availability heuristic. Television and print news reports preserved recent events in the American mainstream. Love Canal's entry into the American canon of environmental disasters served subsequently as a reference point for any community that found itself at risk from toxic pollution. Through the 1980s, a search of the town's name in the *New York Times* showed continued reporting on the site's rehabilitation and on pending lawsuits, but the idea of "another Love Canal" was a common refrain. Fifteen stories on Times Beach in the *New York Times* mentioned Love Canal in 1983. Almost twenty more articles referred to both sites through the rest of the 1980s. Between December 1982 and the end of April 1983, the *Philadelphia Inquirer* linked Times Beach and Love Canal six times; the *Chicago Tribune* printed five articles that cited both towns. As the Missouri dioxin scare developed through 1982 before shifting to the evacuation of Times Beach, the *St. Louis Post-Dispatch* was saturated with references to Love Canal. The *Boston Globe*'s reporting on the Woburn cancer cluster (discussed in chapter 6) made regular connections to Love Canal and to Times Beach. In late 1984, one headline reporting on the chemical explosion in Bhopal, India, called it "A Three Mile Island for Chemicals." The story also made reference to Love Canal and to Times Beach.[54]

There's a dirty truth to stereotypes and availability heuristics, inasmuch as they are derived from some kernel of truth or past perception, or, as the Thomas theorem asserts, those perceptions invent their own consequences. Part of toxic fear's passage through the 1980s stemmed from the idea that "another Love Canal" or Times Beach was always on the imminent horizon. Unfairly or not, industry and government found themselves tasked with an uphill battle of trying to diminish what they considered unwarranted concerns. In response to a November 1981 *Washington Post* editorial titled "Poisons on the Loose," Gary Dietrich, director of the EPA's Office of Solid Waste, felt compelled to respond to the charge that "waste disposal is still being carried out under the same (mostly non-existent) rules that produced Valley of the Drums, Love Canal, and countless other less well-known but equally poisonous disasters." Dietrich categorically rejected the claim and proceeded to outline the recent changes and improvements to hazardous waste disposal.[55]

In essence, the media's contribution to toxic fear in the 1980s was the production of hermetically sealed narratives that commit sins of omission and distortion. In crystallizing dominant narratives from Love Canal to the daminozide-sprayed apple orchards, the media's primary role in constructing toxic narratives in the 1980s was to simplify the story for public consumption. At times, that reporting showed a flair for the dramatic at the expense of important information or points of view. Accounts of angry and frightened residents forgot the heterogeneity of local opinions and desires. Evidence of government evasiveness trumped genuine efforts to help from within various agencies. Industrial accidents, anxious mothers, juicy sound bites, cautionary tales. Sometimes rightly, sometimes wrongly, negligence and malevolence were synonymous. Fear was always a story. Print the legend. In others cases, the media was retained to communicate the opposite. When dioxins from a former wood treatment plant in Hollywood, Maryland, were found to have contaminated soils and groundwater in 1985, EPA officials were quick to stress that the dioxins were far less toxic than the ones at Times Beach. "We don't have a Times Beach here," stressed the EPA site coordinator Jerry Heston. "We don't have the same kind of hazard."[56]

* * *

Another metric—but a hopeful one—that confronts the uncertainty that galvanized toxic fear and challenges the perceived notion that fear provokes passivity: The 1980s witnessed a remarkable growth in the number of active environmental groups and their memberships. These ranged from national organizations such as the Sierra Club, whose numbers swelled by 90 percent during the early 1980s, to the smaller, grassroots groups that sprang up everywhere.[57] After the ordeal at Love Canal, for example, Lois

Gibbs established the Citizens' Clearinghouse for Hazardous Waste, which collected and distributed information to other communities and groups at risk. The formation in 1982 of the Silicon Valley Toxics Coalition responded to the discovery that toxic solvents had contaminated local drinking water. The formation of the Warren County Citizens Concerned About PCBs frequently serves as the origin of the American environmental justice movement. Alabamians for a Clean Environment, founded by Kaye Kiker and her neighbors, responded to the discovery that they were living next to the nation's largest commercial hazardous waste landfill in Emelle.[58] Similarly, Citizens Asking for a Safe Environment sprang up in Sumter, South Carolina, in 1985 in an effort to phase out and shut down a hazardous waste landfill in nearby Pinewood.[59] And on and on. And on. Some organizations worked across states and regions, building coalitions between and across multiple groups with shared concerns. Some worked around churches or community centers or neighborhood associations. Others still worked out of basements and were composed of just a few blocks' worth of neighbors. Their goals were as disparate as their composition. Some targeted national or state policies, others wanted a particular pollutant (or polluter) out of their backyard. But a consistent interest united them. As a front-page *Chicago Tribune* article from 1983 noted astutely, "The discovery that hazardous chemical wastes have been dumped near their homes binds them together with the fear that they and their children are slowly being poisoned by the refuse of an industrial society."[60] This was a trend. "The future is going to be a lot more of that—responding to a local problem. . . . You're going to see more and more everyday citizens who will never join the Sierra Club but will fight the degradation they see around them," urban planner Rebecca Faulkenberry told the *Anniston Star* in 1988.[61]

Perhaps it seems a stretch to argue that increased environmental activism represented an explicit expression of chemical fear—and many of these grassroots organizations had little or no interest in toxins—but consider the following. Recall that sociologist Robert Wuthnow has argued that the need to act is a common response to any manner of threat. Moreover, psychologist Robert Holt hinted in the *New York Times* that social support networks and information about risks counteracted much of the depression and anxiety surrounding toxic fears. Sociologists Russell Stone and Adeline Levine found the same thing at Love Canal. Their interviews with residents showed that activists found mutually constitutive support within organizations and "felt somewhat better about themselves and their family relations than did the non-activists." Another psychologist, Shelley Taylor, found that this kind of agency was crucial in adjusting to life-threatening events. In short, environmental groups may have contributed significantly to individual and community resilience in times of intense psychological stress. Put another way, this kind of community building served as a bulwark to counter the individualizing impulses imposed by the neoliberal project.[62]

Further, broader grassroots coalitions began to form. Linda Guillet of Swansea, Massachusetts, wrote to Joan Gipp of the Love Canal's Ecumenical Task Force in 1986 to ask for advice on how to press for political action to address local drinking water contamination. While Swansea residents were discouraged from drinking their water, she noted that the State Health Department had not prohibited bathing, even though their tests had found concentrations of tetrachloroethylene of fifteen hundred parts per billion.[63] The growing network suggested that afflicted communities were not alone. Technical and tactical information was shared across the country. Inasmuch as chemical contamination could be anywhere, support was also omnipresent.

Lois Gibbs wrote in the 1986 Citizens' Clearinghouse for Hazardous Waste's year-end report, "The grassroots movement has become one of the largest and fastest growing movements for social justice in the country. We're changing public policy. We've just won a strong, renewed Superfund. We've shut over 1,000 landfills down. We've helped people block unsafe facilities in every part of the country, and we're forcing both industry and government regulators to make waste reduction a top priority. This same energy and success has expanded to issues like solid waste, nuclear waste and plant discharges."[64]

It was an impressive string of successes—and clear indication of an historical shift in how social and environmental activism in the United States interacted with politics. Community action was pivotal in spurring government agencies to address the environmental security of Americans in their homes and workplaces. But why the shift? Why were Americans taking greater ownership over their environmental concerns? A growing awareness of chemical hazards, of course. But also a retreating presence from government oversight of public health and environmental safety. "When local people in trouble can't count on their own elected officials for support, then you can't say too much for them," Love Canal resident Martha McGranor charged at county legislators. Lois Gibbs, she asserted, "did more than all the local politicians put together." She continued, "Through all the problems and anguish these people have gone through, a lesson is learned: you can't count on politicians for help."[65] Local organizing constituted more than a passing fad—or, indeed, an explicit reaction to the Reagan administration's antienvironmental sentiments. Instead, it seems the expansion of grassroots social and environmental organizing emanated from a larger outsourcing of social responsibility from government to the people. At the same time, that individual responsibility was hard to acquire. If the public—individually or collectively—could not turn to the insurance industry to protect or underwrite the risks inherent in environmental contamination, then collective organizing and prevention of hazards was the lone recourse for many.

This was the primary neoliberal imperative of the 1970s and 1980s: to absolve government of being responsible for public security. The strategy played both ways. Where the neoliberal project worked to cleave individuals and communities from public dependence, it served the concomitant practice of stimulating popular distrust in government and its agencies. The divorce gave the appearance of being a mutual separation. Distrust was a key feature of toxic fear. The sociologist Michael Edelstein traced the decline in social trust among victims of toxic incidents. "It results," he concluded, "from a gradual breakdown of the assumption that others, particularly those in government, will aid toxic victims to make their lives once again whole."[66] Distrust was born out of the stigma associated with living in a contaminated community and the inversion of normal safety paradigms.

On April 5, 1979, Love Canal resident Grace M. McCoulf testified before the Senate Subcommittee on Toxic Substances and Chemical Wastes. Her statement expressed equal parts fear, anger, and resolve. "We must watch our families deteriorate and our health suffer. Our children are sick, our homes are valueless and we have boarded up homes for neighbors. The entire meaning of family has been corroded." McCoulf powerfully captured the essence of trauma. But while she pleaded for government action, she also warned that her poisoned community had become a politically potent machine. "We have grown from a tattered neighborhood group to a real national power," she asserted in conclusion.[67] Combined, the two statements marked the expanse of the political landscape surrounding environmental fear. Love Canal became the national symbol for toxic contamination—and with it, chemical fear. On the one hand, afflicted communities were frightened and felt abandoned. On the other, a growing sense of empowerment suggested a rebirth within American environmentalism: one that was built from the grassroots and offered a community-based counterpoint to the larger, increasingly litigious big conservationist movements that had dominated American environmental activism.

CHAPTER SIX

Death Inside Me

I've got death inside me. It's just a question of whether or not I can outlive it.
—Don DeLillo, *White Noise*

The pivot for Don DeLillo's troubling, darkly farcical 1985 novel *White Noise* is the "airborne toxic event." The book's blurb referred to the "menacing cloud" as "a more urgent and visible version of the 'white noise' engulfing the Gladney family—radio transmissions, sirens, microwaves, ultrasonic appliances, and TV murmuring—pulsing with life, yet suggesting something ominous." After a train car accident outside fictional college town Blacksmith releases Nyodene Derivative into the air, protagonist Jack Gladney is confronted with his own mortality. During their evacuation, Jack is exposed to the poison when he stops to fill the family car at an abandoned gas station. (Recall the fears associated with anticipating flight in the second chapter—jammed service stations—or how people in precarious places worried about having enough gas in the tank in case an emergency should strike overnight. In less precarious, middle-class spaces, such betrayal of safety is such a relative novelty that it invites its own horrors.) Gas tank filled and back on the road, the family witnesses the chemical cloud in close proximity. "The enormous dark mass moved like some death ship in a Norse legend. . . . We weren't sure how to react," Jack observes as the plume-turned-billowing-cloud-turned-full-on-airborne-toxic-event rolls over them. "It was a terrible thing to see so close, so low, packed with chlorides, benzines, phenols, hydrocarbons, or whatever the precise toxic content."[1]

In a macabre exchange at the evacuation site—an abandoned Boy Scout camp outside of town—Jack learns that a computer has determined his exposure constitutes a "situation." A young SIMUVAC technician, part of a team engaged in simulated evacuations and thrust into the real thing by the airborne toxic event, happily explains the computer's results: "I punch in the name, the substance, the exposure time and then I tap into your computer history. Your genetics, your personals, your medicals, your psychologicals, your police-and-hospitals. It comes back pulsing stars." Jack is "generating big numbers." He won't die today or tomorrow. Maybe they will know more in fifteen years. But he has been exposed. "You are the sum total of your data," the young man tells Jack matter-of-factly. "No man escapes that." This is the inescapable logic of risk and toxic fear in the modern era. A statistical inevitability hides within the uncertain noise that surrounds it. And it bounds the debate in important ways: for risk analysts in one manner and for individuals and lay publics in another. The data are universally accepted as irrefutable. What the data mean, however, is open to some interpretation. This is also the novel's definitive turning point.

> I stood absolutely still. If they thought I was already dead, they might be inclined to leave me alone. I think I felt as I would if a doctor had held an X-ray to the light showing a star-shaped hole at the center of one of my vital organs. Death has entered. It is inside you. You are said to be dying and yet are separate from the dying, can ponder it at your leisure, literally see on the X-ray photograph or computer screen the horrible alien logic of it all. It is when death is rendered graphically, is televised so to speak, that you sense an eerie separation between your condition and yourself. A network of symbols has been introduced, an entire awesome technology wrested from the gods. It makes you feel like a stranger in your own dying.[2]

In its humor, its paranoia, and its irony, *White Noise* captures the quintessential contradictions of the 1980s. Jack Gladney finds himself immersed in a world where the science used to articulate risk is the same science that created it in the first place. It is a world in which the debate over these newly discovered risks precipitates social and individual anxieties, and a world where it is more profitable to respond to disaster after the fact than it is to anticipate it.[3]

This chapter and the next combine the two sources of Jack Gladney's paranoia—latent risk and latent death (in reverse order)—to highlight the politics of expertise as seen through the public fear of cancer incidence and the risks imposed by toxic hazards. In spite of the availability heuristic's tendency toward explosive starts—at Three Mile Island and at Elizabeth, for example—toxic fear is typically a slow disaster. It festers to crescendo behind the scenes. Funny smells in the air or water; residents experience curious health symptoms; disbelief that real harm is possible; unease—malaise—runs through the community. Time passes. Slowly, the identification of a potential source for these problems emerges. Such discoveries could come from government authorities or agencies after they had conducted numerous tests. Sometimes industry would warn of a leak or an error. Sometimes citizen sleuths, driven by concern caused by exposures from living, working, playing, breathing, drinking on the front line, would raise the alarm. But time passes and fears transude. "Fire and explosion were not the inherent dangers here," DeLillo writes. "This death would penetrate, seep into genes, show itself to bodies not yet born."[4] That the initial hazard would take years to manifest itself as disease and/or death only intensified the fear in the short term. Similarly, risk analysis and risk management introduce a language for processing chemical calamity that is inherently ostracizing to toxic victims. Jack has a "situation." His exposure to Nyodene D. increases his chances of getting a "nebulous mass," but "knowledge changes every day." The data are conflicting, says a specialist after running blood tests. Jack is exasperated. Modern science and medicine are supposed to mediate risks and explain things, but Jack is no closer to understanding his fate. DeLillo ekes out what little humor is possible in such a scene. "What can [the nebulous mass] do in terms of worst-case scenario contingencies?," Jack asks the specialist. "Cause a person to die" is the first straight reply Jack receives from any expert in the novel. "Speak English, for God's sake. I despise this modern jargon."[5]

* * *

The two most common responses to uncertain hazards are "excessive overreaction and utter neglect."[6] There is rarely a goldilocks compromise in between. The virtue of a sudden disaster is that it requires immediate action. Big fires need to be put out. Concern for its gravity and significance can follow in due course, but in the short term the required response is obvious. The 1980 explosion at the Chemical Control Corp. facility in Elizabeth, New Jersey, demanded a reaction. At Love Canal, however, uncertain risks meant that a rapid evacuation in the late 1970s might have been unnecessary. Moldering fires do not spark the same kind of reaction, even if their catastrophic potential remains high. Instead, they inspire a watchful unease. Regardless, where Elizabeth and Love Canal share common ground is in the psychological stress surrounding exposure. How many residents near each site worried that their data would come back pulsing stars—that they had a "situation"? And what did that even mean? In Elizabeth, those fears were raised in the immediate aftermath of the explosion, which brought with it its own toxic cloud. At Love Canal, in the absence of a rallying flashpoint, that uncertainty percolated over an extended period of time. No action, no reaction, no response. Just unknowing. Uncertainty is the second part of slow disasters. Where the previous chapter intimated that slow disasters have long histories that precede their flashpoint, all disasters also have an aftermath. Part of that aftermath is the remediation. The other part is reflection on the long-term effects of the disaster.

The prevailing toxic fear—the most visceral type of slow disaster—was a fear of cancer. This chapter needs to reckon with the American preoccupation with cancer, especially as it manifested itself in the 1980s. "Cancer is a scare word," asserted an editorial in the *Woburn Daily Times* in late 1979 as fears mounted that carcinogens had entered into the town's wells.[7] Though the 1980s coincided with the discovery of AIDS and the panic it incited, a fear of all things cancer reached its climax as well. Cancer's latency meant that exposure could result in disease in the distant future. As carcinogenic fears promulgated with increasing numbers of contamination, cancerphobia and chemophobia became intertwined. Indeed, fear of cancer and modern American environmentalism have fallen into lockstep since the end of World War II. During the 1950s and 1960s, concerns over the carcinogenicity of radioactive fallout from nuclear weapons testing ignited American fears of human-made poisons.[8] Rachel Carson's highly influential *Silent Spring* (1962) followed and made explicit the connections between some industrial chemicals and cancer prominent in mainstream environmental discourse. *Silent Spring* is best remembered for its striking imagery surrounding a season without birdsong and an indictment against chemical biocides, especially DDT. "Cancer" and "carcinogen" were invoked frequently throughout the text. Carson's own death from cancer in 1964 only reinforced the link between environment and cancer.[9]

Inasmuch as it was revelatory, *Silent Spring* relied on earlier work on cancer as an environmental disease. During the 1930s, the German émigré Wilhelm Hueper produced groundbreaking work on the relationship between bladder cancer incidence and aniline dye manufacturers. His 1942 *Occupational Tumors and Allied Diseases* became highly influential in epidemiological studies on cancer. In the more reader-friendly pamphlet "Environmental Cancer"—*Occupational Tumors and Allied Diseases* was a monstrous 896 pages—Hueper warned that synthetic organic chemicals posed serious carcinogenic threats to factory workers but also the public at large. "Safety procedures," he asserted, "should include not only protection of the individual workers by enclosing the manufacturing processes, but also protection of the whole plant and the community at large by preventing the escape of carcinogenic wastes into the atmosphere, the water, or the soil."[10] That idea was taken up in the 1950s by the Irish pathologist John Higginson, who proposed that 70 to 80 percent of all human cancers were derived from environmental factors. This assertion became a common refrain within the World Health Organization: "The majority of human cancer is potentially preventable," it declared in 1964 in its expert committee report, *Prevention of Cancer.*[11] And in 1975 the British physician John Cairns declared, "Almost all cancers appear to be caused by exposure to factors in the environment."[12] Cancer was famously regarded as a disease of civilization: Many types of cancer were more prevalent in developed countries. Hueper, Higginson, Cairns, and others seemed to be indicating that industrialization had come at a high and unanticipated cost.

But "environment" is a vague category. According to the epidemiologist Phillip Cole, the category needed to be qualified somewhat in response to the growing interest in carcinogens derived from pollution. In epidemiological circles, "environment" was understood to cover all of it: air, water, workplace, diet, drinking habits, smoking, and other factors. Under such an umbrella, Cole acknowledged that "80 percent to 98 percent of cancer might be called environmentally caused." But cancer caused by environmental pollution was another matter. Even by the 1980s, accounting for cancer incidence from environmental pollution remained an unknown.[13] The argument surrounding environmental cancers, such as it was, stressed that cancer could be curtailed before it appeared and that public, policy, and medical energies should be redirected toward prevention. But the idea didn't gain traction. Instead, in 1971 President Richard Nixon declared a national "War on Cancer," bent on finding a cure for the disease. State support for a long-standing popular effort and discourse, fueled by such philanthropic luminaries as Mary Lasker, reflected that enduring American optimism that a war could be won without any industrial sacrifice to "progress." The National Cancer Act funneled millions of dollars into medical research that promised cures. And the American public—participants and casualties of the War on Cancer and now learning indirectly that cancer was an environmental disease—misinterpreted the message and assumed that everything was carcinogenic.[14]

"Everything," pop singer Joe Jackson sang jauntily in 1982, "gives you cancer." Americans were very explicitly afraid of cancer and convinced that it was an increasingly pervasive threat. Toxic and cancer discourses and their reach contributed to those fears. The availability heuristic again: Glyn Caldwell of the Centers for Disease Control described the nature of changing contexts for worry: "In the 50s and 60s we got little old ladies calling in complaining about smells from their oleander bushes. Then with the environmental movement, the calls switched to concern with chemicals and other environmental agents."[15] The growing sense of cancer's ubiquity and universality changed the nature of toxic fear. If known carcinogens were slipping, spilling, seeping into neighborhoods, then fear, stress, and anger all made sense. After Times Beach became the second nationwide chemical disaster story and toxic-induced evacuation of the 1980s, the palpable question and cause for concern in neighborhoods across the United States was who or where was next? If there was ever cause for intense, chemophobic hypochondria, the discovery of contaminated communities was it. Every headache, every child's asthma or cough could be a harbinger of chemicals escaping improper emission or disposal. The thrust of most horror stories involves inverting or undermining basic assumptions about security. Perverting the places we consider most safe and the gross corruption of innocence are common themes. Most sacred are the innocence and welfare of children (hence the almost requisite music box soundtrack to horror films). Add a dose of mystery to the horror and you have a perfect storm. So it is little surprise that contaminated communities at Love Canal or Times Beach provoked such intense angst on the ground and received such widespread media attention.

* * *

Of course, many towns had been experiencing such conditions throughout the sixties and seventies. The childhood leukemia cluster in working-class Woburn, Massachusetts—twelve miles north of Boston—was one of them. Between 1969 and 1979, Woburn residents counted nineteen cases of leukemia among their children.[16] The rate of incidence defied statistical probability: This was four times the number that might have been deemed "normal" in a community of this size. Another nine children contracted leukemia between 1983 and 1990.[17] After Love Canal became a national story as a contaminated community whose remediation was stalled in fear and inertia, the Woburn case received more media attention. In part, this was the availability heuristic at play. But the two were intimately connected. As early as 1980, Love Canal and Woburn appeared in newspaper articles together, alongside the toxic waste contamination in Jackson Township, New Jersey, and the excessive dumping of tridichlorobenzene and the resulting lung damage near Bumpass Cove, Tennessee. In 1980 reporting, however, the elevated rates of leukemia in Woburn were blamed on tannery wastes—arsenic, chromium, and animal hides—from a previous industrial generation.[18]

In 1956, the state's Department of Public Health had ordered the Riley Tannery to clean up sludge in an area known locally as "Death Valley" because of the dead trees that lined the site. According to a February 1972 Aberjona River Commission report to the Woburn Town Council, its watershed was "so polluted that it is extremely difficult to separate the many different factors contributing to the pollution."[19] In 1975, Woburn's Board of Water Commissioners requested a change in the chlorination methods for two of the town's wells (G and H). The state Department of Health approved the change, but recommended against relying on the water from these wells because of their high concentrations of minerals and salts. Throughout the 1970s, "the putrid odor of old animal hides" bothered residents as the buried remnants of the tanning industries became exposed to the air.[20] And Woburn had its own, local illicit dumping events, such as the discovery of 184 barrels surreptitiously dumped at the Massachusetts Bay Transportation Authority depot on Mishawum Road in 1979.[21] But while the drums were not deemed an imminent hazard, just two weeks later the city of Woburn declared an "extremely critical" emergency over contamination in two of the eight wells that fed residents' homes.[22] On May 22, 1979, officials from the Massachusetts Department of Environmental Quality and Engineering ordered the immediate closure of wells G and H in East Woburn after identifying trichloroethylene, a chlorinated solvent and carcinogen, in the water. The presence of trichloroethylene in the water supply made it clear that new toxicants—not just nineteenth-century tanning detritus—were at work in threatening the community's health.

The immediate local concern at the beginning of summer was a water shortage. After the two wells were taken offline city authorities beseeched residents to cut any nonessential water consumption. But as the 1980s dawned it became one of the most important case studies on toxic contamination because of its contributions to the contentious epidemiological science surrounding the identification of cancer clusters.

As with Love Canal, a breakdown in communication provoked unnecessary angst. In July 1979, an Environmental Protection Agency investigation found high concentrations of arsenic, chromium, and lead persisting in an abandoned lagoon near the site of a former chemical company in North Woburn. Federal drinking water standards marked acceptable arsenic levels at 0.05 parts per million; some samples from the lagoon contained concentrations exceeding 1,000 parts per million.[23] The EPA communicated the discovery to the state's Division of Environmental Quality Engineering, but the state agency failed to inform city officials for two months. "You'd think they would notify us when they find something like that," Woburn Board of Health Chairman Francis O. Ryan told the *Woburn Daily Times*.[24] While this prompted some interjurisdictional tension, it also bred public distrust in officials, which was only exacerbated when it transpired that state authorities had originally been informed about the contaminated lagoons in 1972. Indeed, the Division of Environmental Quality Engineering had requested that the Army Corps of Engineers help them to prevent a landfilling operation in the area by a private company because of question marks surrounding the lagoon's safety.[25] This claim came from Mark Phillip Realty Trust, the company whose landfill was being held up. Its spokesperson charged that they filed for state permits that explicitly acknowledged the presence of the chemicals in question. For their part, the DEQE vehemently denied such early knowledge of the arsenic contamination.[26]

* * *

In most environmental disasters, culpability can wait. The first order of business is invariably to ascertain the safety and well-being of residents exposed to toxic chemicals. And the source. Amid the finger-pointing, a *Woburn Daily Times* editorial urged all parties to "find some answers." Was the chemical contamination in North Woburn contaminating the groundwater and infiltrating the now-shuttered wells in East Woburn? In addition to better understanding the prospective hazards and determining whether or not the arsenic and other metals had entered into the wells, the newspaper called for state and federal agencies to coordinate free blood tests for any residents who may have been exposed. "If anyone has been contaminated, then now is the time to find out, not in 10, 20, 30, or even 50 years when the long term effects of these poisons could make themselves painfully evident."[27]

Testing water quality was a direct legacy of urbanization and industrialization. Terrified of cholera and other bacteria-based, water-borne diseases, public health officials going back into the nineteenth century had carried out tests on wells and drinking water to ensure their safety. Until the late 1970s and early 1980s, however, these common and regular tests searched only for coliform bacteria and not the industrial chemicals that were becoming commonplace in the environment. In Woburn, for example, nobody knew how long arsenic had been sitting in the lagoon or whether it had infiltrated the now-condemned wells. Similarly, trichloroethylene—in production in the United States since the early 1920s—would long have escaped the basic efforts to ensure safe drinking water. Further, nobody really knew what the prospective threats were to such low-level, long-term exposure. This is the key component to the story of chemical contamination during the second half of the twentieth century and the primary source of toxic fear in the 1980s. The history of chemophobia is less an account of chemical trespassers and inept, mendacious authorities, but more a story about the chastening effects of new discoveries, the difficulties associated with addressing unprecedented troubles with a social and political infrastructure unequipped for such challenges, and the broader social, political, and economic systems that were shifting away from state responsibility in preserving the security of the citizenry. At the time of the Woburn crisis, Massachusetts did not have any hazardous waste regulations, so authorities were scrambling to resolve problems without any kind of precedent or protocol or jurisdiction in place. This also meant that they—and local residents—were working under a sobering shadow of uncertainty. Nobody could quantify the risks associated with pollution in Woburn. "All I can say," one DEQE engineer told the *Woburn Daily Times* in 1979, "is there is a potentially hazardous situation existing out there."[28]

To hearken back to Don DeLillo and *White Noise*, Woburn had a "situation." The uncertainty surrounding its severity provoked fear, which was compounded by a suspicious cluster of childhood leukemia cases. New evidence showed that cancer deaths between 1974 and 1978 had increased in Woburn by 17 percent over the previous five-year study. That was enough for some epidemiologists to take note. There were more incidences than there should have been for a population of that size—without some kind of external influence, that is. Air pollution from traffic fumes was one possibility; the city was cordoned by I-93 and Route 128. An aging population might help explain the higher cancer rates. Migration of people from outside Woburn could also be significant. Workplaces could contribute. But the immediate fear was that the increase was associated with chemical pollution, and that prompted the DEQE to seek substantial funding to conduct a "'definitive study' of the toxic waste problems in Woburn." DEQE toxic waste coordinator Dick Chalpin justified the project: "We think it's worth looking at either to allay fears or to see if there is anything to it."[29]

Two events ran concurrently but, for the most part, separately: the search for cancer-causing agents in the environment, on the one hand, and worries about the presence of cancer in Woburn's people. Ongoing studies and concerns about toxic waste in Woburn appeared in news stories as studies tested the water, councilors worried about nasty odors in the air, and various community groups met with state and city officials over the safety of their drinking water. Woburn's drinking water was deemed safe and beyond reproach in December 1979.[30] Wells G and H stayed closed. Meanwhile, concerns over the growing cancer incidence began to escalate. Reference to Woburn's environmental problems received mention here and there, but the links between the two health issues were hardly incontrovertible. Rarely were they presented that way. Among the rare exceptions was a series of tempered editorials in the *Woburn Daily Times*, which engaged the statistics behind cancer epidemiology and professed caution about jumping to conclusions.[31] "There is no way of knowing at this point whether there is any connection at all between the high rate of cancer in this city and the toxic wastes in north Woburn or the chemicals found in the wells in East Woburn," it insisted in its second editorial. "But, because cancer is on everyone's mind anyway, the combination of dangerous chemicals and a high rate of that disease has caused a great deal of worry and fear."[32]

In February 1980, the *Boston Globe* reported that three former workers at the Tabby Cat Food factory, adjacent to the industrial complex, were diagnosed with kidney cancer.[33] Possible coincidence, the article acknowledged, but the fire had been stoked. Information meetings became commonplace in Woburn over the next several months. Information was not always forthcoming. In one meeting following a study that found that workers near the toxic waste site suffered more headaches and fatigue, Kevin Johnson, who worked on the Industri-Plex site, complained, "We know [the contamination is] up there. We're up there every day and breathing it and we don't know if it is doing anything to us."[34] By April, Woburn residents learned in a town hall meeting that the state had formally requested the federal government for assistance in investigating the potential public health problems associated with the city's contaminated air and water. Over two hundred people attended the meeting, where the Department of Public Health indicated that the Centers for Disease Control, based in Atlanta, would send a team of epidemiologists to conduct a series of studies. In addition to leukemia, they would also investigate liver and kidney cancers.[35]

This is where trying to read cancer incidence as proof of environmental harm becomes fraught. That Woburn had a high incidence of leukemia was incontrovertible. What that meant, however, was subject to debate. Working backward from the effect—and in the absence of a consistent and indisputable source—made it difficult to determine where to identify the cause. But there are rarely direct cause-and-effect explanations for cancer. Explaining definitively how cancer selects its victims or how human susceptibility varies across a population remains somewhat mysterious. The carcinogenic process constitutes a "daunting complexity" that defies scientific certainty and breeds a mystique of popular terror.[36] It is even harder to determine the existence of cancer clusters. In her study on the Woburn crisis, Paula DiPerna describes clusters as the "mysterious medical phenomenon loosely defined as an apparent outbreak of disease clumped in time, place, or both."[37] While epidemics of communicable diseases naturally tend to cluster in time and place, cancer clusters provoke an uncomfortable riddle: Statistically, cancer should not cluster unless some hidden cause is spurring it. Because of its latency, it is difficult to pinpoint cancer's point of origin. Too many variables creep into trying to link a particular exposure to an illness that occurs sometimes decades later. This is like starting to chase after bank robbers long after the heist's trail has gone cold. As a result, epidemiologists refer to "associations" rather than explicit links. They discuss the statistical likelihood—or probability—of these associations. Childhood leukemia offers special insight into cancer clusters. Identifying clusters in adults is trickier business. People move from town to town and are exposed to any number of different carcinogens. In contrast, childhood leukemia works on a much faster timeline, and that allows epidemiologists a slightly clearer view of the disease's trajectory and parameters. An abnormally high concentration of leukemia patients in a small area—and especially with the same type of leukemia—is rare. Nevertheless, while it might hint at a suspicious cause, it might also be a fluke. The average incidence of leukemia without a known cause is 3.74 cases per 100,000 children. In Woburn, a town of 36,000, 26 cases were diagnosed between 1979 and 1985, and most of these were from residents of East Woburn in neighborhoods that drew water from wells G and H. The statistical likelihood of this being a freak occurrence was more than 100 to 1.

Woburn's statistical improbability drew the attention of epidemiologists because it met the anomalous criteria of being a geographical or residential cancer cluster. Rather than coming from a controlled source as in a specific workplace that uses a known carcinogen, a geographical cancer cluster in the wild is far less common—and far more difficult to ascertain. That is what made Woburn special. But the trigger was missing. A statistically improbable number of cancer incidences is insufficient to determine a cluster's existence. In the controlled setting of an industrial factory, as among Hueper's dye factory workers who shared a common workspace and exposure conditions, this was more easily done. In the wilds of suburban America, the possibilities are almost endless, reinforcing the prospect of a fluke occurrence. "The only 'proof' of a cluster is another cluster, exactly the same diseases happening under exactly the same environmental circumstances," notes DiPerna, implying that such work more or less needs lightning to strike twice in order to achieve any kind of confidence in their claims.[38] Further, Woburn is historically significant *because* causes for the cluster were more or less identified: the tanneries, the illicit dumping, and so on. But myriad potential sources muddied the waters. For example, almost every American household had a can of benzene, a solvent with useful properties for paint stripping and furniture refinishing. Benzene had a known association with myelocytic leukemia. In 1983, epidemiologists also showed links to lymphocytic leukemia. Such conditions made pinpointing a singular environmental source with any degree of certainty difficult: If cancer incidence could be spurred by numerous different sources inside *and* outside the home—or any combination of numerous different sources—determining specific causes was next to impossible.

The fear of cancer clusters also worked to situate toxic fear in specific geographic locales. As evidenced by the challenges to epidemiology, place mattered. To overcome the charge that random chance was at play, concentrations of disease needed to be tightly refined and persuasive explanations for a contamination's origins needed to be nearby. Fundamentally, there was nothing new about the backyard politics of environmental pollution. Nobody wanted to live next door to a toxic waste facility or an industrial factory. Not only did local residents succumb to fear of illness or future illness, hazardous waste sites were a pox on real estate values and local businesses. While industrial manufacturing plants were often an employment boon in depressed areas, poor practices and bad press could reverse the economic advantages of living close to such factories.

Indeed, not all denialism of toxic fears originated from interests unsympathetic to environmental salubrity. Woburn's Mayor Thomas M. Higgins rejected the suggestion that the City Council had demonstrated insufficient concern for the toxic threats facing the town. "This administration is not in the business of alarming the public," he intoned after some critics charged that the council appeared intent on hoping that the problem would just go away. Higgins insisted that the appropriate agencies were at work, but reiterated his desire for calm until all the facts were known. "For anyone with little or no authority to give the impression that there is a major health problem within the confines of the city without factual evidence to back their statements is totally irresponsible."[39] Wait and see is a tough sell in cases of potential environmental contamination, particularly when childhood leukemia might be involved. But in many respects, Higgins reflected the same kinds of calls for calm that emanated from local and state officials at Love Canal at around the same time. Fear, however legitimate, could create even more detrimental panic and chaos. Higgins also reflected concerns that trouble elected officials in other contaminated towns: He worried that the fears might have been exaggerated, and that threatened to hurt the town. Stigma was a real issue. Recall that Times Beachers lamented being pariahs: "They treat you like you've got a disease."[40] New industry might stay away, too. Property values would decline. "What do I care about property values?" Anne Anderson shot back: Her son Jimmy was one of Woburn's leukemia victims. "I have an empty room."[41] For Anderson and other parents who had lost a child, fear was likely the wrong emotion. Or, at least, fear had evolved into grief or anger. As the historian Michael Laffan observes, "Even if it is experienced in the present moment, one might argue that fear is inherently of the future; that it is the pervading sense of uncertainty about an inherently unknowable condition that could potentially visit pain on the body or loss of what one holds dear."[42]

* * *

"Clusters tug at the national sleeve, pointing out the huge hollow between scientific knowledge and the national need to protect public health and control environmental contamination," writes Paula DiPerna in her book on Woburn.[43] A cluster—real or imagined—indicates that public safety has been compromised. Distrust of industry and scientific authority—brought about by a sense that officials dragged their heels when responding to toxic hazards—fostered another expression of fear that warrants attention: citizen or street science, or what the sociologist Phil Brown has called "popular epidemiology."[44] Brown adopted the term in reference to his work on the response to the leukemia cluster at Woburn. Popular epidemiology "is the process by which lay persons gather scientific data and other information, and also direct and marshal the knowledge and resources of experts in order to understand the epidemiology of disease."[45] Its citizen action constitutes another expression—as with similar community efforts at Love Canal and in other communities across the United States—of toxic fear as a collective experience.[46] Woburn's popular epidemiology efforts were mobilized when Reverend Bruce A. Young, rector at Woburn's Trinity Episcopal Church, wrote a letter to the editor of the *Woburn Daily Times* to invite parents with children diagnosed with acute lymphocytic leukemia or acute myelogeneous leukemia since 1964 to an evening meeting at the church hall on October 4, 1979. "The purpose of the meeting," he wrote, "is two-fold: 1. to obtain the most accurate statistics about the incidence of leukaemia as possible, and 2. see what doors those facts open and close."[47]

Coincidentally, Young's letter was published within a week of the arsenic story—which likely compounded local environmental fears—but Young had been tracking leukemia cases for some time. In the early 1970s, when one of his parishioners was diagnosed with leukemia, Young helped the family in getting the five-year-old boy to his regular treatment at Massachusetts General Hospital. A couple of years later, Young learned of another case of childhood leukemia in his parish. In his trips to the hospital, Young recalled seeing other Woburn residents coming in for treatment. "We don't have a large parish," Young told the *Woburn Daily Times* when the story picked up steam in December 1979. "There aren't that many people, so when two cases of leukemia turned up, I became concerned."[48] The Boston physicians treating Young's parishioners showed little interest in his sense that Woburn was overrepresented in their clinics. Further, there was no established method of charting cancer incidence beyond the kind of happenstance that Young had stumbled upon. "Since leukaemia is not a communicable disease, it is not a 'reportable' disease," he wrote in his letter. "Therefore, to the best of my knowledge, there is no central agency or health data bank to provide statistics on the incidence of leukaemia among children in Woburn."[49] His observation that a disproportionate number of his parishioners and neighbors were visiting hospitals outside of Woburn was a fluke that prompted further investigation. To Young this increase seemed noteworthy.[50] Concern is justified by shared experience. In town, there was enough shared experience with leukemia to want to learn more about its causes. Already, Anne Anderson had counted five or six children with leukemia in Woburn since her son Jimmy's diagnosis. Those meetings fostered collaborations with epidemiologists and produced a new form of grassroots knowledge gathering and social activism.

In its main guise, popular epidemiology was not a challenge to established science or scientific authority, but rather a focused complement. Even in the wake of the renewed interest in chemical controls introduced in the 1970s, too many chemicals in the environment had been "grandfathered" into new TSCA protocols and been left untested, deemed safe. Moreover, for all the studies that had been conducted, most engaged in a molecule-by-molecule accounting of toxins that did little to ascertain their safety in the wild, when confronted and commingled with other chemicals. Chemical synergism suggested that combining two (or three or four or five) innocuous chemicals often had the potential to create highly dangerous cocktails. Ensuring the safety of all these synergisms was impossible: It would require an infinite number of tests, an infinite number of scientists, and an infinite budget. At the same time, faced with a potential disease cluster, local residents invested time and energy to identify its source by proceeding with their own epidemiological studies.[51]

Starting in January 1980, volunteer residents canvased Woburn's neighborhoods under the newly formed organization For a Cleaner Environment (FACE). By early 1982, the EPA had completed a hydrogeological study, which identified two distinct contaminant sources in the water but did not point to the culprits. In May 1982, armed with their data, thirty-three Woburn residents (representing the families of eight leukemia victims) launched a class action lawsuit against W. R. Grace's Cryovac Division and Beatrice Foods' Riley Tannery, whom they held responsible for the contamination of the wells and, by extension, their community's cancer cluster.[52] Technical support from Harvard University's School of Public Health enriched the data, the results of which were completed after the trial had begun. The survey covered more than four thousand pregnancies between 1960 and 1982 and found little evidence that the water from wells G and H had contributed to marked birth defects or spontaneous abortions prior to 1970. After 1970, the study revealed some associations with perinatal deaths, and childhood health disorders involving kidneys and urinal tract and respiratory problems.[53]

On July 26, 1986, a jury found that W. R. Grace had been negligent in illegally dumping toxic chemicals on its property. Beatrice Foods was acquitted. The next stage of the trial would have involved the plaintiffs needing to prove that W. R. Grace's actions had caused leukemia, but the judge ordered a retrial because he felt the hydrogeological data had been poorly understood by the jury. Before the new trial could begin, Grace settled with the residents, paying damages totaling $8 million.[54] It might seem crass to the historical actors at Woburn—especially to those who lost loved ones—to measure Woburn's historical significance in terms other than right and wrong, aggrieved and culpable, assaulted and negligent. But situating Woburn's contributions to the process of grassroots activism is worthwhile: both in terms of its place in the larger story of the American toxic crisis and as an object lesson in how communities come together to confront a faceless corporate, industrial power. Another important facet of Woburn's story stems from the popular epidemiology practiced by local residents in response to local contamination. Due to the state's refusal to test water and an absence of official confirmation that Woburn constituted a cancer cluster, residents took it upon themselves to shed light on the uncertainty that plagued their case. They sought to build a body of information, seeking answers for themselves and ammunition that could be used in a court of law. At Woburn, the final data were never actually used in the legal proceedings because W. R. Grace settled before the trial proceeded to the point of connecting their contamination of the wells to the cluster of cancer cases in the town. But there is some speculation that the judge ordered a retrial because he was aware that an out-of-court settlement was imminent.[55] In many respects, the popular epidemiological work had put Woburn residents in a position of power.

In working-class Woburn, residents clearly understood they were on their own against the polluting industries. Reverend Young, an early ally in Anderson's search for environmental answers to her son's illness, noted the obstacles to their struggle: "For seven years we were told that the burden of proof was upon us as independent citizens to gather the statistics. . . . All our work was independent of the Commonwealth of Massachusetts. They offered no support, and were in fact one of our adversaries in this battle to prove that we had a problem."[56] Given the obstacles, that Woburn became a national story and that their popular epidemiological work served as a model for subsequent communities across the United States reveals the importance of activist power in contending with toxic fear and challenging polluters. Confronting state and federal agencies—and meeting resistance at every turn—must have been frustrating, but the lack of support resulted in the Woburn activists becoming more independent. They conducted their own investigations, collated that information, and mastered the knowledge it provided in order to accuse W. R. Grace and Beatrice Foods of being culpable for the sickness and deaths in the community. Similar popular epidemiology occurred at Love Canal as well. And across the entire spectrum of grassroots environmental activism and struggles for environmental justice, local community groups have organized to collect their own health data to bring to authorities as a means of pushing for remediation. To the historian outsider, there is something very moving about local productions of knowledge, run frequently out of neighborhood basements or church or community center halls. They are exercises in community empowerment that reflect a commitment to children, to family, to neighbors, to place, and to the future.

However, citizen science is also a clear indication that the state has failed in its responsibility to ensure the security of its citizenry. By all accounts, Woburn is a critical and positive case study in the history of American citizen action. But it also reflects the slippery slope of the 1980s' neoliberal turn. On the one hand, participatory democracy invites and even requires public activism and interaction as a part of the political discourse. On the other hand, its nature changed during the neoliberal shift to the political right that occurred in democracies around the world during the 1980s. Social problems became individual problems: Their solutions required individual fixes. By design, the onus of responsibility moved from government and government agencies to a public that had in the previous decade turned environmental oversight and the necessary scientific literacy over to experts who were now finding themselves underfunded or ousted from government offices and agencies.

The rise of popular epidemiology, as evidenced in Woburn, represented the breakdown in the traditional political contract. That contract asserts that government bears the responsibility to keep its citizens safe from toxic threats as well as enemies, foreign and domestic. FACE engaged in epidemiological data collection not to assist an underresourced state or federal agency, but rather to conduct work that they thought officials—experts—should have been doing in the first place. At the same time, that neoliberal outsourcing of responsibility made no room on the ledger for the emotional costs associated with the fears that promulgated action nor for the stresses associated with struggles in scientific, legal, and political forums that were typically unfamiliar.

* * *

More often than not, the source of a potential cluster was less of a mystery than it had been in Woburn. The "something in the environment" tended to have a more obvious source. Labor was at the front line of vulnerability. Workers in chemical factories and their families who lived near the plants were also the first to experience environmental fears and to sense the potential for disease clusters, as Wilhelm Hueper's epidemiological work had shown. Bladder cancers concentrated in aniline dye workers. In chemical towns across the United States—in chemical corridors from the Texas Gulf Coast to Louisiana to New Jersey to southern Ohio—trading good jobs for bad health was a common refrain. Hopewell, Virginia, used to be proud of its title as "Chemical Capital of the South." After Kepone was discovered to have contaminated the James River in the 1970s, those signs came down.

But Hopewell remained a chemical hub. In addition to Allied Chemical, numerous other factories were sited there. In 1988 eight factories in Hopewell released more than a quarter of Virginia's statewide total of hazardous materials into the environment. The community remained relatively mute. "I suspect they may be afraid," suggested former Mayor Hilda Traina. But while toxic fear prompted some factory workers to move outside the city and away from the noxious smells, Traina was referring to a form of economic fear. Even when they moved farther afield, most stayed on at their jobs. "I'd say this town would be a ghost town without the chemical companies," acknowledged one longtime chemical factory worker. Twenty-five hundred people from Hopewell and its surrounding towns worked for the chemical companies.[57] Hopewell and towns like it, which forced upon their inhabitants the impossible choice between economic and bodily health, constituted another form of slow violence that rendered the stark divisions between the producers and the consumers—or the casualties and the beneficiaries—of American abundance. Indeed, an industrial map of factories, waste sites, and environmentally vulnerable spaces overlays tidily upon maps that chart socioeconomic standing and racial lines. Local confrontation, popular epidemiology, grassroots organizing all became driving forces behind the emerging environmental justice movement. Much of the struggle for environmental justice and against environmental racism failed to resonate in national media stories the way that Woburn or Three Mile Island or Love Canal did. While cancer mortality rates certainly skewed along socioeconomic lines, the fear of cancer most certainly did not. But what was evident across the socioeconomic spectrum was that individuals and small neighborhood groups and even physicians were contacting their state health agencies and the national Centers for Disease Control main offices in Atlanta to report cancer incidence in their neighborhoods.[58] In reporting potential cancer clusters to state and federal health agencies in unprecedented numbers, Americans across the country were doubly seeking information and communicating not-so-subconscious anxieties. Cancer and the prospect of clusters showed ways in which fear intersected with bodies and the environment, an important mingling of emotional and physical healths.[59]

Calls to state or federal agencies to report a potential cancer cluster work somewhere between the availability heuristic and another cognitive bias known as the confirmation bias. The confirmation bias asserts the tendency to search for and favor information that confirms one's preconceptions. If contaminated communities across the United States rendered more Americans sensitive to the availability heuristic, the confirmation bias ensured that people were actively looking for (and finding and being fearful of) cancer links. By 1977, the Centers for Disease Control communicated to states that asbestos in schools could be hazardous. The following year a draft summary from the National Cancer Institute and the National Institute of Environmental Health Sciences warned of an imminent asbestos-related cancer epidemic. Past occupational exposure to asbestos "is expected to result in over two million premature cancer deaths in the next three decades." The study anticipated that asbestos would account for "roughly 17 percent of the total cancer deaths in the next three decades."[60] In this manner, toxic fear posited in its starkest terms the way in which fear was a future-oriented emotion. The absence of any immediate harm did little to dissipate popular anxieties around contaminated neighborhoods. For a public wrestling with uncertainty, toxic fear surrounding cancer was shaped by the prospect that "many more pollution-induced cancer clusters may be out there, but we don't see them and we rarely even bother to look."[61] But in spite of all the difficulties in proving a true cluster, consider the alternative, frightening conclusion: that environmentally caused cancer clusters are much more common than we realize. In 1987, scientists found disturbingly high levels of gasoline and cleaning solvents in drinking water that supplied the Marine base Camp Lejeune in Jacksonville, North Carolina. The base received Superfund designation in 1989. By 2018, the *Wilmington Star News* collected over 150 accounts from servicemen and -women and their families who had lived at Camp Lejeune since the 1960s.[62] In the multiple testimonies came various ailments. Amid various cancers, tremors, aches, and clinical depressions, the lone common denominator was the base and its water. And while the contaminated water may very well have contributed to many if not all of the illnesses in question, a cancer cluster requires not just a common source but also a common disease. Breast cancer, however, recurred in the testimonies in alarming numbers.[63] This is where fear enters into the equation. The emotional stomach punch that accompanies a cancer diagnosis definitely forces patients and their families to seek causes and explanations and allocate some kind of blame. And the politics of such a disaster are just as stark. The important debate is less over whether or not a particular site constitutes a cluster or not, and more about whether a grouping of illnesses could be (or could have been) prevented. If cancer's triggers are largely, somewhat, or even partially environmental, then what social, technical, political, and industrial obligations exist to minimize its risk? And to what extent is any risk of exposure justified?

CHAPTER SEVEN

Securing Knowledge

In a crisis the true facts are whatever other people say they are.
No one's knowledge is less secure than your own.
—Don DeLillo, *White Noise*

In common parlance, risk is typically defined by the challenge harm poses to its opposite: safety.[1] Risk is the potential for harm. According to the sociologist Ulrich Beck, risk is also the embodiment of modernity.[2] Deborah Lupton, another sociologist, describes risk as "assemblages of meanings, logics, and beliefs cohering around material phenomena, giving these phenomena form and substance."[3] Just about every work on risk prefaces its analysis with the assertion that risk is a function of everyday life. A risk-free society is a unicorn. Driving, crossing the street, and skydiving—normal stuff—involve making choices that require some conscious or unconscious consideration of the inherent hazards. Historians, likewise, insist that risk aversion—fear—is historically situated, and it changes over time.[4] Engagement with risk is also historically situated. Professional risk analysis is a product of the 1960s.[5] A new emphasis on acknowledging risk promoted a greater dependence on the new kinds of experts tasked with assessing, managing, and mitigating potential harm. In a 1969 watershed paper published in *Science,* Chauncey Starr—an engineer typically credited with founding risk analysis as an academic discipline—promoted a quantitative method for measuring cost-benefit analyses. This became the template for risk quantification, and it established the shape of risk practice and its knowledge authority hierarchies that have persisted ever since in policy circles. Statistical quantification, motivated and calculated by economic concerns, was the prime mover of this new, professional risk analysis. The research was still in its infancy. Starr conceded that his risk analysis could not yet distinguish "what is 'best' for society from what is 'traditionally acceptable,'" but this would become the project of the 1970s, as risk experts sought to quantify all manner of technological threats as a means of anticipating hazard and prioritizing danger.[6] Risk could be quantified, could be isolated, measured, and theorized. Risk assessment became a clinical venture. Removed from the messy realities and repercussions of culture and society and put under the microscope, risk could be diagnosed.[7]

But where risk analysts worked to determine the contours of acceptable risks, a populace exposed to new hazards found themselves creating their own less overtly hierarchical algorithms, which insisted that hard data be complemented with psychological, sociological, and cultural contexts. The distinction between science and emotion—calculation versus feeling—became an ingrained feature of toxic fears during the 1980s. The character of that tension was articulated in a series of sociological studies in the late 1970s and early 1980s, which sought to identify the specific criteria that contributed to heightened risk aversion. As the sociologist Lee Clarke argued at the end of the 1980s, risk analysis was conducted by agencies and organizations. These institutions use scientific data to qualify acceptable risk.[8] However, Clarke was quick to point out that the political results rarely advantaged "that portion of the public that bears the disproportionate burden of such risk assessments."[9] In addition to the dichotomy between experts and publics—between the math and the lived experience—the science and technology studies scholar Sheila Jasanoff stressed the importance of parsing the language that shaped risk perception and risk analysis. She argued that the seemingly simple differentiation between risk perception (what publics do) and risk analysis or assessment (what experts do) undermines the lay experience. Compared with the apparent rigor of scientific data gathering and analysis, perception can be dismissed as perspectives "shaped by the ignorance, prior beliefs, and subjective personal experiences of non-experts."[10] I would submit that the ways experts have wielded the availability and confirmation bias heuristics work in a similar vein to diminish the standing and merits of subjective, lived experience. Problems with this social hierarchy played a critical role in the manifestation of chemical anxieties across the 1980s.[11]

The debate over what constituted "acceptable risk" was contentious ground that toxic fear was instrumental in shaping. Surveys found that regardless of how infrequent or how potentially harmful a hazard, Americans were less likely to accept risk under the following circumstances:

1. Involuntary exposure to a risk
2. Lack of personal control over outcomes
3. Uncertainty about probabilities or consequences of exposure
4. Lack of experience with the risk (fear of unknown)
5. Difficulty in imagining risk exposure
6. Effects of exposure delayed in time
7. Genetic effects of exposure (threatens future generations)
8. Infrequent but catastrophic accidents ("Kill Size")
9. Benefits not highly visible
10. Benefits go to others (inequity)
11. Accidents caused by human failure rather than natural causes[12]

Each of these aspects of greater risk aversion intersected with fears surrounding chemical exposure. Indeed, each criterion has featured as an organizing principle for toxic fear (in different forms and orders of priority) in every case study examined in this work. Few would have ranked so highly in a comparable survey of risk experts.

* * *

Starr was right to infer that risk analysis would become a project of the 1970s. By the middle of that decade, the Environmental Protection Agency had started implementing various risk assessment protocols and practices in its operations. Risk assessment was no formalized process, but the EPA recognized that some kind of evaluation of health risks and economic impacts was a necessary function of any kind of rigorous planning. The watershed moment for risk assessment came just after William Ruckelshaus returned to head the agency. In 1983, the National Academy of Science produced *Risk Assessment in the Federal Government: Managing the Process*, published eight days before Anne Gorsuch resigned. Commonly known as the Red Book for its cover, *Risk Assessment in the Federal Government* was produced in response to the recognition that the new environmental and policy landscape had changed markedly, first with the series of strong environmental laws introduced in the 1970s, then with a growing technological capacity to detect and understand the nature of chemical contaminants and their threat to human health, and finally with the callous and cavalier disinterest in environmental health from those at the head of the EPA during the first years of the Reagan administration. "Cancer, birth defects, and other conditions were seldom seen as preventable by government intervention," the authors opined in the introduction. "Only in the last 15 years has the potential extent of the linkage between such conditions and toxic substances been revealed."[13] These developments presented a new species of challenge for the EPA: "Public policies are not immediately adaptable to rapid changes in social priorities and scientific advances. Many of the fundamental difficulties of regulatory risk assessment result from attempts to bend old laws and policies to fit newly perceived risks."[14]

The Red Book proposed risk assessment guidelines that the EPA quickly adopted as a means of digging its way out of the crisis it experienced during the Gorsuch years in charge. This involved restructuring risk assessment to avoid the kind of political or industrial influences that had shaped earlier decisions.[15] The study's first recommendation was a clear separation between the assessment of risks and the consideration of risk management—a means of distinguishing between scientific findings and policy judgments, on the one hand, and "political, economic, and technical considerations that influence the design and choice of regulatory strategies," on the other.[16] Greater transparency—making risk assessment studies public accessible—was another key pillar in the Red Book's recommendations. Public assessments also needed to articulate the boundaries between scientific and political motivations for the EPA's decisions. In addition, independent science advisory panels would be called upon to evaluate risk assessment reports before major regulatory action could be taken.[17]

This standardization of the EPA's protocols toward risk assessment and risk management constituted an important and largely positive institutional step forward. But its shift toward a more objective, more transparent kind of risk analysis did little to mitigate environmental fears; the media machine, the mounting number of contamination alarms, and perhaps its own transparency and communication—giving language to and fodder for popular anxieties—meant that the new EPA, "an agency that is structurally embedded in controversy," faced a continuing uphill battle to win back public trust.[18] Further, the quantitative turn may have helped to depoliticize environmental policymaking, but it did little to reconcile the distance between objective data and lived experience, between risk analysis and risk perception. The driving question that strikes at the tension over toxic fears in the 1980s and works to explain the kinds of popular epidemiology practiced in Woburn and elsewhere is who owns risk, the actuaries or the prospective victims? This question needn't be quite such a binary, but it is important to reckon with the distance between the two ends of the spectrum. Risk is at once "objective and scientifically knowable" as well as "subjective and socially constructed."[19] It is a probability: a statistical inference. It is also a consequence of deliberate social actions. Frequently, its histories engage with the discovery of a new problem and the worries for prospective harm that they pose. Alternatively, they examine disasters and the lessons learned (and not learned) from them. In either case, the idea of risk hinges on the uncertainties derived from new or unforeseen occurrences. Those uncertainties created a dissonance between experts who evaluate risks and publics exposed to them. More often than not, the experts who analyzed risk quantitatively in government agencies, in academic think tanks, or in epidemiological studies were not part of the publics exposed to those potential harms.[20] For example, staffers of health and environmental agencies exercised a strikingly different relationship with the risks at Love Canal than did the community's inhabitants. After their work, they were free to remove themselves from Love Canal; the residents enjoyed no such luxury.[21]

In this regard, the 1980s witnessed a contest between state expertise and local experiences in the debate over risk from contaminations. Chemophobia emerged as the playing field. In simplified terms, the dispute arose over objective and subjective readings of risk. Where state expertise practiced a kind of risk analysis—quantifying the extent of a potential hazard—local experiences worked in risk perceptions—a more qualified assessment of what potential hazard meant to them. Risk analysis could interpret generic risks, but it could not dictate to individuals or groups of individuals at risk what constituted acceptable harm. That was a public discussion that transcended scientific expertise and state authority. This tension served as the heart of Beck's groundbreaking 1992 work, *Risk Society*.[22] According to Beck, risk society was "an inescapable structural condition of advanced industrialization."[23] Modernity introduced countless social and technical advances, but also a series of unavoidable risks that became entrenched (or were becoming so) in everyday life and public discourse. New high-technology industries, for example, created new environmental problems they were ill-equipped to contain—or fully understand. In *Risk Society*, Beck chastised management experts for the contempt they showed toward public perceptions of risk. Hard data needed to be softened with psychological, sociological, and cultural contexts. Because of a relative breakdown in communication, public perceptions of new environmental pollutants gravitated toward increased fear over the course of the 1970s, climaxing with a culture of toxic fear in the United States in the 1980s.[24]

The debate, as it played out in mainstream discourse, consisted of critics lambasting public risk perception as being reactionary, overblown, and dangerous. One 1979 *Wall Street Journal* editorial urged caution:

> This is not to say that the precise connection will not be found at some point between these phenomena and human disease; but the uncertainties do provoke a special distaste at the political circus that's now developing over both the radiation search and the dioxin issue. The anti-nuclear organizations and the environmental groups and the antiwar-based veterans organizations and tort liability lawyers are now in the ring, filing their own lawsuits and encouraging suits and claims by others; such groups are palpably happy to be able to use the current public fear of environmental poisons in support of their various causes. The TV documentary makers are out in force, claiming that they've established one lethal connection or another and scaring their viewers.[25]

Risk certainly existed, critics contended, but the discourse had blown its reality out of proportion. If twentieth-century practice had turned risk management over to experts, then surely the experts were the best arbiters of what constituted legitimate danger. Permitting an expansion of debate undermined scientific authority and exacerbated the prospect of irrational fears interfering with rational decision-making. A big part of this problem stemmed from the popular assumption that risk and danger were effectively synonymous. Rather, risk was the possibility or measure of danger, not a practical peril in itself. Inasmuch as risk constituting a kind of latent harm certainly galvanized popular fear of chemical pollution, critics of popular risk perception objected to the idea of responding to or banning everything that went bump in the night. Fear was its own disease. As conservative critic of environmental fears Edith Efron argued in *The Apocalyptics* (1984), "Cancer in a culture is a far more devastating disease, and possibly more incurable, than cancer in an individual."[26]

* * *

Statistics and chance—complexity and uncertainty—contributed to the difficulties in positively linking localized contaminations and cancer clusters. But for all the epidemiological challenges, the 1980s also witnessed an uptick in the amount of noise that cluttered local and scientific toxic discourse. The decade marked an unprecedented high point in antienvironmental rhetoric, most of it coming from the right. After a decade of groundbreaking environmental legislation in the 1970s, the pushback against what many conservatives perceived as being the apotheosis of big government interventions and a series of regulations that inhibited markets and trade acquired momentum across the spectrum of environmental issues. Consider Arizona Senator Barry Goldwater's 1979 complaint that EPA regulations "have added hundreds of billions of dollars to the cost of our mineral products, electric power, highway construction, food, automobiles, and housing."[27] Cancer and public health were equally in the conservative crosshairs. Antienvironmental sentiment rejected the notion that public health was really at risk from environmental transgressions. Indeed, as fears of cancer clusters featured in 1980s environmental discourse, counterarguments downplayed the threats posed by environmental contaminants. Efron's *The Apocalyptics* was one of many books that worked to stem the tide against intense fear of chemicals. Indeed, it was the backlash against Americans' fears of chemical contamination that transformed chemophobia from a cultural phenomenon into a derogatory term. That was part of the antienvironmental blueprint from within American conservative circles. Painting environmentalists as hysterical, mendacious malcontents bent on disrupting American freedoms became a common mainstream strategy, and one that added considerable noise to public discourse.

As American politics began shifting to the right in the 1960s and 1970s, Edith Efron was among the first wave of successful conservative authors to combine an effective voice with a compelling polemical style. She was, briefly, a contributor to Ayn Rand's *The Objectivist,* before splitting with Rand. She subsequently moved to writing celebrity profiles, political columns, and editorials for Walter Annenberg's *TV Guide* and ghost-wrote Treasury Secretary (and "Energy Czar") William E. Simon's 1978 book, *A Time for Truth.* At *TV Guide,* Efron was a contemporary of Pat Buchanan and a number of other conservative thinkers who challenged the liberal media bias they perceived in American programming. In her editorials and behind the scenes, she sought to expand the rightward range of the political spectrum on the airwaves. Rather than promoting greater political objectivity in news reporting, she encouraged more coverage of right-wing perspectives to provide a counterbalance. The traditional conservatism that did appear on mainstream news shows was too centrist to reflect the ground shift on the American right as evidenced by Goldwater's ascension in the 1960s.[28] Efron's bestselling 1971 *The News Twisters* condemned what she saw as a liberal crusade within the media against Richard Nixon during the 1968 presidential campaign. During the final weeks of the campaign, she argued, television hewed an "elitist-liberal-left line in all controversies."[29]

By the mid-1980s, Efron had developed a similar critique of American environmental politics, putting particular emphasis on the relationship between toxicity and cancer, and the fears they provoked. Americans had been "so thoroughly besieged by myths, errors, and falsehoods about environmental cancer that they have been plunged into a neoprimitive pathology."[30] The perpetrators of this pathology were the apocalyptics of her title, jeremiad-touting environmentalists who wanted to bring industry to its knees. Their support from cadres within the scientific establishment resulted in nothing short of a gross misinformation campaign about cancer and carcinogens that were provoking widespread chemophobia. Environmentalists were fear mongers, peddling a message that hindered psychological health that constituted nothing short of "a complex corruption of science and a prolonged deception of the public."[31] Cancer was a tool, she argued, used by the left to provoke fear and to assert the importance of greater and centralized governance. Environmentalists were hysterical pawns in that gambit, promoting the existence of a horrific toxic society.

Efron took up the challenge of the toxic society. Cancer risks had not changed, she argued. "Natural" carcinogens and other factors, not new chemicals, were responsible for the spike in cancer incidence. She began her book by invoking what she called the "paradox of Rehn." In 1895, a Frankfurt surgeon named Ludwig Rehn identified a link between bladder cancers and aniline dye manufacturers. Subsequent research in the following decades established more connections between cancers and new synthetic chemicals. As the chemical industry continued to discover and produce more synthetic chemicals, a legitimate concern grew among occupational health specialists that many of these new compounds might be carcinogenic. Progress could unwittingly create a massive cancer epidemic. Animal testing found that many of the new chemicals were, indeed, carcinogenic. And yet—here was the paradox—no massive escalation of cancer incidence had occurred.[32] Efron noted that in December 1975, Irving Selikoff revisited the question in the context of asbestos in the environment: "Do experiences with vinyl chloride, bischloromethyl ether, chromates, etc., demonstrate that the prophecies were really correct, merely premature?"[33] Selikoff left the question open-ended, but in the mid-1970s it was a question worth asking. In Washington, on January 12, 1976, Samuel Epstein warned a House of Representatives informal symposium on the environment that a cancer "epidemic" was on the rise, driven by "chemical carcinogens in the environment." His fellow panelist, Ralph Nader, intoned that the world was entering "the carcinogenic century." Both insisted that lawmakers and federal agencies act to rein in polluting industries.[34]

The timing was auspicious. Scientists and regulatory bodies warned of widespread chemical contamination and its potential hazard right before the major chemical crises of the 1980s—Love Canal, Three Mile Island, Woburn, Times Beach, New Jersey. To Efron, this was a perfect example of a national disaster spun, using the availability heuristic to foster its panic and spread. Every headache, every case of dizziness, permitted confirmation biases to run rampant, drawing connections to the last contamination. "In one month," she mused, "Selikoff's ignorance had turned into Epstein's statistics and Selikoff's paradox of Rehn into Nader's 'carcinogenic century.'"[35] Cancer rates *were* going up, but for Efron this was a sign of progress. Cancer was a disease of the aged. Advances in public health and medicine meant that Americans were living longer. Their regular exposure to low-level doses of harmful chemicals suggested not risk but rather an evolving tolerance to these substances.

Moreover, Efron contended that the cancer epidemic was a manufactured hysteria in order to push through new environmental regulations and impose greater government control over industry. Environmentalists and scientists had taken over government agencies and were using public hysteria over cancer to push through antibusiness (and anticapitalist) restrictions. The "carcinogenic century . . . arrived in a form that Congress may not have anticipated: that of an unintelligible menace." For Efron, this unintelligible menace was the real source of toxic fear, and that fear was unwarranted:

> An unintelligible menace did not inspire human beings with intellectual self-confidence. It did not trigger thought at all but, rather, emotional response. The fearful were severely afflicted, trying desperately to make

> little lists of what was safe to eat, to drink, to do. A certain number paid no attention to the unintelligible menace once they ascertained that it was unintelligible. Others converted it into morbid humour: "Everything causes cancer." Yet others liked to imagine themselves knowledgeable, which is to say that they blindly repeated the latest formulae on the unintelligible menace from trusted sources. And, finally, some came slowly to suspect that the menace was unintelligible because those who had deposited it on the public agenda did not understand it themselves.[36]

Set aside for the moment that the vagaries of "unintelligible menace" and "toxic airborne event" sound eerily similar (Efron's *The Apocalyptics* and DeLillo's *White Noise* were published six months apart). Chemophobia, Efron contended, was a deliberate form of fear mongering, motivated by an environmental, left-wing conspiracy. Or even a communist plot. It was a blatant attack on the United States. A particularly damning review of her book in the *Washington Post* dismissed the notion as conspiracy theory from the lunatic fringe: "If paranoia is the antidote to hysteria, then *The Apocalyptics* is indeed a valuable book."[37] But to reject *The Apocalyptics* out of hand imposes an intellectual dichotomy that, for the purposes of this study, problematically assumes caricatured black hats and white hats to fairly flat historical actors. In so doing, it does an injustice to history and to the complicated politics of victimhood that an analysis of toxic fear seeks to interrogate. Moreover, there was an interesting strategy to Efron's polemic, frequently overlooked when opposing interests argue past each other. Throughout *The Apocalyptics*, Efron made a concerted claim to reason and science, two pillars typically claimed by more progressive arguments. She stressed the importance of objectivity in presenting her findings, citing thousands of sources and interviewing more than two hundred scientists.[38] This was an especially interesting tack since Efron also conceded she was not a scientist, but a humanist. Further, as many reviews pointed out, her work was hardly an effective survey of the scientific literature—or, rather, it cherrypicked material, much of it more than a decade old by the time the book was published.

If there was a place for debate on the risks of chemical contamination in American communities, it eroded over the course of the 1980s. Distrust in government created adversarial tension in many contaminated neighborhoods that left many citizens unwilling to participate in studies or respond to surveys. Underresourced agencies rendered many genuine efforts to engage with potential problems slow or inept. That they were potential hazards until experts could assert a proper taxonomy established stark and uneasy hierarchies of knowledge authority that excluded local inhabitants. Finally, obstructionism and ad hominem attacks from a growing antienvironmental movement—emboldened by the Reagan administration's determination to cut and deregulate recent environmental gains—became increasingly charged. Where Efron referred to "radical environmentalists" intent on subverting American industry and politics by scaring the public as "the apocalyptics," Elizabeth M. Whelan, the founder of the pro-industry advocacy organization American Council on Science and Health, went further, labeling them "toxic terrorists" in her 1985 book, *Toxic Terror: The Truth Behind the Cancer Scares*.[39] Such semantic escalation persisted well beyond the 1980s and into the new century. Toxic fear turned the space between the two sides debating chemical risk and safety into a chasm. The debate itself was often vitriolic. There is an irony here. Where both sides fought to claim reason as the commanding heights, the rhetoric from the right became more and more shrill, oppositional, and derisive. Debate and discourse require a back-and-forth: abuttal, rebuttal, and surrebuttal. They require interaction with competing ideas. There is very little evidence that by the end of the 1980s listening to counterarguments was something that happened with any regularity. Instead, opposing sides created separate echo chambers composed only of those inclined to confirm their position. This, in turn, resulted in a fierce tribalism of ideas that profoundly wracked American polity and civility.

In such isolation, two oppositional rhetorics do not make a debate. Moreover, their noise interfered with addressing real fears from communities on the ground. Government agencies found themselves caught somewhere between this growing divide. Their mandate to respond to environmental irregularities put them on the front line of testing and remediation ventures. But their lack of resources and propensity for caution and not provoking alarm—good things on paper—frequently gave the appearance that they were siding with industry more than communities. Americans afraid of chemicals in the environment reacted strongly against governing authorities and industries that seemed to turn an unsympathetic ear to their concerns. From a certain distance, clear dichotomies could be discerned. In response to grassroots concerns, an energized and increasingly antiregulatory "right" denounced the culture of dependency that clearly stressed the need for a strong, responsible central government. Similarly, it appeared as though "experts" from distant laboratories lined up against communities with "emotions." Or that frightened local residents opposed "industries' intent on profit. But such divisions rarely played out so cleanly on the ground, where grassroots groups typically relied on scientific research and many industrial neighbors worked with community groups to allay local concerns.[40] Instead, the critical lens through which to frame pollution debates is over risk understandings and the cultural significance of uncertainty as an organizing principle. At stake was a political debate that pitted statistical significance against public health significance as the preeminent risk authority. In between was a wary and frightened populace.

* * *

The growing focus on cancer as environmental bellwether was also a problem that likely did disservice to better understanding the state of environmental contamination. Lost amid popular fears of cancer clusters and charges of cancer hysteria were the litany of non-cancer-related health problems associated with environmental contaminants: depression, infertility, miscarriages, birth defects, developmental challenges, hormonal imbalances. Love Canal mothers had raised the prospect of a high number of miscarriages in the area surrounding the waste site. Fears surrounding—and the identification of—hormone-disrupting chemicals were still a decade away. But as antienvironmental critics isolated their arguments around the relationship between chemophobia and cancerphobia, the focus on cancer incidences and deaths as the only statistics worth counting problematically narrowed the frame of environmental engagement. The public debate over the American environment—renewed in 1970 with the first Earth Day and powerful legislation to confront widespread pollution problems—was dead before the 1980s had drawn to a close.[41]

So back to the driving question: Who owns risk? In his landmark essay, Starr asked the question another way, from a risk manager's perspective: "How safe is safe enough?"[42] The answer depended on whom you were asking. More often than not, the experts and agencies brought in to evaluate the risks at Love Canal or, more recently, the long-standing water quality issues in Flint, Michigan, do not typically live with those slow-burning, persistent contaminations. Nor do the antienvironmental critics. The separation between irrational hysteria and legitimate fear might best be understood by distinguishing between expert probabilities and situated possibilities. For outside experts, negligible risks or hazards still brought with them the *possibility* of harm for those exposed to them. This tension was further amplified by the uncertainties inherent in any kind of judgment, professional or popular. Moreover, as local communities retained their own science professionals to conduct air and water quality studies, to assist with popular epidemiology projects, the welter of scientific knowledge was hardly skewed in favor of government agencies. Everybody had their own science. And, frequently, it made competing claims that intensified debate and entrenched differences. Information was incomplete, but it was hardly insufficient. Rather, Daniel Sarewitz has reflected on the challenges of having too much knowledge. Rather than too little knowledge, chemophobia cases typically experienced the opposite, what he calls "an excess of objectivity." Sarewitz writes, "We are not suffering from a lack of objectivity, but from an excess of it. Science is sufficiently rich, diverse, and Balkanized to provide comfort and support for a range of subjective, political positions on complex issues such as climate change, nuclear waste disposal, acid rain, or endangered species."[43] This makes sense. It suggests that uncertainty is the result of too much noise rather than insufficient data. Others have observed similar developments. But combined with the neoliberal assault on the welfare state and an imposed culture of dependency, too much noise and not enough oversight created a series of new risks that nobody properly understood. Fears persisted.

Whatever the solution to the information oversaturation, the historical lesson is clear. In debates over individual risk, possibility, however minute, always trumps infinitesimal probability. This is not a castigation of public fears or some inherent irrationality of the masses. Rather, it is perfectly normal. Throughout this book, toxic fear has wrestled with two incommensurable realities. The first is that humans are biologically hardwired to err on the side of caution. This is a basic survival mechanism. As with birds scared out of a tree by a sudden noise, or ungulates on the savannah bolting at a rustle in the long grass, the knee-jerk social response for desiring greater security comes from an uncertain evaluation of an unclear problem. Flight is a safer proposition than lingering to determine whether or not the risk is real. In cases of toxic fear, the availability heuristic—that recent, similar experiences help shape individual and collective responses to uncertainty—

magnified the growing sense of chemical urgency across the country. Of course people were frightened. And of course they wanted to escape the chemical threats in their communities. The second reality is that modern industry is economically hardwired to be bold and disruptive. Politics and economies cannot function properly amid an overweening flight mentality. In the case of a possible toxic contamination, running tests, identifying the pertinent chemicals and their risks, determining the health hazards, and developing an action plan can take months. It is perhaps no surprise that local residents pushed vociferously for remediation or evacuation—or action of some kind, any kind—on timelines that were incompatible with authorities' efforts to understand the nature of the problem. For the public, the uncertainty was terrifying. In Love Canal, in Times Beach, and elsewhere, not knowing was tantamount to dangerous exposure, and they wanted out. But for the various branches of government agencies, coping with a new species of trouble and in the absence of clear protocols and response mechanisms, care and accuracy took time. At the height of the Missouri dioxin fears, EPA officials beseeched local residents not to conduct independent tests. "The accuracy of tests is very, very important," Fred Lafser told concerned citizens at a November 17, 1982, hearing in Jefferson County. Private companies, he warned were less reliable and might only provoke further fears. Another official noted that some private laboratories had won contracts to test for dioxin privately and then contacted the EPA to learn how to do it.[44] Even though skepticism and hesitation in the face of uncertainty are the correct responses from scientifically grounded health and environment officials, we need to acknowledge that local fears were exacerbated by these protocols and the apparent delays in gathering and communicating information. Authorities championing diligence weren't the ones at risk.

Add historical and political context to this tension and it becomes easier to realize the true nature of the perfect storm that constituted toxic fear in the American 1980s. There are two key elements here. The first is the relative novelty of ubiquitous local contamination. Toxic pollution had very much been on the social and political radar during the 1960s and 1970s. It was an essential lesson from Rachel Carson's influential *Silent Spring*, from 1962. "For the first time in the history of the world," she admonished, "every human being is now subjected to contact with dangerous chemicals, from the moment of conception until death."[45] Over the next twenty years, that fact sank into the American psyche. During the 1970s, Americans introduced some of the most advanced chemical control laws of the time. But neither fact prepared Americans or administrators for the hazards confronting them at Love Canal, at Times Beach, or at the countless other toxic waste sites around the country. Carson and laws such as the Toxic Substances Control Act (TSCA) might have been tacit recognitions that Americans had a pollution problem, but that wasn't the same as knowing what to do when those pollutants were found to have seeped into the water table or were turning up in drinking water reservoirs. Environmental remediation was a new concept—and one that no government agency could really fathom, especially not at the scale and scope of the emergent disasters during the 1980s. As New York State Health Commissioner David Axelrod acknowledged in a letter at the height of the Love Canal crisis, "While we have found no lack of criticism from a host of self-anointed experts from the federal, private, and political spheres, we have become increasingly aware of a virtual poverty of an understanding of the complexity of the problem."[46] Juggling responsibilities and jurisdictions between different health and environmental agencies did little to calm frightened residents. To locals on the ground, government scientists and officials were uncaring, inefficient, and incompetent. In regional offices, they were overwhelmed, understaffed, underfunded, and learning new ropes. In short, the various county, state, and federal health and environmental agencies that populate this work lacked real experience in confronting the toxic tsunami that crested at the very end of the 1970s.

* * *

During the 1980s, chemical-propelled fear and anxiety become palpable elements of the everyday experience, and upset social and personal methods of understanding the world for many Americans. The uncertainties surrounding exposure to carcinogens and the palpable worries around the creations of cancer clusters merged cultural and political discourses. Disruption and disconfirmation compose the baseline tenets of toxic fear. As the sociologist Michael Edelstein observed in the late 1980s, "Toxic exposure directly assails several fundamental social beliefs: that humans have dominion over nature; that personal control over one's destiny is possible; that technology and science are forces of progress only; that risks necessary for the good life are acceptable; that people get what they deserve; that experts know best; that the marketplace is self-regulating; that one's home is one's castle; that people have the right to do what they wish on their own property; and that government exists to help."[47] Put another way, uncertainty—bred by disruption to and disconfirmation of existing patterns of health and safety—is a social manifestation and a product of the risk society. Uncertainties "proliferate," the science studies scholar Helga Nowotny declares, because of "the relentless pursuit of the novel through innovation." The spread of toxic chemicals provoked fear, not just because of their potential health hazard, but because of their novelty. As a result, fear and uncertainty emerge "by not only challenging but also changing established ways of doing things."[48]

The "airborne toxic event" in *White Noise* is an exercise in the proliferation of novel uncertainties. Jack's conversation with the SIMUVAC technician concludes in an unsatisfactory manner. Trying to reassure Jack, the technician tells him "I wouldn't worry about what I can't see or feel. . . . I'd go ahead and live my life. Get married, settle down, have kids. There's no reason you can't do these things, knowing what we know."[49] In essence, the technician dismisses any discernible disruption to Jack's lifescape. But the upset has already occurred. If Three Mile Island, Love Canal, Times Beach, and Woburn rattled the national faith in technology and authority, subsequent findings warned that the toxic pollution threat was likely to endure. While the Times Beach evacuation was underway, the *New York Times* reported that toxic waste landfills across the country were inherently unsafe. Putting hazardous chemicals underground but failing to seal them effectively for the duration of their toxicity was tantamount to promising an inevitable crisis in the future.[50] These kinds of toxic hypotheticals—toxic possibilities—were examples of "slow violence," an explanatory tool for "slowly unfolding environmental catastrophes [that] present formidable representational obstacles that can hinder our efforts to mobilize and act decisively."[51]

Epidemiology and risk were decisively indecisive tools for confronting the new slow disasters. They required clinical care, of course, but they were also inherently prone to political influence. When experts talked of risks, they calculated complex actuarial algorithms and extrapolated averages, norms, and probabilities that appeared abstract and foreign to the nonspecialist. Similarly, epidemiologists seemed to be constantly intent on complicating their analyses of potential disease clusters. The smaller a study, the more subject it was to random chance. The larger it was, the greater the chance that a real cluster was diluted to the point where it became as invisible and indecipherable as the trace chemicals that seeped into groundwater or escaped factory plants and spread on the wind. Neither was democratic in vocabulary or practice. Expertise created a kind of scientific hierarchy that diminished local voices, experiences, and fears. In many respects, expert authority posed its own challenges to local, lived experience by taking ownership over communities with contamination risks.[52] And where DeLillo's fictional character was encouraged to set aside the airborne toxic event and carry on with his life, in the real world that was not always possible. The week after eleven-year-old Patrick Toomey died from leukemia in Woburn in late March 1981, *Daily Times and Chronicle* reporter Charles C. Ryan captured the essence of local chemophobia and the tension over the ownership of risk in a column titled "They Are Not Statistics." Ryan reminded readers that Jimmy Anderson had been buried just a few months earlier. Jimmy liked to watch *The Dukes of Hazzard*, "when he was well enough to stay up a little later than normal." Patrick took trombone lessons. At the end of March, another local child—a four-year-old girl—was diagnosed with leukemia. The rhetorical thrust of Ryan's article hinged on the question that accompanied any cancer diagnosis or premature death: Why? "Some politicians, many businessmen, a handful of scientists, too many doctors would say it is all just a statistical coincidence. People die from leukaemia, cancer, auto accidents, and a thousand other causes every year. Where and when it happens is just a matter of statistics, they say." Correct, but this fact was no consolation, and it missed the point. "Jimmy and Patrick are not statistics," Ryan intoned. "No child is just a statistic."[53]

Dan Fagin notes that "mystery and dread have always been the close consorts of cancer."[54] In terms of suspected clusters, mystery and dread were amplified by the responsible and irresponsible authority practiced by experts. Afflicted communities were especially distraught by what appeared to them as ineffective communication or conflicting information as it was relayed to residents. Lamenting growing concerns over New Jersey's "Cancer Alley" as the American Cyanamid site in Bridgewater Township revealed itself to be a long-standing and illicit toxic waste dump, Robert Bukowcyk of Somerville railed against the "Three Mile Island syndrome" he saw in protective agencies. "One day, the state says that our water is contaminated; the next day, it says it's not. Does Alice live in Wonderland or in New Jersey?" he fumed.[55] Fears and edifications swung like a metronome in the balance.

Risk and uncertainty galvanized citizen action. Local efforts to acquire knowledge, data, information mark an important shift in social empowerment and in environmental politics. Grassroots activities became a direct response and challenge to government deregulation and antienvironmental sentiments. Both popular epidemiology and the rise of grassroots activism transformed American environmental fears or returned them to kitchen tables, church basements, and front porches.[56] As Brown points out, lay actors frequently have better access to information about their daily lives and health histories than do scientific experts.[57] What they frequently lacked—but quickly discovered—was the political nous to make their fears heard. Fear was no longer a passive emotion: a response to something that happened. Those who feared were not hapless victims anymore. In environmental politics, fear replaced slogans and jeremiads and propelled public health and environmental safety into mainstream discussions, many of which remain prevalent in contemporary debates over climate change.

But where the politics of probabilism dictated expert risk analysis and the politics of possibilism shaped community fears, traumas, and grief, other interests sought to craft a different kind of narrative by crafting a much more optimistic—risk-free—vision of the future. Frequently in the crosshairs for being responsible for producing the chemicals that provoked fears, the chemical industry sought to bolster government attempts to release industry from the legislative shackles that slowed production. For DuPont chairman Irving Shapiro, focusing on risk and blame was unproductive. Sticking to the wonders of chemistry—better things and better living, as the longstanding DuPont advertisement promised—meant resisting the impulse to be cautious. Since the Industrial Revolution, the predominant American ethos had been one wedded to unquestioning technological progress. Shapiro stuck to that message. "Let's start with today, not worry about who did what in the past. Government and industry should work together rather than get emotional. We've got to get going rather than sitting around trying to figure out who's wearing the black hat and who's wearing the white hat."[58] Past transgressions be damned; industry should be free to forge ahead; lessons needn't be for learning; obsession with novelty should not be restrained by caution surrounding its consequences. Looking back on the past four decades of toxic fears, disease clusters, uncertain risks, and vitriolic debate, it might be fair to conclude: and that's exactly what they did.

The Nature of Plots

All plots tend to move deathward. This is the nature of plots.
—Don DeLillo, *White Noise*

I have resisted mentioning 9/11, climate change, and COVID-19. That was a deliberate choice on my part to dampen the distortion of how subsequent American fears may have cast a pall over my treatment of toxic fear in the 1980s or distracted from the topic under investigation. I preferred to examine the problem of pollution anxieties in the 1980s without keeping one eye trained on what happened next. But I think there is also some historical justification for focusing on what feels like a more concentrated kind of social fear—at least in the manner in which it was manifested in the 1980s. Existential fears surrounding planetary-scale catastrophes or globalized violences are intimately related, of course, to the chemical affront imposed on human health and well-being by the chemical industry, which has its own planetary history.[1] But the pollution anxieties that animate this work are a function of time and place, and it is important to start with situating them in that milieu. The potential for comparison is obvious, however, and I leave the reader to consider whether or not my discussion of the 1980s informs contemporary understanding on fear writ large. I would submit that it does, and I hope that this conclusion makes a nod toward that case: The manner in which popular fear and the state have become constant, interminable interlocutors in modern history suggests a degree of continuity and hints at the merits of treating fear in its various guises as an important subject for historical study. Fear is an ingrained, implicit, and all-consuming feature of our environmental discourse to such an extent that Americans are frequently incapable of identifying or extricating it from the component parts of political debate. Americans have lost sight of the relationship between fear and risk. It is just there: the noise that clouds our environmental signals.

Perhaps, too, the persistent presence of chemical fears has somewhat desensitized fears or made them a tricky component of the social and environmental landscape to pin down. In the 1920s, the developmental psychologist Mary Cover Jones introduced the practice of conditioning patients to overcome their fears. Her celebrated Little Peter studies consisted of regularly exposing her subject in low doses to the anxiety-inducing object in a controlled environment. It was a kind of psychological immunotherapy.[2] Over time, the fears would subside. The South African psychiatrist Joseph Wolpe pursued Jones's work, and in the 1950s he coined the term "systematic desensitization." The alternative to systematic desensitization was called the flooding technique, which involved exhausting the senses through intense immersion to that fear. After an intense fear, the patient would become exhausted, thereby reducing the response.[3] Both these treatments engaged individuals suffering from specific phobias to the point of depletion, but is it possible to imagine some kind of similar, uncontrolled version of these practices blanketing American toxic discourse in the period after the 1980s? Some case studies suggested that toxic fear was subsiding. In 1984 United Farm Workers' founder César Chávez launched a second grape boycott against the use of five pesticides that coated the fruit and constituted a health threat to workers in the fields. Whereas a 1966 table grape boycott had generated widespread attention to and support for California's field workers, the 1984 strike did not resonate, in spite of renewed efforts in late 1987, when consumer advocate Ralph Nader publicly supported the cause. "People are getting numb to the issue of chemicals in the environment," conceded Ron Pembelton of the California Public Interest Research Group in 1988. The *New York Times* concurred: "Even some who support the boycott say the union has chosen a futile cause in an age when consumers are bombarded with warnings about the radon in their cellars and the cholesterol in their eggs."[4] Perhaps. Stark labor divisions in the United States had already removed most of middle-class white America—the ones whose plight had resonated at Love Canal and in Woburn—from the most menial workplace jobs and hazards.

Did toxic fear reach a saturation point sometime after the 1980s? Sort of. But I think it might be more accurate to suggest that its mutation persisted in other sources of popular fear. While the intense chemical scares of the 1980s seem less commonplace today, they also appear to have evolved into various concerns about the foods Americans eat, the water they drink, the medicines they are prescribed. In many respects, the new expressions of toxic fear have become more sophisticated insofar as they address specific sources of chemical assaults, rather than the generic fear that captivated 1980s America. Reflecting on the continuing difficulties in confronting climate change and especially the pushback against popular denials, the historian Kari Marie Norgaard offers further fruitful insight to the persistence of chemicals and the fears they provoke. Much like chemical compounds, climate science is a popular abstraction, somehow removed from social, political, and private life. The abstraction permits a kind of popular jumblism of good information and sincere public discourse.[5] This is the space in which chemophobia still exists. But it's also a landscape cohabited by antivaccination fears, fears over genetically modified organisms, and the organic food debate. Breaking this Gordian knot by insisting that "Science" is the lone, right arbiter is problematic, precisely for reasons discussed throughout this book: "Objective knowledge" is never an absolute. Nor is it its own thing, but rather a function of a state power structure that rarely works in favor of those most at risk. Moreover, in reference to late nineteenth-century fears of being buried alive, Joanna Bourke writes "the dignified voice of scientific reassurance was no match for the roar of moral panic."[6] The contemporary rationalist response would be to scoff at such an abject abdication of reason. But the historian needs to show a little more empathy and inquire as to why that gulf between reason and emotion was so broad. In short, I draw a line under the assertion that there is no such thing as irrational fear: It comes from somewhere, and it needs to be addressed fairly and attentively and not dismissively. A phobia is considered an undignified weakness. That is a big part of the problem.

Nevertheless, the fear industry remains alive and well. Chemical concerns endure, but they frequently seem crushed under the welter of other issues that Americans are told should frighten them. In 1970, Alvin Toffler opined that Americans were less likely to suffer the totalitarian fate portrayed in George Orwell's *1984*, where Big Brother's singular message was the lone, repressive signal. Toffler's bestselling book proposed that the more likely outcome was quite the opposite: *Future Shock* warned of a point where so much noise was present that the signal would be completely lost.[7] Looking back over the past half century's history of information and communication, it is not difficult to be persuaded that the proliferation of noise is a fundamental characteristic of the United States in the 2020s—

and why shades of authoritarianism and its false promise of order might appeal in some corners of the unimaginative mainstream. The availability heuristic amplifies popular American rhetoric and fear over terror, crime, immigration, gay marriage, personal safety.[8] The cultural divide among Americans has become so vast that something of a cold civil war is taking place over fears about the future, and those fears are turned into angers. Traditional conservative anxieties about youth have been recast as a vitriolic fear about sexuality: homophobia and transphobia are expressed—even in mainstream media—as threats to the bulwark of American society. Latent racisms, antisemitisms, and xenophobias are emboldened in contemporary discourse. This all marks a quantum shift from the toxic fears covered in this book, but they are intimately related in terms of form and history. A conclusion may be no place to introduce new problems and diagnoses, but I would submit that the idea of the United States has been transformed into a key battleground in which debate over the evolution of American fears (writ large) has raged. The tragedy, of course, is that the American idea seems more important in that debate than the United Statesian people who inhabit it. The more ground fear gains, the less room remains for civil discourse; the decline of civil discourse, twentieth-century history tells us, serves as preface to violent threats to civil liberties.

* * *

In history, no narrative ends, full stop. Instead, aftermaths, but-it's-more-complicated-than-that caveats, renewed and revised consequences, and re-analyses jostle for the final afterword. Conclusions are difficult. This book makes three attempts at closure while also asserting that the toxic fear of the 1980s is a past that has not passed. The first conclusion steps beyond American borders to briefly consider the transnational story of toxic fear not taken up in this book. The second conclusion offers a coda to the 1980s by moving into the 1990s and the new millennium. Finally, the third conclusion makes an attempt at articulating the history of fear's contemporary relevance, and why toxic fear in the 1980s should matter to readers and to environmental politics in the 2020s and beyond. Before all that, the easy, concluding assertion to this history of toxic fear is to observe that differences between expert risk *quantification* rarely reconciled with more *qualitative* risk perceptions from public groups and individuals. The rational metrics used by risk experts enjoy little traction in the polis, and that is no failing of the public. Expert risk management flatlines nuance and detail in order to render a cost-benefit analysis based on the law of averages. But just as Woburn or Love Canal or Times Beach were Everytown, USA, nobody and nowhere is the representative average. One of the enduring failings in responding to global environmental problems is the insistence that the ecosphere be made to conform to economic interests. In risk analysis, asking a public to accede to a numerical value driven by what the market will yield is equally problematic—and tone deaf to the real fears experienced by locals on the ground.[9]

That's the easy part. Another concluding assertion posits that society should take fear more seriously. Wendell Berry has written about the importance of developing a vocabulary for nature because people are more inclined to protect what they can name, what they love.[10] By way of counterpoint, this book makes an argument for developing a more sophisticated vocabulary for fear—and more importantly expand the channels of communication—so that citizens may better understand and confront the hazards to which they are exposed. Fear also needs to be recognized as a socially active and relevant component of contemporary politics. Expressions of chemophobia constituted "a test of American democracy," the biologist Barry Commoner told residents around Three Mile Island on the first anniversary of the meltdown scare. "You people are doing your best to make democracy live under difficult conditions."[11] When addressing moments of catastrophe—in the wake of a new disaster—when panic and emergency breed distinct brands of fear, knowledge communication needs to be a carefully conceived and multilateral activity. The community at risk needs to be a part of the process, rather than recipients of outside expert information. Research and studies should be shared with teachers, clergy, and doctors to make sure that information is disseminated, but more importantly consumed along more personal conduits. But even here, there exists the danger of treating environmental fear as an issue in need of a top-down solution. The implicit suggestion is that an uninformed public is suffering from a deficit of knowledge, experience, and understanding.[12] Privileging lived, embodied experience acknowledges that environmental stakes are not evenly distributed. And it permits more balanced dialog. But this is the low-hanging fruit. A proper exit needs to establish some kind of historical closure.

1. The Transnational Perspective

There was no American monopoly on toxic fear. In July 1976, a toxic dioxin airborne event hit the small town of Seveso in Lombardy. The cloud left a wake of destruction behind it. Locals complained of rashes and chloracne, 20,000 hectares of soils were contaminated, and 80,000 poisoned cattle were slaughtered.[13] Scientific inquiries into the genetic and carcinogenic hazards posed by dioxin accelerated after the Seveso chemical plant spill in July 1976. In the aftermath of the spill, uncertainty reigned supreme. Long-term health risks posed by dioxin compounds could not be ascertained because the science did not exist.[14] Seveso became the availability heuristic for European chemical fears. Two years after the Seveso disaster, for example, a couple of German policymakers published the provocatively titled "Seveso is Everywhere—The Lethal Risks of Chemicals." In May 1983, the German newspaper *Der Spiegel* renewed the alarm with a front page reminder—"Seveso Is Everywhere"—after it had become clear that dioxin was widely present in German landfills.[15]

Don DeLillo's *White Noise* was published in January 1985, in the immediate wake of the Bhopal disaster. The novel was already in page proofs on December 2, 1984, when the Union Carbide plant released mass quantities of methyl isocyanate into the air after pressure built up in the storage tank faster than the scrubber could neutralize the toxic gas. Early reviewers, however, noted the eerie similarities between the cloud that afflicted Bhopal and the toxic airborne event that terrified Jack Gladney, his family, and his neighbors.[16] *Time* magazine offered a most perverse interpretation of cost-benefit analysis for American readers: "The citizens of Bhopal lived near the Union Carbide plant because they sought to live there. The plant provided jobs, the pesticide more food. Bhopal was a modern parable of the risks and rewards originally engendered by the Industrial Revolution." *Time* hardly dismissed the tragedy of the event, but its reflection on the disaster constituted a callous, rather grotesque, shrug of the shoulders and the 1980s version of "thoughts and prayers": "If the world felt especially close to Bhopal last week, it may be because the world is Bhopal, a place where occupational hazard is modern life. History teaches us that there is no avoiding that hazard, and no point in trying; one only trusts that the gods in the machine will give a good deal more than they take away."[17] The relationship between give and take was hardly even. "In 2001," Rob Nixon writes, "Union

Carbide disappeared through that act of corporate necromancy known as the merger. Dow Chemical bought out Union Carbide, and so the name indelibly associated with disaster evaporated, further confounding the quest in Bhopal for environmental justice, compensation, remediation, and redress."[18] There was no concomitant necromancy for chemical anxieties. They persisted. Bhopal became a palpable symbol of slow violence on a globalized planet. An American company outsourced its manufacturing and hazard to the developing world, where it had set up shop in a space where regulations were lax and labor was cheap. Reduced costs and externalized risks increased profit margins. For American consumers and stockholders, environmental damage was invisibilized by dint of being away, over there. On the ground, though, the horrors of the pesticide leak were far more palpable, and so were the fears associated with the disaster.[19]

The costs of keeping the modern industrial regime were, indeed, quite high. And the risks of failure were great. The impact of the near meltdown at Three Mile Island, for example, resonated across the world's emerging nuclear energy regime. In France, Jan Bucquoy and Jacques Santi collaborated on *Mourir à Creys-Malville* (Dying at Creys-Malville), an apocalyptic graphic story dealing with the aftermath of a nuclear catastrophe near Lyon. In their comic book, a reactor disaster has wiped out the entire region; entering and exiting the contaminated zone is prohibited.[20] The comic's publication coincided with the real-life opening of the Superphénix fast breeder reactor at Creys-Malville. Opposition to the reactor preceded its opening and the disaster at Chernobyl, but the comic book reflected ongoing anticipatory fears surrounding nuclear power plants, even in France, which had committed to atomic energy more wholeheartedly than any other country.[21] But where the prospect of nuclear catastrophe weighed on populations near every nuclear power facility in the world—not least at Three Mile Island—the prospect of disaster turned into the real thing in Ukraine on April 26, 1986, when a chain reaction in the reactor core precipitated an explosion that ripped through reactor 4 and spread nuclear radiation across Ukraine and Belarus and much of Northern Europe. Fears linger. That is the nature of slow disasters. And make no mistake: Even the most explosive environmental catastrophes were slow disasters. The historian Kate Brown contends that radiation poisoning from Chernobyl was far worse than previously realized—and that authorities concealed the real rates of contamination. Regardless, Chernobyl was "an exclamation point in a chain of toxic exposures that restructured the landscape, bodies and politics."[22]

The American waste crisis of the 1970s and 1980s also became a global issue in that chain of toxic exposures. As mounting consumption and the stiffer controls imposed on hazardous waste disposal left landfills bursting at the seams, Americans searched for solutions by trying to export solid and toxic wastes. The famous 1987 visuals of a barge carrying 3,100 tons of New York City waste looking for a dumping ground as it trundled down the eastern seaboard and into the Gulf of Mexico—where it was turned away by Belize, Mexico, and Cuba, before it returned to Brooklyn to have its cargo incinerated—became an international story. Nevertheless, its hapless trek masked the fact that Americans were outsourcing their hazardous waste in growing quantities during the 1980s and 1990s. In January 1988, after more than a year at sea, the *Khian Sea* illicitly dumped more than four thousand tons of incinerator ash from Philadelphia on a beach in northern Haiti before later dumping another ten thousand tons at sea when numerous countries refused to receive its cargo. The growing trend of rich countries exporting their waste to poor countries in growing quantities was a catalyst for the United Nations Basel Convention on the Control of Transboundary Movements of Hazardous Wastes and Their Disposal, which sought to put strict controls on the global waste economy. The United States signed but never ratified the Basel Convention.[23]

Indeed, a key component of the contamination landscape after the 1980s is its globalization. The anthropologist Arjun Appadurai has long been interested in more contemporary elements of what he calls risk-taking and risk-bearing, themes that should track reasonably well across this book's seventh chapter. There is an inverse relationship between those who create risks and those who suffer them. American affluence during the final third of the twentieth century ensured that Americans were risk producers who enjoyed the capacity to outsource hazards to poorer nations desperate to generate revenue by absorbing risks. But where Appadurai's interest in "risk society" is marked by a broadening of this social disparity (in the context of this work, between those who contaminate and those who are contaminated), he also stressed its geographical expansion. Indeed, productions of and exposures to risk have not only separated people but also connected them across "national and market boundaries."[24] In addition to international waste disposal, these connections have involved interesting chemical life cycles: chemicals manufactured in the United States, even though their use is banned. The chemicals are exported to countries that tolerate their use, where they are used in agricultural and manufacturing processes before being returned on produce and in goods that are cheaper than American-made alternatives. This circle of poisons constituted another version of the outsourcing of risk—or diverting risk, hazards, and fears elsewhere.

Read from the United States—or read from American media sources—the transnational conclusion feels like a tragic abstraction or theoretical conjecture on the worst-case scenarios. In a curious twist that DeLillo might appreciate, disasters abroad were almost reassuring. Bhopal and Chernobyl were proof positive of American technological ingenuity. Such explosive disasters were decidedly un-American: human errors caused by poorly trained operators, or technical failures inspired by inadequate maintenance routines. Such problems were bound to occur, but they could never happen here, the argument went. The greatest benefit of this argument was the manner in which it promoted a kind of amnesia that quarantined American science, technology, and expertise from any error or hubris. Of course, disasters did happen in the United States. Months before Chernobyl, millions of Americans watched in horror as the *Challenger* shuttle exploded shortly after takeoff. This was no chemical disaster, but its tragedy undermined the technological prowess that served as a kind of American calling card. That Union Carbide could also experience a leak at its West Virginia plant just months after Bhopal almost passed without comment. Trust in technical progress had been a key defense against spills, leaks, and slow disasters.

2. Coda to the American 1980s

A second conclusion examines the aftermath of the American 1980s. It compares the chemophobic landscape of the early 1990s with that of the 1970s: the discovery of endocrine-disrupting chemicals and new frames for engaging with contamination. "Apocalypse is the single most powerful master metaphor that the contemporary environmental imagination has at its disposal."[25] During the 1970s, as environmentalism entered into mainstream American politics, many of its leaders adopted a rhetorical jeremiad that intoned death and destruction was imminent. While the jeremiad seemed to lose some of its power as the 1970s turned into the 1980s—another kind of cultural desensitization—the discovery that many chemicals disrupted hormonal systems served as grounds to suggest that perhaps some of the more vociferous environmental rhetoric hadn't gone far enough.[26]

Further, the chemical landscape—or at least the scientific understanding of its risk to human health—shifted. Lost in much of the story of chemophobia, where historical actors expressed concerns about specific sources of contamination, is that scientists in the 1980s were discovering that pollution was synergistic. Frequently, combinations of two or more toxic substances posed a greater threat than either one on their own. This chemical synergism reared its head in fears over cancer clusters at Woburn and elsewhere. It also featured renewed concern about a series of persistent organic pollutants that were produced during the twentieth century before their harm was properly understood. Many of these chemicals were so widespread across industrial manufacturing and had escaped in such great quantities into the environment and were so prevalent that their study became problematic because epidemiologists struggled to find uncontaminated populations to function as benchmarks. In the 1990s, new scientific discoveries found that these legacy contaminants posed serious albeit uncertain threats to human hormonal and reproductive systems. Much the way chemicals could fire specific neural receptors to spark fear, new findings showed that synthetic chemicals were firing all kinds of hormonal responses. The groundbreaking work that brought these discoveries to a mainstream audience and introduced endocrine-disrupting chemicals as another new species of trouble was titled *Our Stolen Future*. Its author and protagonist was Theo Colborn, a zoologist and health analyst who began piecing together bits of scientific findings and eventually uncovered the conduits through which hormone-disrupting chemicals were upsetting sexual development and reproduction. A collaboration with the environmental scientist John Peterson Myers and the environmental journalist Dianne Dumanoski to communicate Colborn's findings, *Our Stolen Future* dropped a psychological atom bomb on the state of environmental contamination. If there were distinct turning points in the history of toxic fear, the epistemological shift after *Our Stolen Future*'s 1997 publication is one of them. Colborn's warning was as earth-shattering and as grave as Rachel Carson's had been thirty-five years earlier: "No young person alive today has been born without some in utero exposure to synthetic chemicals that can disrupt development," the authors asserted.[27] Cancer continued to provoke popular fears, but the risks of hormonal disruption were terrifying. Their prospect posited myriad new harms or potential hazards around health, child development, and reproduction. Because many of these new understandings posed distinct health risks to women and children and motherhood, hormone-disrupting contaminants gendered popular productions and consumptions of toxic fear. It is important to reiterate, then, that toxic fear—and fear writ large, for that matter—was intensely gendered in its expression. Studies on the aftermath of chemical pollution events pointed toward an imbalance between how women and men responded to toxic hazards. These tended to follow old stereotypes of more risk-averse women compared with risk-taking, stoic men.[28]

But scientific questions and uncertainties persisted, as they do, and that invited a more concerted attack on public fears and environmental controls. The debate over dioxins, flagged as a health concern in the late nineteenth century, serves as a good case study. The dioxin fears emanating from the Times Beach evacuation were muted as the decade progressed. Remember that dioxin was regarded in the 1970s as one of the most dangerous human-made chemicals in existence. During the 1980s and into the 1990s, the science on dioxin vacillated, though not nearly as excessively as the media's reporting on it did. Where dioxin was deemed wildly hazardous, subsequent studies tempered the early alarm. "While [dioxin] is undoubtedly toxic, the evidence that's been brought forward so far of a link between it and birth defects is impressionistic, and of a kind that is specially vulnerable to error."[29] By 1994, however, the EPA had revised its standards again, renewing concerns that dioxin constituted a severe toxic threat. A draft copy of the new study claimed, "A picture emerges of dioxin and related compounds as potent toxicants producing a wide range of effects at very low levels when compared to other environmental contaminants."[30] The study also reflected a shift in environmental health monitoring. Rather than concentrating on dioxin's carcinogenic potential, the EPA expanded on risks associated with stunted fetal growth and the suppression of immune and hormone systems.[31] Antienvironmental criticisms of the science and concomitant policies persisted. Environmentalists were disparaged as "Chicken Littles" and doomsayers hoping for environmental collapse. In his 1993 book *Ecoscam: The False Prophets of Ecological Apocalypse* (one of many such titles), Ronald Bailey charged that "modern ecological millenarians, impatient with waiting for the flash of thermonuclear doom, now claim there is a 'global environmental crisis' threatening not just humanity, but all life on earth."[32] Neither his tone nor his florid prose was divergent from the trend in most antienvironmental rhetoric. Also by the early 1990s, pundits widely alleged that the United States was becoming a hysterical victim society. The topic became a literary industry for books on self-help and caustic attacks on the decline of family values.[33] These criticisms of environmental concerns—whether held by government authorities, mainstream environmental groups, grassroots activists, or independent scientists—charged that fear was a mendacious part of the environmentalist agenda. In a 2003 white paper that served as the background for a July floor speech, Senator Jim Inhofe (R-Okla.) berated climate change as "the greatest hoax ever perpetrated on the American people." The popular debate, he insisted, was "predicated on fear, rather than science."[34] Inhofe was drawing directly from the playbook outlined in Edith Efron's *The Apocalyptics,* and which has been carefully analyzed in more recent work on doubt and agnotology: dismiss concerns as paranoia and stake a claim (however unsubstantiated) to reason. "Fear" appeared nine times in Inhofe's white paper. As much as ignorance is about what we don't know—or don't know yet—it can also be manufactured through intentional misinformation and misdirection. I am reminded of Thomas Pynchon's 1973 *Gravity's Rainbow* and his Proverbs for Paranoids 3: "If they can get you asking the wrong questions, they don't have to worry about answers."[35] This, I think, speaks as loudly about the state of the present echo chambers of right-wing punditry in the United States as I hope it reflects elements of the confusion, uncertainty, and anxiety surrounding toxic chemicals in the environment in the 1980s. As the physician Henry Vyner noted in 1988, the health effects of chemical exposure were poorly understood. It was not unrealistic, he argued, to compare 1980s knowledge of industrial contaminants in the body to what fourteenth-century Europeans knew about controlling and preventing the bubonic plague.[36] The noise didn't help.

As the old century rolled into the new one, a number of long-standing products were found to contain chemicals that provoked new worries. Plastics were at the forefront. Early in the new millennium fears emerged that bisphenol A (BPA), a human-made chemical that mimicked estrogen in the body, was widespread in a number of commercial products. BPA's presence in baby bottles, used to make hard and resilient plastics, crossed a long-held line in American toxic politics. Since World War II, and under the guidance of James Delaney, a congressman from New York, federal politics had acknowledged the importance of keeping harmful chemicals out of food and food packaging. "BPA free" labels began appearing in pharmacies and on baby bottles across the United States. Another suite of legacy contaminants, polyfluorinated alkyl substances or fluorocarbons, caused a comparable and enduring scare.[37] Where BPA threatened to leach out of consumer plastics, fluorocarbons were present in just about every water system in the United States. Like BPA, however, they posed a series of health risks. Perfluorooctane sulfonate (PFOS) was banned under the Stockholm Convention on Persistent Organic Pollutants in 2009.[38] American perfluoroctanoic acid (PFOA) production was halted in 2015. Both persist in the environment and compose a part of the American toxic past, present, and foreseeable future. The other historical development prompted by these new discoveries is the concomitant discovery of their ubiquity. The story of toxic fear in the American 1980s was framed in case studies where specific contaminants from specific sources posed—or were feared to pose—specific harms, but the twenty-first-century chapter of chemical fear is the ominous realization that chemical pollutants have already infiltrated communities, homes, and bodies. In effect, in the 1980s fear was treated in potentialities that played out in the future tense. The availability heuristic set markers for exposure to contaminants. An historical and psychological shift has taken place; Americans now know that contaminants are omnipresent and inescapable. Exposure has already happened in the past tense.[39]

And while the discovery of endocrine-disrupting chemicals entered the environmental lexicon and challenged the temptation to reduce all environmental harm to the risk of cancer, it is also important to not lose sight of the ubiquity of environmental carcinogens. In 2007, researchers compiled data from five international cancer agencies to produce a study in the American Cancer Society's journal, *Cancer*, that showed that of the 212 organic chemicals known to cause breast cancer in laboratory animals, 203 are synthetic and only 9 are produced by living things.[40] This finding provided further evidence of Sarah A. Vogel's claim that "we are what we make."[41] It is this merging of the natural and the synthetic—frequently inside the human body—that I think serves as the defining epilogue of this book, and as clear a conceptual statement on the state of fear and toxic epistemology in the 2020s. In 2010 the President's Cancer Panel submitted a lengthy report on "Reducing Environmental Cancer Risk," which stressed that "the true burden of environmentally induced cancer has been grossly underestimated." In its preamble letter to the president, the panel continued, "With nearly 80,000 chemicals on the market in the United States, many of which are used by millions of Americans in their daily lives and are un- or understudied and largely unregulated, exposure to potential environmental carcinogens is widespread."[42]

New sources of harm and fear also had a profound impact on American environmentalism. The struggle for environmental justice and against environmental racism adopted strategies and principles from grassroots movements for public and urban health, peace, civil rights, and gender equality to frame the most pivotal expression of American democracy in the 1980s and thereafter. Environmental justice is one of the most important developments in American participatory politics, not least because its struggle against disenfranchisement has highlighted the extent to which many Americans have been excluded from presiding over their own environmental futures because of their race or socioeconomic standing. No book—let alone a passing reference in the conclusion of a short one—can do justice to the proliferation and variety of local and grassroots movements across the United States that shared common political marginalization. Robert Bullard's *Dumping in Dixie*, published in 1990, showed that people of color were exposed to environmental hazards at a rate disproportionate to the American population as a whole.[43] In 1991, the First National People of Color Environmental Leadership Summit convened in Washington, D.C., where it entered environmental racism firmly into the American environmental vocabulary. Opposition to environmental injustice, as Bullard noted in his book, was an expanding product of the 1980s response to chemical concerns. The public outcry from residents of Emelle, Alabama, opposing the siting of a hazardous waste facility in their community, and from opponents to an incinerator being built in East Los Angeles, was clearly part of a comparable tendency in American environmental politics from below. Further, the emergence of a national trend can also be discerned from the variety of efforts to create a national anti-toxic movement outside of the established and mainstream (read: white and middle-class) environmental movement. In 1983, Love Canal catalyst Lois Gibbs established the Citizen's Clearing House for Hazardous Waste; its newsletter, *Everyone's Backyard*, sought to disseminate information from the myriad contaminated communities across the United States in an attempt to build solidarity and share resources. And in 1988 the

National Toxics Campaign began publishing the *Toxic Times* in an effort to coordinate disparate groups and concerns.[44] But each movement has its own actors, priorities, idiosyncrasies, and complexities that historians would do well to take seriously and bring to the fore. That fear of exposure and a lack of access to information may have been consistent features of so many cases of environmental justice activism during and after the 1980s should be a departure point for engaging with the particularities of specific events rather than the last word.

3. Contemporary Relevance

The coda to the American 1980s also needs to acknowledge the tectonic shift from fear to terror at the beginning of the new century. The "war on terror" transformed American discourse at the beginning of the twenty-first century, even if terror had long been a driver of cultural fears.[45] I have resisted the temptation to discuss 9/11, in large part because I think it marks an important turning point in contemporary American fear, and that it represents a problematic reference point for a more careful reading of the chemophobia of the 1980s inasmuch as it likely sucks all the contextual oxygen out of popular and scholarly discourses.[46] The intensification of airport security across the country and the widespread prevalence of cement barriers in Washington, D.C., and other major urban centers set the pretext for living with new fears of terror that didn't fully subside in the twenty years that followed.

It would take a completely different book to evaluate the extent to which 9/11 has transformed American fears in general and toxic fears more specifically. Chemophobia is still very much with us; fear writ large is the preeminent political conceit of the twenty-first century. The third conclusion seeks to tackle the "so what" question by pointing to the topic's contemporary relevance. Understanding the popular response to chemical pollution warrants our attention. If *Our Stolen Future* provoked further chemical fears, it was justified in pointing out that chemicals were even more widespread in the 1990s than they had been in the 1980s. Or that our understanding of their threat had become more sophisticated. Contemporary body burden analyses reveal that all Americans are walking chemical cocktails. And lest critics assert that endocrine-disrupting chemicals are the latest attempt to drive Americans to hysteria, new and better science has quite recently revealed that cancer incidences from Three Mile Island are higher—and more precisely identifiable—than previously imagined.[47] And recent scientific studies suggest that air pollution, notably nitrogen oxide and PM2.5, is killing more people across the planet than smoking—and more than AIDS, diabetes, and traffic accidents combined.[48] In short, there remains a place for fear, anxiety, and concern in environmental politics.

That place, however, is contentious and mired in so much noise that it is difficult to identify any specific signal. Indeed, all fears exist on some kind of multidimensional cultural spectrum, where AIDS, Cold War, nuclear radiation, the *Challenger* disaster, chemical pollution, and countless other fears intersected and overlapped based on their chronology and availability heuristics driven by media reporting. The toxic fears of the 1980s have, in different ways, contributed to and stoked anti-vaccination fears and worries about genetic engineering and genetically modified foods. Each has its own history and its own lobbies (though many of these overlap). While I want to reassert that no fear should be treated as a pejorative emotion, the amount of competing information and misinformation available to Americans—Toffler's future shock—can make any statement about the importance of empathy seem like a naïve idea.

This is where the neoliberal project reaches beyond balance sheets to help explain the cultural evolution of American fears. Just as Americans were learning about the hazards inherent in many of the new technologies that promised them greater affluence—and, it should be noted, suffering the first economic crisis to post–World War II prosperity—neoliberalism's architects were at work cutting ties between the market and the institutions in place to ensure public security was preserved. During the 1970s, the economist Milton Friedman in *Newsweek* advocated abolishing the Food and Drug Administration, giving Americans the freedom to choose their own medical treatment.[49] That ambition never took. But it indicated the extent to which neoliberalism was keen to reject history. The Food and Drug Administration was founded in 1906 as a countermeasure against the kind of uncontrolled free market that Friedman wanted. That previous iteration of unbridled "progress" had introduced a host of new industrial problems: labor exploitation, insalubrious living and working places, dangerous foods and drugs of dubious merit, lots and lots of pollution. The measures introduced during the Progressive era at the beginning of the twentieth century—of which the creation of the Food and Drug Administration was one—aimed to bring greater social order to industry, and firmer controls over what was and was not permissible.[50] For Friedman, bureaucracy and government intervention were only obstacles to unshackled progress; the reasons or historical motivations for controls were immaterial. Lost in this debate, neoliberalism's efforts to reduce bureaucracy, promote autonomy, and foster creativity seem to have produced the opposite. Brutal insistence on adhering to the neoliberal model has engendered conformity. Privatization has encouraged fierce competition and killed cooperation. The capacity for dialog has been lost; hyperindividualized interest is at least partly to blame. More than any specific policy, neoliberalism's unyielding breakdown of social support and community networks has been the contemporary world's primary engine for expanding fears. Put another way, this fearful uncertainty was not a bug but a feature of the neoliberal project.

"How is it," asks the anthropologist Joseph Masco, "that Americans, residents of the most powerful country in human history . . . have come to feel so precarious and vulnerable?" His question and answer are interested in a broader catastrophic psyche than environmental contaminations in the 1980s and the fears they provoked, but they engage with similar formulations of political, cultural, and material interactions. "The demise of the large social engineering projects of the twentieth century, and the rise of an unrestrained neoliberalism in their wake, combine to create a vision of a market-driven future that can only produce profit by generating boom-and-bust cycles and extraction regimes that leave ruin in their wake."[51] That vision, I have proposed, was an American state vision that overlooked, mistook, and underappreciated the significance of popular fear. In general terms, I think Masco and the historian Daniel T. Rodgers offer a compatible and compelling description of the social and cultural "fracture" that occurred in the late stages of the twentieth century. It would be imprudent to single out neoliberalism as the singular and sole source of American fears over pollution during the 1980s; Rodgers argues, recall from chapter 2, that the age of fracture "was not a single, dominant idea—postmodern, new right, or neoliberal—but a contagion of metaphors," and Masco's analysis is far more nuanced as well.[52] At the same time, both contend that out of these competing visions there emerged the one metaphor to rule them all: the market. I think that the lesson derived from reflecting on pollution fears during the 1980s is that these uncertainties were manufactured by a government system intent on undoing public safety regulations to relieve cost burdens on the industrial interests that funded and supported them. New and tireless media engines enlivened and capitalized on the same anxieties by promising and failing to resolve them after the next commercial break (don't go away, we'll be right back). A captive audience became a captive society with no recourse to diminishing agencies unprepared and ill-equipped to manage the scale of the toxic disasters.

I don't know that I am equipped to offer a solution—or even a roadmap toward one—for this problem of growing fears and diminishing public participations. I am equally unsatisfied with what often feels like the alternative, nihilistic impotence that in my more optimistic moments I frame as the historian's duty just to bear witness. I take some hope from the guidance of scholars such as the economic geographer J. K. Gibson-Graham, who demonstrates how capitalism is not a monolith and that the relationships between power, capitalism, and environment are historically fluid.[53]

* * *

Grafting together these three conclusions invites inquiry into what this all means and what history can teach. I am reluctant to prescribe any high-minded takeaways based on the work. Part of me would be satisfied simply with historians and other scholars acquiring a deeper appreciation for emotions in the work they do. However, I believe chemophobia's history from the 1980s does offer some basic steps that are worth investigating well beyond the academic arena.

We live in a world where fear needs to be recognized as a legitimate human emotion, and that acknowledgment requires empathy and humility in political discourse. This is a surprisingly difficult conclusion to fully justify. Numerous scholarly tracts assert the ubiquity of fear in the twenty-first century. But a lot of this fear is a product of a resurgence in the "paranoid style," which the historian Richard Hofstadter famously articulated in the mid-1960s, first in a *Harper's* article and then in a book. "American politics has often been an arena for angry minds," Hofstadter argued.[54] The invention or exaggeration of enemies or the threats they posed fermented animosities; Hofstadter's Cold War–era angry minds frequently gave the appearance of being frightened or cornered because their traditional way of life was under siege. The root of their ambivalence was a sense that they felt dispossessed. "The paranoid spokesman sees the fate of conspiracy in apocalyptic terms—he traffics in the birth and death of whole worlds, whole political orders, whole systems of human values. He is always manning the barricades of civilization. He constantly lives at a turning point."[55] The rise of right-wing populism in the contemporary United States fits this description perfectly. This is really a discussion about dignity, and the backward assumption that dignity is a finite resource that cannot be surrendered, shared, or accorded to others. Against the tsunami of such vilifications of constructed fears and angers and paranoias, it is difficult to find space to justify that there is more to fear than fear itself. Hofstadter's paranoia is compounded by the sociologist Frank Furedi's interest in a sort of fear paradox: The less there is to be frightened of, the more frightened people are. In the contemporary world, there is a tendency for people to fear progressive changes: vaccinations, genetically modified foods, genetic research, and so on.[56] The story of chemical pollution as it manifested itself after World War II fits Furedi's category of an invisible, hypothetical risk. In these treatments, fear is a pejorative emotion. But there are too many instances of chemical pollution causing real harm—in rapid, explosive form or slowly, at low levels of exposure—to reject toxic fears in so cavalier a manner. People were afraid and their fears were justified on too many occasions to ignore. During the toxic waste crisis at the beginning of the 1980s, federal officials were loath to dismiss local fears as unwarranted. As the EPA's Midwest deputy chief told *Time* in 1980, "Every time we go into these cases, we find it's worse than we thought."[57] Local experiences of fear have a place alongside expert risk managers. In mainstream culture, distinguishing between fear and paranoia can be a tricky business. And even where fears can be (and are) manufactured and stoked for specific gain, it is important to practice deeper understanding and to search for the roots of their anxieties. This is hardly a satisfying conclusion, but public discourse is losing its capacity to engage in dialog. Starting by asking *why* people fear and how the uncertainties that provoke those fears are left to fester is an important departure point. Moreover, fear has an aftermath. Too many cases of environmental catastrophe have been measured in deaths, cancers, and other physical illnesses. Psychological trauma rarely enters into the equation. This is problematic, to say the least. Where mainstream media is reporting on rises in anxiety and depression among Americans, it would be wise to heed more sensitively the potential for psychological trauma from environmental events. This is especially important since trauma can linger long after moments of crisis.

We live in a world of knowledge hierarchies, but it could be reconfigured to establish better access to knowledge and privilege lived experience. Reducing risk to a problem for expert deliberation misses the profoundly social dynamic of how toxic chemicals were received—and, taken in tandem with the previous prescription, it risks intensifying both noise and fear. Fear of chemicals was never wholly irrational, nor was it uninformed. Rather, it was, at least in part, a response to the perversion of how risk and chemical dangers were rationalized as an inevitable feature of modernity. The key lesson in this study is that hazard is never a purely technical issue. The story of toxic fear in the American 1980s explains why. In the final analysis, every citizen assessed fear on two competing spectrums. In the abstract, the overwhelming majority of Americans understood and accepted the traditional cost-benefit analysis conducted by risk experts and government agencies. While strong criticisms of industrial practices and of the economic system that encouraged them might have rattled the cage from time to time, these bulwarks of modern capitalism persisted through the 1980s and into the twenty-first century unruffled and unabated. Pollution was seen as the cost of doing business: the price of progress. But in the visceral immediacy of chemical risk affecting individuals quite directly, that attitude changed. When the potential for hazard emerged—often quite literally in the backyard—broader appreciations of the cost-benefit analyses went out the window. It is easy to gamble with other people's money.

We live in a chemical world, but it could be a safer one. I want to be clear on how and where to place the blame for these fears. I am unconvinced that hazardous chemical production and disposal can be conducted in a completely benign and safe way. The one historical constant of hazardous materials is their capacity to escape human control. Accidents can always happen. The 1985 Union Carbide spill in Institute, West Virginia, for example, came after several months of safety upgrades. But the ubiquity of chemical disasters and contaminations during the 1980s and after suggests that a certain industrial cynicism was also a prevalent trend. Controlling spills and emissions—by retrofitting plants, installing scrubbers and filters, and monitoring materials more carefully—costs money. Too frequently, chemical companies saw greater profit in paying retributions should their transgressions be identified. Lawyers—already on retainer—delayed, challenged, and obfuscated in courtrooms all over the country and worked to divide communities at risk. If poor health was a tragedy, the shuttering of jobs would be a disaster. The false dichotomy that bounds the debate in this way masks both the capital gains and the social and environmental costs. The economy-environment divide is a false one, but it is an effective plank in the foundation of the neoliberal handbook. In brief, the current economic system, the one that created the current chemical regime, has been instrumental in systematically removing the checks and controls on spills and accidents while simultaneously absolving chemical disasters' perpetrators from responsibility for their trespasses. History also teaches us that the chemical industry is either unable or unwilling to police itself. Safe production is an afterthought. And it will only ever be an afterthought if the margins between profits and penalties remain so vast. More rigorous controls, stiffer penalties, greater, more careful oversight, and more rigid enforcement. Through much of the history in this book, better government oversight was a virtual impossibility: Overtaxed agents were looking for needles in haystacks. Legal and governmental systems require an overhaul, and the burden for those costs should come from the industries. What Americans might learn from radical efforts to put liability and responsibility back onto its pollution and by-product producers is that many polluting technologies are not actually more profitable than cleaner technologies. Remove the external diseconomies that drive polluting practices, punish transgressors.

We live in a capitalist world, but it could be a more humane one. In some respect, this is a reiteration of the previous prescription but articulated from a vantage point influenced by capitalist realism.[58] One of neoliberalism's tenets is a devotion to high modernism, the ideological concept introduced by David Harvey—and developed by James C. Scott—to explain Western societies' unconditional faith in scientific and technical progress since industrialization, particularly in how it defers to the market.[59] Above and beyond the creation of contaminated environments, I contend that toxic fear constitutes a significant social crack in the veneer of its unbridled optimism.

But high modernism has no time for local complications, which is exactly what Love Canal, Times Beach, and other disasters were. The idea that the contemporary moment exists in a mindset where it is easier to imagine the end of the world than the end of capitalism is indicative of just how entrenched existing economic systems and power structures have become. At the same time, no economic theory provides a viable alternative to air, soil, and water as the lifeblood of human life, social organization, and civilization.[60] On a slightly less cosmic scale, one might also inquire into how it came to this—where the rise of public concern emerged only after the clear and present environmental danger that was driven by profits and share prices. I suspect that a big part of the answer is consistent with the neoliberal fracturing of the kinds of methods that might help to counter threats. Reflecting on the last quarter of the twentieth century, Rodgers observes, "One heard less about society, history and power, and more about individuals, contingency and choice."[61] Politics and markets enjoyed greater independence while ideas of what public and the public interest meant were confused and curtailed. Solutions for these problems are to be found in the practices and emerging vocabularies of the movements for social and environmental justice all over the world. The peoples who live, work, and play at the front lines of environmental precarity reject—and have been rejected by—the economic imperative to concentrate wealth and dismiss human well-being as a motive for shaping their operations. The driving force for progressive changes within subaltern environmentalisms and movements for social and racial justice has been to pull back the curtain on the deliberate and unapologetic slow violence of the neoliberal project.

* * *

Measuring risk in a postmaterialist world in deaths and dollars seems antiquated, especially since chemical fear is a quality-of-life issue that does not register tidily in either column. Body counting is an especially vulgar method of bounding the debate. And maybe this strikes at a much larger question than chemical pollution, but it seems as though the economic metric also fails insofar as it does little to assuage fear, while also putting economics first in an Anthropocenic world where environmental policies need to undergo a radical shift to acknowledge that economies must be shaped around ecological carrying capacities, rather than the other way around.

Modern society needs to become better at living with uncertainty. Uncertainty is inevitable. But where political theorists going back at least to Niccolo Machiavelli and Thomas Hobbes, who embraced fear in the sixteenth and seventeenth centuries as a means of bolstering a tenuous social order, have recognized fear as a potent political tool, uncertainty does not have to be an obstacle. Indeed, in the right contexts, it can be a salve. In the binary politics that frame so much contemporary debate—where the confession "I don't know" is anathema—uncertainty offers a poignant third way, a retreat from such essentialist thinking. Dialog beginning with the acceptance of uncertainty as a legitimate starting point—a sort of humility long absent from modern political discourse—downplays the polarity that drives current discourse at the expense of fruitful exchange.[62] And it permits space for local knowledges, experiences, interests, and priorities.

At the same time, embracing uncertainty as a legal defense against future toxic trespasses simply reinforces the current neoliberal regime. Buzzing around in the background of this work is a tacit interest in the precautionary principle, a long-standing feature of European environmental policy, and a long-standing taboo in American environmental policy. The precautionary principle holds that "there is a duty to prevent damage to human and environmental health even when evidence of harm is inconclusive."[63] The argument against the precautionary principle is that it runs against the grain of American exceptionalism: the bold, the industrious, the innovative, the incautious embrace of risk, profit, and production. The precautionary principle, its opponents contend, is expensive, and American industry cannot—will not—countenance the bureaucratic red tape and costs in delays that such careful measures would impose. At the same time, the source of toxic fear comes directly from a lack of control and the uncertainty that revolves around possible hazards and their potential for coming into contact with human bodies. Whether this means more careful adherence to a precautionary principle or a more radical means of reimagining our relationship with the production of toxic hazards, recognition that there are psychological impacts associated with chemical harm that have not been addressed in expert analyses demands more attention.

Regardless of how precaution is or is not practiced in the United States, expertise needs to be less remote. If this sounds like an invitation to democratize knowledge, it's a cautious one: The scientific method remains the best or most consistently reliable method of acquiring facts. But science and policy need to be far more inclusive, and there needs to be a place in both for lived experience. Acceptable risk cannot exist without input from people and communities living on the front lines of possible exposure. In addition, both must find ways to be more transparent and accessible to the publics who live with them—and the publics who live with them must have greater participatory access in their imagination and construction, while controlling for the kinds of agnotological noise that have become such a powerful cultural and political tool. This is almost a utopian ideal: impossible in practice. And it is important to note the long and important history of protocols and procedures and freedoms of information that are commonplace in many local planning and decision-making processes across the United States. At the same time, human actions—technological production and consumption—are more far-reaching than ever before. And the consequences of these expanding toxic trespasses into nature have become more rather than less uncertain. That environmental outcomes are increasingly unknowable—that is frightening.

To live is to risk. Channels of interaction between scientific experts, risk managers, policymakers, and emergency response teams must take time and find ways to include the public in their communication of toxic hazards. Teachers, clergy, community leaders need to be given more—and more accessible—information to share with their constituents. While this might constitute a basic right-to-know argument, it also acknowledges that public fear undermines effective and efficient remediation of environmental harm and that trust in experts and in government has been so eroded that effective knowledge communication must be tailored for front porch or town hall politics and delivered through trusted community members. But this is a two-way street. Publics have the same duty to be involved in participatory politics, informed on issues, and proactive about community interests, rather than waiting for some unknown problem to emerge. That same public also needs to combat creeping social and scientific illiteracy as a means of bridging the gap between expert vocabularies and their own. In essence, this is a lament for the devaluing of public education and the ease with which shrill supersedes substance in contemporary, socially mediated discourse. Sadly, in a world ridden by unceasing online social media white noise and orchestrated misinformation tactics and cuts to public education and growing rather than receding waves of social and private fears and anxieties, that ship may have sailed.

Born (Scared) in the U.S.A.

So in America when the sun goes down and the generic food (white packages, plainly labeled) in the supermarket aisles are the only goods that haven't been rearranged and there is no underlying logic to discern from why anyone thought they should be shuffled in the first place, these aisles of processed abundance (and of nothing) briefly made up the new open roads of a fluorescent-tube- and cathode-ray-lit America until the internet's conduits further entrenched the lonely anonymity of consumerism; where a home is a fortress (guarded by assault weapons) and not a castle, there is in all of this not just a cult of individualism and commodification—twin pillars of the culture of narcissism that the historian Christopher Lasch wrote about in 1979, before the 1980s had even arrived and neoliberalism hit its full stride—but also a deep-seated fear of discomfort in all its various guises, and this is not a lament for a (bygone) resilient society to make great again, but a call for one that is perhaps more agile in and sensitive about acknowledging difference—of opinion of color of nationality of faith—and to come to terms with and not be overrun by the discomfort of competing emotions, feelings, ideas: squashed by the singularity of "market imperatives" and to do the work of looking for collective hope, because the eighties almost killed us all, or they're still killing us (and who is we?)—Tracy Chapman's fast car is a story of the past folding in on itself, or of the wash, rinse, repeat of personal lives trapped in a national cycle of hope, but confusing hope and optimism: This is a lesson I learned from the Irish poet Seamus Heaney (I think he said he got it from Václav Havel), who said that optimism is the belief that things will turn out well—from which one might infer that optimism is the basis for that American sadness—but optimism and hope are different and hope is the conviction that there is a good worth working toward—read that again: Hope is the conviction that there is a good worth working toward—and the trick is to have an earnest, informed social discussion about the correct principles that might help to move things toward that good, but American optimism—heartbeat of United Statesian exceptionalism—is only interested in the unconsidered ends, not the considered means, where Europeans learned in the twentieth century that ends superseding means are what wrought the twin authoritarianisms and horrors of fascism and communism and their consequences, and so at the end of a book on United Statesian fear as it played out forty years ago over chemicals, it seems appropriate for me to note, first, that everything is connected to everything else, and, second, that I am afraid of and afraid for the United States of today (and tomorrow) and its toxicities—from the water* in Flint, Michigan, to the angry, unrepentant streets of every United Statesian city where George Floyd can be (and is) murdered and white supremacy is emboldened, to the silent, unspoken opioid crises afflicting whole communities of scared, angry, pained—uninsured—people in smaller and bigger America, just out of sight of the interstate throughways where liberals slap COEXIST bumper stickers on the backs of their Teslas (or at least I assume that's what's happening: a decade ago those stickers seemed like they were plastered on every Subaru and Prius in the country) and feel they've done their part, as they whizz from one place to another in air-conditioned comfort, latest favorite podcast playing, dodging (hiding from) Least Heat-Moon's blue highways to avoid exposure to anything that might counter their vision of an American dream and the green-manicured lawns pouring out from their decks and barbecues in their suburban havens—*we paid more for the kitchen reno than we wanted but the granite countertops really pop in the light from the new bay window and the contractor assured us they'd retain their value if we ever decide to put the house up for sale*—and meanwhile, just two school districts away, with whole neighborhoods foreclosed in between, children are made to perp-walk through metal detectors into asbestos-riddled, decaying buildings with no books and no resources where, honestly, neither hope nor optimism is on the curriculum anyway—and this can't be a viable way to run a civilization, and there's no wonder that people are afraid, are conditioned to be afraid: from Fitzgerald's East and West Egg (and so we beat on . . .) to Naylor's Linden Hills (they let it burn . . .), then: no green light but no less desire—that world is fractured and cut adrift from its tethers (if it ever had any) and drawn ever deeper into a vortex of hyperreality—a blurred state, Baudrillard posited when he visited in the middle of the

1980s, that hyperreality, spread across massive intersections cornered by fast food and gas stations, where it has become ever more difficult to separate reality from simulation, and that I think is how and where fear (of life of death of discomfort of sickness of others of self of everything) is manifest-ed.

ACKNOWLEDGMENTS

I'm glad you're here. This is not the book I was trying to write or the one I expected you to be reading. It was supposed to be a survey of what I called the "Toxic Century," which refers to the contamination of the entire planet since World War II. My premise was that the synthetic chemicals defining this century (1945–2045) have become a ubiquitous feature of the human footprint on the global landscape. The Toxic Century was a historical investigation from within, where "within" referred to the fact that we are still living in the Toxic Century, and also that this was an embodied history that explored the history of the toxins we carried around inside us.

The preliminary outline for that project served as the basis for an undergraduate survey course, which I offered at McMaster University in 2013. An early in-class group project asked students to collect around five hundred newspaper articles in digital form in order to conduct some low-stakes data visualization and noticing work. Students compiled their articles into a single, text-searchable file, and ran them through some web-based reading and analysis tools. Their assignment involved developing a series of word clouds in order to chart change and continuity in the Toxic Century's vocabulary over time to see if their analysis could identify trends in that vocabulary. Each group would create a chronological suite of word clouds (1950s, 1960s, 1970s, for example) in order to "see" trends in the articles they had collected. I should stress that these words clouds did not mean to offer anything but a bird's-eye view of a singular primary source while introducing first-year students to the library's historical newspapers databases. The exercise was less about acquiring any conclusive historical understanding about a particular time or event. Instead, I introduced this process as a method of *starting* inquiry into a new topic. Noticing change and continuity, I told them, could provoke historical questions for subsequent research and analysis. Which brings me back to "toxic fear" and the origins of this book project. To provide a mock example and case study for the class to take them through the assignment, I conducted a search for *New York Times* articles between 1950 and 1990 that searched for [toxic

AND (fear OR anxiety) AND (chemical OR pollution)]. The search parameters were far from perfect, and I had to weed out some articles that debated marijuana use in the 1970s. But a cursory scan of article titles suggested there was not too much noise, nonrelevant results that would interfere with the data visualization. I added the 1980s since we had just covered Bhopal and Chernobyl in a lecture, and I thought it would be interesting to determine if we could "see" American coverage of these international crises. I had associated fear of toxic chemicals with the Age of Ecology writ large, a story where Rachel Carson's *Silent Spring* would serve as popular catalyst in the American story. Of the 729 articles that met my search criteria, 504 (69 percent) were from the 1980s. Further tweaking of the search parameters and keywords returned similar results. I had not expected to observe such a disproportionate emphasis in the news media attention in the 1980s as distinct from the 1960s and 1970s, especially. Even the more conservative *Wall Street Journal* skewed heavily toward the eighties. The resulting project was one that turned its attention squarely on the 1980s.[1]

Even if the focal point of the work shifted to concentrate on toxic fears in the United Statesian 1980s, the steadfast encouragement and direction from the following people have been instrumental in its preparation and completion. This book began in the classroom, and the classroom also became an active laboratory for its ideas. As a result, I need to start by thanking over a decade's worth of undergraduate students for their questions, patience, and curiosities. Special mention, I think, is required for my doctoral students, many of whom suffered much of my inner wranglings while trying to cohere argument and narrative. Michael Clemens, Valeria Flores Zambrano, Hayley Goodchild, Mica Jorgenson, and Nevcihan Ozilge might find some of our conversations on these pages—and they will definitely be the better pages. It almost goes without saying (but should be said) that my career is much richer for the privilege of having spent time in each of their orbits. Similarly, I am grateful to the small army of MA students with whom I worked while drafting and revising the manuscript, especially Duncan Chambers, Peter Gardhouse, Mark Leeming, Tosh Miller-Francis, Phillip Morgan, Sarah Perry, Gavin Rees, Salomé Rodriguez Solarte, Caleb Wellum, and Alex Zavarise.

David Brande (big brother) and Nick Pearce read early manuscript drafts, and furnished me with notes on how to refine voice, story, and message. Two anonymous readers at the University of Georgia Press provided thoughtful specialist and organizational feedback. During the summer of 2024, a group of McMaster University students—Samuel Abbott, Sophie Banwell, Valeria Flores Zambrano (again), Matthew Monrose, Carter Neale, Sharang Sharma, Eva Shepherd, and Manahil Shonaiber—contributed to a reading workshop, reading the revised manuscript chapter by chapter and offering notes and recommendations over a series of smart, thoughtful, rambunctious, and irreverent meetings.

Also at McMaster, I have been fortunate to be surrounded by terrific colleagues who showed investment in and support for me and this project, notably Karen Balcom, Jennifer Bonnell, Nancy Bouchier, Ken Cruikshank, Kim Dej, Myron Groover, Stephen Heathorn, Art Heidebrecht, Stuart Henderson, Celeste Licorish, Debbie Lobban, Rodrigo Narro Perez, Viv Nelles, Jessica Van Horssen, and Philip Van Huizen. Early in the project, colleagues at the Sherman Centre for Digital Scholarship—Dale Askey, John Fink, Mica Jorgenson (again), Bryor Snefjella, and Andrea Zeffiro—provided guidance, navigating my tentative forays into digital humanities visualizing techniques. Further afield, my intellectual community has shrunk a good deal since 2016, when I curtailed my travels to the United States. Nevertheless, I am richer for interactions and conversations and correspondences with Angeliki Balayannis, Scout Blum, Claire Campbell, Mauricio Cardenas Reyes, Jeff Crane, Sara Dant, Agustín Doncelar, Andrew Duffin, Kai D. Fan, Mohamed Fetaih, Leif Frederickson, Wyatt Galusky, Roger Gaudreau, Dale Goble, Jacob Darwin Hamblin, Marc Hanvelt, John Hausdoerffer, Amy Hay, Toshihiro Higuchi, Krys Hines, Paul Hirt, Nathalie Jas, Dolly Jørgensen, Finn-Arne Jørgensen, Christine Keiner, Melanie Kiechle, Damian Kuehn, Nancy Langston, Alan MacEachern, Kevin Marsh, Michelle Mart, Elan Mastai, Stuart McCook, Patrick McCray, Gregg Mitman, Simone Müller, Kate O'Neill, Lisa Picone, Liza Piper, Sara Pritchard, Libby Robin, Rachel Rothschild, Lise Sedrez, Christopher Sellers, Sverker Sörlin, Ellen Griffith Spears, William Turkel, Jessica Varner, Paul Warde, Kristoffer Whitney, and David Wilkie. A long list of names hardly does justice to my gratitude, and this list is surely incomplete. I leave a space for old friends and colleagues who don't appear above to write in their own names, because I do appreciate the altruistic sharing that makes communities of learning such vibrant places. Thank you to ______________________________.

Rebecca Altman deserves special mention for several years' worth of (mostly remote) enthusiastic conversations over email and social media. I can't begin to count the number of good references and recommendations I owe to her counsel. I am similarly indebted to Jody Roberts. He and Ben Cohen have been a part of this project since before its inception. I miss that great pleasure derived from energetic, intellectual, and stimulating conversations and correspondences. My fondness for both—and their great wit and good humor—is hidden throughout this book. More evident are their smart insights, many of which I would have stolen if they hadn't been so freely offered. No acknowledgment of colleagues-turned-friends would be complete without Adam Sowards, whose critical eye and exasperation for my penchant for overlapping, extraneous clauses and run-on sentences, has been a stalwart and imaginary (he was never actually standing behind me tutting as I wrote—not that I recall) constant throughout the writing and revising processes. From students to colleagues to friends: I am better for the people mentioned above. So, too, is this book, though its enduring flaws are no reflection of their smarts or generosities.

This project benefited from grants from the Social Sciences & Humanities Research Council of Canada, a McMaster Incentive Grant, and further support from McMaster's Arts Research Board. Archives and special collections are the magical kingdoms of historical research, but they cannot exist without good funding and the terrific people who make them go. This book was made possible by the friendly assistance of staff at the Tufts University Archival Research Center, the Special Collections at the University of Buffalo, and the Buffalo History Museum's Research Library. Early drafts of this work were presented at the 2014 "Framing Nature" conference in Tartu, Estonia, and the 2016 American Society for Environmental History annual meeting in Seattle, USA. Fellow panelists and audience members asked good questions that helped to reframe and crystallize the work's contours and themes. Further conceptual variations of the question of environmental fears were published in edited volumes. I am grateful for the steady editorial hand offered by Hannes Bergthaller, Jeff Crane, Char Miller, and Peter Mortensen. At the University of Georgia Press, Mick Gusinde-Duffy has been a terrific shepherd for this project, full of encouragement and sympathy for all the British/Canadian u's left on the cutting room floor.

I have the ridiculous good luck to be surrounded by excellent people I get to call family. This book is dedicated (in part) to my mother, Susanna. My father, Kieran, died just as this book was being prepared for peer review.

Both read variations on introductions, chapters, and proposals. Janice read through this manuscript at least twice, during which time we also co-translated *The Contamination of the Earth* for MIT Press. We share a different but abiding respect for languages (their constructions, their precisions and imprecisions, their beauty), which makes it all the more puzzling that I should find myself rendered speechless when reckoning with my gratitude. Our children—Ciarán, Jordan, and Meredith—constitute our best collaborative work. Each possesses and exhibits the kinds of commitment and courage (and tremendous company) that make me hope for the future.

NOTES

Introduction. The Eighties Almost Killed Me

1. The traditional account of risk as an expression of public safety has been well treated by historians. See, as a representative study, Mohun, *Risk*. For an important analysis of risk in American environmental governance, see Demortain, *Science of Bureaucracy*. Somewhat related to this, a growing literature on the history of risk highlights the intricacies of risk's relationship with capitalism, corporations, and American social and economic history. See Levy, *Freaks of Fortune*, and Bouk, *How Our Days Became Numbered*. See also Porter, *Trust in Numbers*, as a foundational study. Little of this work, however, has engaged with risk perception, and especially in terms of exploring environmental risks from technological hazards.

2. Erikson, *New Species of Trouble*, 144.

3. Slovic, "Perception of Risk."

4. Sensory history is pivotal to this story of toxic fear in the 1980s. I am grateful for the conceptual guidance provided in Kiechle, *Smell Detectives*; Van Horssen, *Town Called Asbestos*; Alaimo, *Bodily Natures*; and Parr, *Sensing Changes*.

5. In his essay on "Toxic Discourse," Lawrence Buell rightly observes that the discourse of toxicity has not received extensive attention, largely because discourse might be perceived as a low priority when individual and public health are in immediate jeopardy. Buell, "Toxic Discourse." In the immediacy of disaster, Buell writes, "not even the most humanistic intellectuals might agree with Emerson's dictum that the most abstract truth is the most practical" (640). Buell's essay is now more than twenty-five years old, and it seems more than past time to put toxicity, fear, toxic discourse, and the 1980s under the microscope of historical attention. And perhaps a historical perspective—trying to situate the emergence of toxic fear in context—provides the right resolution for investigating how that discourse has become all-consuming. It is manifest not just in contemporary concerns about air and water quality or individual pollution sources, but also in mainstream conversations about healthful living and food consumption. Writing about interpretations of risk in contemporary fiction, Ursula K. Heise describes an "urgent search for the aesthetic of uncertainty." Across numerous literary genres, she argues, risk and hazard lack complexity—or at least the fictional fails to do justice to the real-world nuances that drive the modern risk society. Heise, "Cultures of Risk and the Aesthetic of Uncertainty," 41.

6. Resting mostly in the background through this study is the intriguing notion that anxiety is a future-tense emotion: that it provokes worry about something that might or will happen, rather than something that is happening or has happened. Much as fear and emotions have traditionally received short shrift from historians, the omnipresence of the future and thinking about future are underrepresented aspects of historical narratives. Two good exceptions on the history of environmental futures are Masco, *Future of Fallout*; and Pietruska, *Looking Forward*. The idea of how people imagined the future over time—a kind of history of the future—interests me very much. Since 2008, I have been teaching variants of an undergraduate course titled "History of the Future" at McMaster University. One of the key themes in that class is reminding students that there is a chasm between historical events and what historical actors thought might happen—and that serves as an important reminder to the history student that they, unlike their subjects, know what happened next.

7. I am grateful for the instructive guidance I found in Rivera Garza, *Grieving*; and Cavarero, *Horrorism*. Both these scholars treat fear through the phenomenology of violence, a few steps beyond the kinds of "slow violence" familiar to many scholars working on environmental topics and examined in Nixon, *Slow Violence and the Environmentalism of the Poor*. Their engagement with the aesthetics of fear, violence, and the state resonates with some aspects of American toxic fears in the 1980s, not least Cavarero's efforts to establish a vocabulary of violence and Rivera Garza's meditation on neoliberalism and the "visceraless state."

8. The public silencing and ridiculing of environmental fears was part of the environmental rhetoric in the 1980s, certainly, and they receive attention in this study, but there remains a dangerous tendency to interpret fear as pejorative or as a sign of weakness. That tendency could not be further from my intent in this work. Nor do I mean to plot out some objective metric for evaluating the severity of past chemical fears. New work is starting to develop algorithms for "reading" emotions more effectively. See Davies, *Nervous States*. This is not a book about justifying or dismissing some fears as they arose in different places, at different times, and under different circumstances. Social anxieties are almost never irrational—they have a history that deserves attention. Inasmuch as chemophobia acknowledged a social or technical breakdown in measures designed to keep people safe, many instances of fear bred resilience. And in the proper contexts it provoked action and remediation.

9. Robinson, "Fear."

10. There is an established and growing body of scholarship on the history of emotions with its own rich historiography. Foundational work in the 1980s from Carol and Peter Stearns initiated engagement with "emotionology." In the following

decade William M. Reddy introduced "emotional regimes" and "emotives" into this inquiry, which sought to highlight the relationships between power and emotions. Around the same time, Barbara H. Rosenwein developed analyses of "emotional communities," which stressed the evolution of emotional norms. For a crash course on the history of emotions, see Stearns and Stearns, "Emotionology"; Reddy, *Navigation of Feeling*; Rosenwein, "Worrying about Emotions in History"; and Rosenwein, *Emotional Communities in the Early Middle Ages*. See also Boddice, *History of Feelings*. In addition, there are three recent and excellent surveys of the field that I have found instructive. See Boddice, *History of Emotions*; Rosenwein and Cristiani, *What Is the History of Emotions?*; and Plamper, *History of Emotions*. The primary scholarly challenge implicit in examining the history of emotions is that feelings seem relatively subjective and invisible. As Joanna Bourke observes, the only access historians have "to fearful people from the past is through the things they left behind." Bourke, *Fear*, 7. Typically, these artifacts are words and language, but they can also be actions or performances, as Gerd Althoff has argued in his work on performance as a conduit for studying the history of emotions. This lens is particularly valuable for examining toxic fear. While language analysis is undoubtedly useful in this work, people's actions—their impulses to flee or to decide to speak out and leave some textual trail—are themselves sources that warrant attention. For an excellent summary of Althoff's German work, see Rosenwein and Cristiani, *What Is the History of Emotions?*, 45–49. Much more can and should be done to examine the relationships between environmental history and the history of emotions. I can profess a genuine enthusiasm for what that endeavor might yield, but I concede that this current work commits the intellectual crime of not doing this avenue of inquiry anything even remotely approximating justice.

11. Robin, *Fear*, 27.

12. Aron, *Main Currents in Sociological Thought I*, 20–21. Robin cites this quotation twice. Robin, *Fear*, 9 and 27.

13. Masco, *Theater of Operations*, 2.

14. Mitman, Murphy, and Sellers, "Introduction," 13.

15. Kummerer, "Ecological Impact of Time," 228.

16. Magnuson et al., "Poisoning of America," 58. Richmond is also quoted in Riismandel, *Neighborhood of Fear*, 54.

17. Magnuson et al., "Poisoning of America," 58.

18. Michael H. Brown, "Love Canal, U.S.A.," *New York Times*, January 21, 1979, SM6.

19. Larry Agran, "Toxic-Waste Dumping: What We Don't See *Is* Bothering Us," *Los Angeles Times*, February 3, 1980, F5.

20. Magnuson et al., "Poisoning of America."

21. I blogged about the rise of the media response to toxic fear in the 1980s here: https://eganhistory.wordpress.com/2014/10/31/the-80s-almost-killed-me-toxic-fear-in-america/ (last accessed June 19, 2025).

22. Lloyd-Smith and Sheffield-Brotherton, "Children's Environmental Health."

23. Magnuson et al., "Poisoning of America," 61.

24. Harvey, *Brief History of Neoliberalism*, 3. See also Gerstle, *Rise and Fall of the Neoliberal Order*. Lurking behind the scenes of this argument is a long-standing economic debate about the role of the state in modern societies. The welfare or insurance state grew out of the Enlightenment ideal that the state's role was to protect its citizenry. As it evolved during the economic boom that followed World War II, federal governments managed risk and provided for pensions, education, health care, and income support. Critics declaimed a "culture of dependency," wherein entrepreneurialism was shackled and discouraged and individual responsibility was minimized. Theory and practice came to a head during the financial crises of the 1970s; neoliberal governments sought to promote free enterprise through deregulation and shifting risk and responsibility onto the individual. These transitions eroded social welfare nets. An excellent recent intervention in this history is Wellum, *Energizing Neoliberalism*. For the persistence of neoliberalism's influence, see Monbiot and Hutchison, *Invisible Doctrine*; and Brown, *Undoing the Demos*.

25. I am indebted to the late Michael Fellman for the *Wall Street* comparison. In the early 1990s, one of the final lectures of his U.S. History survey at Simon Fraser University (HIS 213) consisted of an examination of capitalism, neoliberalism, labor, and culture told through excerpts from that film. On a personal note, I might mention that his style and approach to teaching history was formative in inspiring my own teaching praxis.

26. The fear of radioactive fallout and nuclear war in the 1950s is a worthwhile historical corollary, but nuclear threats engendered solidarity in ways that are less immediately characteristic of responses in the 1980s.

27. I owe this comparison to H. V. Nelles, who proposed it as part of an informal seminar on "Remembering the 1980s?," McMaster University, March 11, 2015. Frederick Buell hints at a similar comparison in *From Apocalypse to Way of Life*, 6–8.

28. Rome, "What Really Matters in History?" See also Sutter, "World with Us."

29. Hays, *Beauty, Health, and Permanence*.

30. Beck, *World Risk Society*, 119.

31. Beck, *Risk Society*, 22.

32. Beck, *Risk Society*, 155–234.

33. In a 2018 blog post, Alex Zahara outlined the important distinctions between perception and understandings in the politics of knowledge: "When public

understandings of risk are framed as 'perception' as opposed to knowledge, public concerns and insights about contamination are often ignored." Zahara, "Against Risk Perception." My reading of the 1980s suggests that public understanding was broadly regarded as a more derogatory "perception." My work follows Zahara's path: I mean to treat fear as a critical lived experience and one that frames chemical anxiety as an instructive form of knowledge.

34. Clarke, *Acceptable Risk?*, 178.

35. Hepler-Smith, "Molecular Bureaucracy," 3.

36. Jasanoff, "EPA's Regulation of Daminozide," 116.

37. This fact and the burgeoning popular awareness of and response to these toxic burdens serve as the plot line for this study of the American 1980s. It constitutes a key chapter in the embodied history of the "Toxic Century."

38. Ericson, *Crime in an Insecure World*.

39. Tversky and Kahneman, "Availability."

40. This is the point where emotional and environmental skeptics note that the availability heuristic's capacity for fostering hyperbole grossly exaggerated the extent of the hazard posed by chemical materials. But exposure and fear of exposure are two different things; hazard should be measured in a sober, quantifiable manner, away from the noise of a hysterical populace. In scientific terms, that would be the laboratory. But in cases of chemical contamination, the residents of polluted communities were the unwitting lab rats.

41. "Fears of Another Love Canal Spread Through Memphis Area," *Lakeland Ledger*, April 14, 1980, 7A.

42. James Coates, "Denver Suburb Fears It's 'Love Canal West,'" *Chicago Tribune*, November 5, 1984, 6.

43. Glassner, *Culture of Fear*, xii.

44. Stearns, *American Fear*, 4.

45. Quoted in Bourke, *Fear*, 189. Freud was taking his cue from Danish philosopher Søren Kierkegaard, who applied fear to the specific while anxiety did not have a specific object. In his analysis of Kierkegaard's *Concept of Anxiety*, Arne Grøn makes the interesting distinction between fear and anxiety: "When using the term 'anxiety'—as opposed to 'fear'—for the future, it is because anxiety has both a more undetermined and more wide-ranging character than fear. It is an anxiety about catastrophes where life as we know it ceases to exist and maybe where even the possibility of human life disappears." Grøn, *Concept of Anxiety in Søren Kierkegaard*, 3.

46. Bourke, *Fear*, 190. Perhaps the strongest word against specific terms comes from the developmental psychologist Jerome Kagan, who railed against the limitations of language: "Let us agree to a moratorium on the use of single words, such as *fear*, . . . and write about processes with full sentences rather than ambiguous, naked

concepts." Kagan, *What Is Emotion?*, 14, cited in Plamper and Lazier, "Introduction," 59–60.

47. I remain agnostic to the potential merits or virtues of harnessing the big data powers of digital scholarship to quantify fear through sentiment analysis. For the moment, I remain sensitive to the enduring ineffability of individual emotions as well as the potential variabilities associated with tracking fear across race, class, gender, time, and place. I am grateful, however, to Bryor Snefjella for highlighting this as a possible avenue of inquiry. I suspect that further research in this vein might uncover ever richer methods of understanding emotional pasts.

48. I draw inspiration and guidance for a nonlinear organization from Alison, *Meander, Spiral, Explode*. For the distinction between communication and expression in the written word—where the former imparts precise, *literal* information with the intention of it being clearly received and understood, and the latter involves articulating something more abstract and *figurative* (feelings and thoughts, for example) to convey a sense, a mood, a direction—see Baricco, *Barbarians*, 53.

49. Gensburg et al., "Mortality Among Former Love Canal Residents."

50. Glassner, *Culture of Fear*.

51. Paula DiPerna, "Leukemia Strikes a Small Town," *New York Times Saturday Magazine*, December 2, 1984, 100–108.

52. Sellers and Melling, "Towards a Transnational Industrial Hazard History," esp. 414–419.

Chapter One. The More Primitive the Fear

1. For an excellent treatment of Three Mile Island, with a substantial interest in fear as an historical driver, see Zaretsky, *Radiation Nation*. For competing readings and analyses of nuclear fears, see Schwab, *Radioactive Ghosts*; and Weart, *Rise of Nuclear Fear*.

2. Zeigler, Brunn, and Johnson, "Evacuation from a Nuclear Technological Disaster," 3.

3. Bob Dvorchak, "Residents Near Nuclear Plant Are Urged to Remain Indoors," *Kane Republican*, March 30, 1979, 1.

4. "Evacuation Alert for Plant Area Continues," *Huntingdon Daily News*, April 4, 1979, 16. The story reported that Greyhound ridership had subsided to normal levels by April 3, 1979.

5. Erikson, *New Species of Trouble*, 140.

6. On nuclear fears, see Zaretsky, *Radiation Nation*; Weart, *Rise of Nuclear Fear*; Schwab, *Radioactive Ghosts*; Boyer, *By the Bomb's Early Light*; Masco, *Nuclear Borderlands*; Masco, *Future of Fallout*; and Brown, *Plutopia*.

7. Frances Cerra, "Evacuation Planning at Shoreham Studied," *New York Times,* April 15, 1979, LI1.

8. Philip Shabecoff, "Residents Tell of Fears," *New York Times,* May 3, 1983, A17. See also Shabecoff, "E.P.A. Evacuating Trailer Site Near Asbestos Mine," *New York Times,* April 16, 1983, L6. For Imperial, see Robert Reinhold, "Claims in Missouri Show Complexity of Toxic Waste Cleanup and Buyouts," *New York Times,* May 4, 1983, B8.

9. Office of Public Health, Department of Health, State of New York, "Love Canal: Public Health Time Bomb" (special report, Robert P. Whelan, Commissioner, September 1978).

10. The literature on Love Canal is extensive. See Thomson, *The Wild and the Toxic;* Hay, "Recipe for Disaster" (PhD diss.); Hay, "Recipe for Disaster"; Hay, "New Earthly Vision"; Mazur, *Hazardous Inquiry;* Blum, *Love Canal Revisited;* and Newman, *Love Canal.* Also important are the accounts of one of the key protagonists of the Love Canal struggle, Lois Gibbs. See Gibbs, *Love Canal: My Story;* and Gibbs, *Love Canal: The Story Continues. . . .* I also want to highlight two older works: Levine, *Love Canal;* and Brown, *Laying Waste.* They are interesting for a couple of reasons. First, with respect to the literature on Love Canal, they highlight the prevalence of public fears in much greater detail than do more recent studies. Second, Levine and Brown were both on the ground at Love Canal as the story evolved. Levine conducted some of the earliest sociological studies on the effects of the pollution scare; Brown was the first to break the story (he worked at the *Niagara Gazette;* his articles became the basis for the book) before it became a topic of national interest. That they should put a greater emphasis on fear is important and deserving of notice. Levine's papers—dispersed between the University at Buffalo Special Collections and the Research Library at the Buffalo History Museum—also constitute essential resources.

11. Kolata, "Love Canal," 1239.

12. In her analysis of Love Canal, Jennifer Thomson addresses environmental health as a perceived right of citizenship. She also challenges the scholarly preponderance of stressing the community's foregrounding of their own health rather than treating the question of health as an evolving landscape subject to change. I think my treatment of Love Canal follows a similar, if less ambitious examination: the way fear and anxiety contributed to that debate. See Thomson, *The Wild and the Toxic,* 43–70.

13. Hernan, *This Borrowed Earth,* 71.

14. Chlorinated hydrocarbons refer to a variety of chlorine-, carbon-, and hydrogen-based compounds known for their prolonged persistence, high toxicity, and tendency to cause cancer. DDT, PCBs, dioxins, and furans are among the more notorious and toxic chlorinated hydrocarbons.

15. Levine, "Psychosocial Impact of Toxic Chemical Waste Dumps," 16.

16. In 1972, nuclear physicist Alvin Weinberg lamented that responses to social problems "hang on answers to questions which can be asked of science and yet *which cannot be answered by science.*" The best scientists could do was extrapolate averages at which they felt confident that minimal hazard might occur. To some degree, this was educated guesswork. There was no magic number after which exposure should be taken more seriously. But public risk perception (a topic to which I return in chapter 7) was steeped as much in qualitative moral values and fears as it was in quantifiable scientific empiricism. To Weinberg, this was a "trans-scientific" question because its answer transcended—or demanded more than just—science. Weinberg, "Science and Trans-Science," 209. I discuss this kind of scientific engagement with "crisis disciplines" in the 1970s. See Egan, "Survival Science." The biologist Barry Commoner played an important role in the evolution of science communication as a key to public participation—I called this the "remaking of American environmentalism"—after World War II. See Egan, *Barry Commoner and the Science of Survival.*

17. Adeline Levine, "Love Canal: Scientific Controversy and Policy Dilemma" (presentation, Institute of Environmental Health, University of Cincinnati Medical Center, April 19, 1983), 10, Adeline Levine Collection, Buffalo History Museum, 12.2. Also quoted in Vyner, *Invisible Trauma*, 14.

18. Levine, "Psychosocial Impact of Toxic Chemical Waste Dumps," 16.

19. Hernan, *This Borrowed Earth*, 74.

20. "Worried Mothers Feel They're Stuck," *Niagara Gazette*, August 2, 1978, 1.

21. Brown, "Cheers Greet Word of Relief," *Niagara Gazette*, August 5, 1978, 1.

22. Stone and Levine, "Reactions to Collective Stress."

23. Michael Brown, "Evacuation of Kids Urged," *Niagara Gazette*, August 2, 1978, 1.

24. Michael Brown, "Love Canal and the Poisoning of America," *The Atlantic*, December 1979, 33–47.

25. "Adjacent Canal Homeowner Going to Give His House Away," *Niagara Gazette*, November 3, 1978, 1.

26. Michael Brown, "Tons of Dioxin Agent in Canal," *Niagara Gazette*, November 10, 1978, 1. See also Mike Brown, "Dioxin Fear at Canal," *Niagara Gazette*, November 8, 1978, 1.

27. Brown, *Laying Waste*, 51. See also Gary Spencer, "Canal Force Warned About Deadly Chemical," *Buffalo Courier-Express*, November 11, 1978, 3.

28. Brown, *Laying Waste*, 51.

29. "Cancer Scares," *Wall Street Journal*, July 27, 1979, 12; "Dioxin Hysteria," *Wall Street Journal*, May 31, 1983, 28.

30. See, for example, Schwetz et al., "Toxicology of Chlorinated Dibenzo-*p*-dioxins."

31. Dioxin needs a history or biography of its own. Much environmental literature makes passing reference to dioxin, and histories of environmental harm note how it is released from the incineration of PVC plastics. Others note the link between the dioxin family and Agent Orange. One might speculate on the relationship between war and Agent Orange in further provoking the manner in which chemical poisons generated fear. Dioxins are a curious exception to the traditional narrative that marks the history of environmental pollution. Unlike the majority of chemical contaminants whose beneficial purposes came with unanticipated consequences, dioxins were never deliberately produced for market. Rather, dioxins were the incidental by-product of numerous industrial and combustion processes, the cost of doing business. For an introduction to dioxin and its history, start with Hay, *Defoliation of America*; Thornton, *Pandora's Poison*; and Hites, "Dioxins." A diligent researcher would also be well-served to study the dioxins holdings within the Center for Health, Environment, & Justice records at Tufts University. I am grateful to the university's Special Collections staff for their assistance in accessing these papers.

32. Michael Brown, "Canal Protesters Arrested," *Niagara Gazette*, December 11, 1978, 1.

33. Michael Brown, "State Asked to Move More from Love Canal," *Niagara Gazette*, January 23, 1979, 1. See also Thomson, *The Wild and the Toxic*, 52.

34. Brown, *Laying Waste*, 46–47. For an account of a similar incident, of the Stringfellow Acid Pits in Southern California, see Craig, *Stringfellow Acid Pits*.

35. "Increased Dioxin Level Is Called No Health Hazard," *Niagara Gazette*, April 14, 1979, 2A.

36. Quoted in Mazur, *Hazardous Inquiry*, 82.

37. Quoted in Mazur, *Hazardous Inquiry*, 83.

38. "The Killing Ground," ABC News, aired March 29, 1979.

39. "'Every Mother Is Scared to Death,'" *Niagara Gazette*, April 27, 1980, 10A.

40. Brown, *Laying Waste*, 48–49.

41. Brown, *Laying Waste*, 46.

42. Brown, *Laying Waste*, 48.

43. "Love Canal Crisis Grabbed International Attention," *Niagara Gazette*, December 31, 1978.

44. National Wildlife Federation, *Toxic Substances Programs in the U.S. States and Territories: How Well Do They Work?* (Washington, D.C.: National Wildlife Federation, 1979).

45. Robert Reinhold, "Missouri Dioxin Cleanup: A Decade of Little Action," *New York Times*, February 20, 1983, 54.

46. Melinda Beck et al., "The Toxic-Waste Crisis," *Newsweek*, March 7, 1983, 24.

47. Reinhold, "Missouri Dioxin Cleanup," 54.

48. Marjorie Mandel, "EPA Never Interviewed Missouri Dioxin Sprayer," *St. Louis Post-Dispatch*, November 1, 1982, 1.

49. Marjorie Mandel, "EPA Called Too Slow on Dioxin Threat," *St. Louis Post-Dispatch*, November 6, 1982, 1, 3, quotation on 3.

50. Marjorie Mandel, "EPA Crash Program on Dioxin Demanded," *St. Louis Post-Dispatch*, November 11, 1982, 1, 5, quotation on 5.

51. Mandel, "EPA Crash Program on Dioxin Demanded," 1.

52. Martha Shirk and Kathy Rogers, "Do Something About Dioxin, Residents Plead to Officials," *St. Louis Post-Dispatch*, November 18, 1982, 1, 4, quotation on 1.

53. Shirk and Rogers, "Do Something About Dioxin, Residents Plead to Officials," 4.

54. "Dioxin People Speak," November 17, 1982, Richard A. Gephardt Congressional Audio/Visual Collection, 1976–2004, item 542, Missouri Historical Society. Baczynski was referring to the Missouri Department of Natural Resources.

55. William Powell, "Remember Times Beach: The Dioxin Disaster, 30 Years Later," *St. Louis*, December 2012, http://www.stlmag.com/Remember-Times-Beach-The-Dioxin-Disaster-30-Years-Later/ (accessed October 13, 2025).

56. Michael A. Lerner et al., "The Trouble at Times Beach," *Newsweek*, January 10, 1983, 24.

57. Burford, *Are You Tough Enough?*, 193, 188. A pedant (like me) would want to question the American overtendency to equate "Kafkaesque" with universal horror. It is unlikely that Times Beach in the 1980s captured any of the bureaucratic and urban absurdities of Franz Kafka's stories. The Edvard Munch comparison seems similarly dubious.

58. Lerner et al., "Trouble at Times Beach," 24.

59. Powell, "Remember Times Beach."

60. Art Harris, "After the Deluge, a Tainted Town: U.S. May Relocate Missouri Town to High, Uncontaminated Ground," *Washington Post*, January 6, 1983, A1.

61. *Habitability of the Love Canal Area: An Analysis of the Technical Basis for the Division on the Habitability of the Emergency Declaration Area—A Technical Memorandum* (Washington, D.C.: U.S. Congress, Office of Technology Assessment, OTA-TM-M-13, June 1983), 51.

62. These abstractions play a prominent feature of my analysis of fear surrounding cancer and cancer clusters in chapter 6.

63. "A Healthy Life Style," *Washington Post*, March 5, 1987, A26.

64. David M. Mog, "The Paralysis of Chemophobia," *Washington Post*, March 14, 1987, A21.

65. I revisit this question in the conclusion, where I examine the globalization of toxic fear during the 1980s. Naturally, the disaster at Bhopal serves as an especially poignant exception to this claim. It is important to also stress the difference

between workplace exposures to chemical contaminants, which also tended to produce chronic health risks, and workplace accidents, where acute problems could manifest themselves. The labor history of chemical hazard is an important part of the larger history of pollution that, in the main, fell outside the popular discourse of exposure during the 1980s. For a range of suggestive titles that address industrial hazards and chemical pollution, see Sellers, *Hazards of the Job*; Nash, *Inescapable Ecologies*; Doyle, *Trespass Against Us*; Sarathy, Hamilton, and Brodie, *Inevitably Toxic*; Van Horssen, *Town Called Asbestos*; and Fagin, *Toms River.*

66. Wuthnow, *Be Very Afraid.*

Chapter Two. Some Seasonal Perversity of the Earth

1. Gibbs, *Love Canal: My Story,* 1–2.

2. Stone-Mediatore, *Reading Across Borders,* 43.

3. Newman, "Darker Shades of Green."

4. Kristin Butler, "It Was Like Watching an Accident in Slow Motion," PBS *American Experience,* April 11, 2024, https://www.pbs.org/wgbh/americanexperience/features/posioned-ground-accident-slow-motion/ (last accessed August 6, 2024).

5. Newman, "Darker Shades of Green," 22.

6. Kuletz, "Invisible Places, Violent Spaces," 238.

7. For more on Yucca Mountain, see Houston, "Environmental Justice Storytelling"; Kuletz, *Tainted Desert*; Schrader-Frechette, *Burying Uncertainty*; Solnit, *Savage Dreams*; Solnit, *Hope in the Dark*; and Stoffle and Arnold, "Confronting the Angry Rock."

8. Ian D. Zabarte, "View of the Western Shoshone Nation Relating to the Yucca Mountain Socioeconomic Studies" (U.S. Nuclear Waste Technical Review Board, Environment and Public Health Panel, October 16, 1990), https://www.nwtrb.gov/docs/default-source/meetings/1990/october/zabarte.pdf?sfvrsn=e27f505_4 (last accessed August 2, 2024).

9. Kuletz, *Tainted Desert,* xviii. For more on Zabarte, see 166–177. "Nuclear colonialism" was coined in Churchill and LaDuke, "Native North America." For further discussion, see Schwab, *Radioactive Ghosts,* 57–84; and Enders, "Rhetoric of Nuclear Colonialism." Zabarte was hardly the lone voice of dissent against the nuclear repository siting among the Western Shoshone, but I use his testimonies as another example of toxic autobiography. A more expansive collection of voices and perspectives is offered in the various titles presented in this section's endnotes.

10. Boyer, *By the Bomb's Early Light*; Weart, *Rise of Nuclear Fear*; Masco, *Nuclear Borderlands*; Zaretsky, *Radiation Nation*; and Schwab, *Radioactive Ghosts.*

11. Walker, *Road to Yucca Mountain*, 186.

12. Kuletz, *Tainted Desert*, 85.

13. Ian D. Zabarte testimony reprinted in Nahr, *Poison Fire, Sacred Earth*, 168.

14. Houston, "Environmental Justice Storytelling," 420.

15. In an autobiographical reflection on destruction, sacrifice, and invisibility in the preface to her book, Kuletz writes that "throughout my youth in the late '50s, '60s, and '70s Indians—Western Shoshone, Timbisha Shoshone, and Owens Valley Paiute—were invisible. They weren't *not* there, they were simply invisible to most (although not all) of the white scientific research community and their families." Kuletz, *Tainted Desert*, xv. Newman distinguishes between toxic autobiography and geocriticism: "geocriticism rejects environmental policies that divide the world into appropriate and inappropriate dumping grounds." Newman, "Darker Shades of Green," 32.

16. Houston, "Environmental Justice Storytelling," 419. See also Di Chiro, "Living Environmentalisms"; and Rose, *Reports from a Wild Country*.

17. Newman, "Darker Shades of Green," 32.

18. For a discussion of 1980s materialism, see the introduction to Jelfs, *Argument About Things in the 1980s*.

19. The more people aged—and the longer and further they degenerated—the greater the types of interactions with life and death were altered. As a result, experiences of fear and well-being in individuals and societies have evolved over time. Bourke, *Fear*. Further, the historian Arwen Mohun traces the evolution of Americans' sense of risk over the past three hundred years. Where eighteenth-century Americans worried about "organic" dangers posed by fire, disease, weather, and animals, the industrialization of the nineteenth century introduced new hazards through encounters with machinery and manufacturing. The twentieth century, she observes, brought with it a "new gospel of safety" that transformed again the American relationship with risk and, by extension, with fear. See Mohun, *Risk*, 4. It is possible in the 2020s—with recent pandemic and climatological fears raising new anxieties—that this question of degeneration surpassing contagion as a source of mortal fear might not be quite so obvious, but I remain inclined to want to follow Bourke here, nevertheless.

20. See, for example, Markowitz and Rosner, *Deceit and Denial*; Conis, *How to Sell a Poison*; Nash, *Inescapable Ecologies*; and Sellers, *Crabgrass Crucible*. My own work on Barry Commoner reflects on many of these earlier examples that might serve as prolegomena for toxic fear in the 1980s. Egan, *Barry Commoner and the Science of Survival*.

21. Hays, *Beauty, Health, and Permanence*, 13–39; see also 171–206.

22. Hans and Sell, *Evacuation Risks*, 101–153. See also Zeigler, Brunn, and Johnson, "Evacuation from a Nuclear Technological Disaster."

23. Cited in David Sarokin and Warren Muir, "Too Little Toxic-Waste Data," *New York Times*, October 7, 1985, 31.

24. Neil Orloff, "Climbing the Pollution Learning Curve," *Wall Street Journal*, November 5, 1985, 30. As a point of clarification, both benzene and formaldehyde are hydrocarbons.

25. Doctorow, "State of Mind of the Union," 330. In the shadow of that atomic culture rests a parallel and equally unsettling chemical culture, where it has become easier to mitigate chemical disaster than it has to imagine a world in which harmful chemicals are controlled so that they do not cause harm.

26. Patterson, *Restless Giant*, 205.

27. David Brand, "Yuri Andropov, Ex-KGB Chief, Emerges from Shadows to Vie for Top Kremlin Post," *Wall Street Journal*, November 12, 1982, 18.

28. Andrew and Mitrokhin, *Sword and the Shield*, 214; and Jenkins, *Decade of Nightmares*, 219.

29. Quotations are from Jenkins, *Decade of Nightmares*, 207.

30. Alma Guillermoprieto, "Epidemic of Fear: D.C. Homosexuals Face AIDS," *Washington Post*, June 5, 1983, A1. See also D'Emilio and Freedman, *Intimate Matters*, 354–367; Shilts, *And the Band Played On*; and Schulman, *Let the Record Show*.

31. Bowser, "Race Relations in the 1980s," 307.

32. "Punishment and Prejudice: Racial Disparities in the War on Drugs," *Human Rights Watch* 12, no. 2 (May 2000), https://www.hrw.org/reports/2000/usa/ (accessed August 18, 2023).

33. Farber, *Crack*, 96.

34. Riismandel, *Neighborhood of Fear*. See also Stearns, *Anxious Parents*.

35. DeLillo, *White Noise*, 114.

36. DeLillo, *White Noise*, 117. For a history of the socioeconomic disparity of American disasters, see Steinberg, *Acts of God*.

37. Brick, *Age of Contradiction*; Rodgers, *Age of Fracture*.

38. Rodgers, *Age of Fracture*, 3. Metaphors in the plural is an important part of Rodgers's analysis. Fracture "was not a single, dominant idea—postmodern, new right, or neoliberal—but a contagion of metaphors." Rodgers, *Age of Fracture*, 10. I mean to reconcile my attention to neoliberalism with this disaggregation by highlighting neoliberalism less as a theory or body of thought and more as a multifarious practice that worked within economic, political, and cultural frameworks to keep the market at the forefront of social discourse and activity. See, for example, Wellum, *Energizing Neoliberalism*; Brown, *Undoing the Demos*; and Mirowski, *Never Let a Serious Crisis Go to Waste*, 325–358. The desired outcome was a weakening of the communal social fabric and a reinforcement of more personal interests. Jennifer Thomson, for example, notes a trend toward more individualist definitions of

health and away from public health during this period of growing environmental fears. Thomson, *The Wild and the Toxic*, 5. See also a literary criticism perspective on similar themes in Houser, *Ecosickness in Contemporary U.S. Fiction*.

39. The 1980s certainly had their own series of global environmental catastrophes to contend with, not least concerns about acid rain, the ozone, and the growing question of global warming. But these issues failed to gain as much cultural currency in the United States as they might have in the previous decade—or, indeed, as they subsequently did in the 1990s and 2000s. In his insightful analysis on American public and environmental health as characteristically local enterprises, Merlin Chowkwanyun rejects the idea of an overarching national health agenda in order to show how intrinsically political the American health system is and has been. See Chowkwanyun, *All Health Politics Is Local*.

40. Maya Pines, "Psychological Time Bombs," *New York Times*, June 13, 1982, 10E.

41. Newman, *Love Canal*, 264.

42. Holden, "Love Canal Residents Under Stress," 1242.

43. Kolata, "Love Canal," 1239.

44. Irvin Molotsky, "Damage to Chromosomes Found in Love Canal Tests," *New York Times*, May 17, 1980, 1.

45. Josh Barbanel, "Homeowners Are Bitter and Fearful as Results of Study are Released," *New York Times*, May 18, 1980, 1.

46. See, for example, Barbara Blum to Barbara Quimby, May 16, 1980, box 1, folder 11, 22/3F/634, Adeline Levine Love Canal research materials (pt. 1), 1953–1981 (1978–1981 bulk), University Archives, State University of New York at Buffalo.

47. Kolata, "Love Canal," 1242.

48. Arthur Page, "UB Genetics Expert Doubts Significance of Chromosome Study," *Buffalo Evening News*, May 20, 1980, 1.

49. "Gobbledygook Bomb at Love Canal," *New York Times*, June 12, 1980, A30.

50. Kolata, "Chromosome Damage," 1240.

51. "Panel Review of Biogenics Corporation Study of Chromosome Abnormalities in Love Canal Residents Members" (June 12, 1980), box 1, folder 3, 22/3F/634, Adeline Levine Love Canal research materials.

52. Kolata, "Love Canal," 1239.

53. Marc Humbert, "Health Department Holding Canal Report," *Niagara Gazette*, June 13, 1980, 6A.

54. "How Not to Cope with a Pollution Crisis," *Lancet* 2, no. 8186 (July 19, 1980): 131–132.

55. Holden, "Love Canal Residents Under Stress," 1242.

56. Michael Cordts, "Love Canal Residents are Heard, Free Hostages," *Oakland Tribune*, May 20, 1980, A9.

57. Barbanel, "Homeowners at Love Canal Hold 2 Officials Until F.B.I. Intervenes," *New York Times*, May 20, 1980, 1. See also Dan MacDonald, "EPA Insists Incident Won't Affect Love Canal Decision," *Buffalo Evening News*, May 20, 1980, 39; and Bob Buyer, "'The People Wanted Answers,' Love Canal Protester Explains," *Buffalo Evening News*, May 20, 1980, 39.

58. Statement by Barbara Blum, Deputy Administrator, U.S. Environmental Protection Agency, at a press conference announcing relocation of Love Canal residents, May 21, 1980, box 1, folder 11, 22/3F/634, Adeline Levine Love Canal research materials.

59. Lawrence Ingrassia and Bryan Burrough, "Toxic Waste Scare 'Killed' Small Town, Its People Complain," *Wall Street Journal*, March 1, 1983, 1.

60. Ingrassia and Burrough, "Toxic Waste Scare 'Killed' Small Town," 16.

61. Baum and Fleming, "Implications of Psychological Research on Stress."

62. This literature is expansive. See, for starters, Gensburg et al., "Mortality Among Former Love Canal Residents"; and Gensburg et al., "Cancer Incidence Among Former Love Canal Residents."

63. Erikson, *New Species of Trouble*, 139–157.

64. Roberts and Toffolon-Weiss, *Chronicles from the Environmental Justice Frontline*, 22.

65. Environmental justice conflicts invariably involve debates over the unequal distribution of environmental goods and exposures to environmental bads. Too frequently, access to information is a key catalyst. This was especially the case in Kai Erikson's analysis of Grassy Narrows, in northern Ontario, Canada. See Erikson, *New Species of Trouble*, 27–57. But the question of access to information—and the uncertainties provoked by limited access—is a common refrain throughout environmental justice literature. See Bullard, *Unequal Protection*. Frequently, struggles for environmental justice begin not with demands for clean living and working spaces, but in efforts to determine the relative salubrity of an environment under threat. This is a key theme in this book's sixth chapter, where I examine popular epidemiology projects in Woburn, Massachusetts. For more on Woburn, see DiPerna, *Cluster Mystery*; and Brown and Mikkelsen, *No Safe Place*.

66. Taylor, *Toxic Communities*, 115–118. See also Čapek, "'Environmental Justice' Frame."

67. Cerrell Associates and J. S. Powell, *Political Difficulties Facing Waste-to-Energy Conversion Plant Siting* (California Waste Management Board, 1984). For scholarly reflection on the Cerrell Report, see Taylor, *Toxic Communities*, 82; Cole and Foster, *From the Ground Up*, 70–74; Walsh, Warland, and Smith, *Don't Burn It Here*, 13–14; Blumberg and Gottlieb, *War on Waste*, 58–60; and Hamilton, "Concerned Citizens of South Central Los Angeles."

68. I revisit this assertion with examples in subsequent chapters.

69. Beck, *Risk Society*, 36.

70. Kuletz, *Tainted Desert*, 95.

71. See Szasz, *Shopping Our Way to Safety*. Szasz introduces the notion of "inverted quarantines," the practice of people insulating themselves from environmental harms rather than preventing the harms. Examples such as buying bottled water to escape local contamination, living in gated communities to escape rising crime rates, and buying only organic food to escape from pesticides point to the neoliberal solution to environmental hazards, which individualizes the threat and how to address it. However, when environmental threats are indiscriminate and cannot be escaped by those with the means to do so—nuclear fallout, lead, PCBs, etc.—the United States has a remarkable record of environmental policy success. Lead deserves a bit of an asterisk here as an example of an ubiquitous hazard. Unleaded gasoline was introduced in the 1970s, and leaded gasoline was completely phased out by the mid-1990s. A twenty-year phaseout might have been slow, but it marked a consistent and considered strategy (and concerted imposition on the auto industry) to eliminate lead from car emissions without putting too much financial hardship on car owners. A similar kind of slow roll occurred with paint, where lead was banned for residential use in 1978, but no legislation could remove it from where it had previously been applied. Lead paint chips and dust persisted, especially in socioeconomically disadvantaged areas where refreshed coats of paint (without lead) might have been less common. For histories of lead pollution, see Markowitz and Rosner, *Deceit and Denial*; Warren, *Brush with Death*; and Frederickson, "Age of Lead."

72. On environmental justice and storytelling, see Barca, "Telling the Right Story." I am conscious, too, of the hazard of asserting narrative violence in environmental history, when professional historians have traditionally been so complicit in grander forms of historical silencing. See, for example, Trouillot, *Silencing the Past*; and Azoulay, *Potential History*. Both make an important and compelling case against the blind spots in professional history constituting sins of omission, but rather sins of commission.

73. Marshall, "Experts Clash Over Cancer Data," 900. Broder's claim supported some National Cancer Institute epidemiological findings published earlier in the year in the *Lancet*. See Davis et al., "International Trends in Cancer Mortality."

Chapter Three. Wear the Same Disguise

1. Another cover on the same theme was printed for the October 14, 1985, issue of *Time*. It was a replica of the 1980 cover, the same white man's face half submerged in a pool of toxic chemicals. If anything, the man's face looked older and more haggard.

2. Hays, *Beauty, Health, and Permanence*. For background on American environmental policy leading up to the critical decade, see Brooks, *Before Earth Day*; and Milazzo, *Unlikely Environmentalists*.

3. Josh Barbanel, "An Explosive Fire in Jersey Causes a Night of Fear," *New York Times*, April 23, 1980, A1.

4. Epstein, Brown, and Pope, *Hazardous Waste in America*, 156.

5. Barbanel, "Explosive Fire in Jersey Causes a Night of Fear," A1. See also Joanne Omang, "Blasts, Fire Hit N.J. Toxic Waste Dump," *Washington Post*, April 23, 1980, A3.

6. Barbanel, "Explosive Fire in Jersey Causes a Night of Fear," B4.

7. "Family Sues Company in Spread of Chemicals," *Eugene Register-Guard*, May 1, 1980, 5A; "S. I. Family's Suit Cites Chemical Fire in Jersey," *New York Times*, May 1, 1980, B14.

8. Barbanel, "Explosive Fire in Jersey Causes a Night of Fear," B4.

9. Epstein, Brown, and Pope paint a slightly more sympathetic picture of Carracino. In correspondence with Brown, Carracino insists he was muscled out of Chemical Control by a bigger company, Northeast Pollution Control, that bought him out. See Epstein, Brown, and Pope, *Hazardous Waste in America*, 157–159. In the interest of historical symmetry, it is also worth noting that Carracino began his waste disposal career at the Kin-Buc waste dump.

10. "Disguising a Lethal Brew," *Philadelphia Inquirer*, September 24, 1979. Senator H. John Heinz III collection, Carnegie Mellon University Libraries, box 100, folder 2.1.

11. Ralph Blumenthal, "Witness Refuses More testimony on Toxic Waste," *New York Times*, February 7, 1981, 24.

12. Rod Nordland and Josh Friedman, "Poison at Our Doorsteps: Some Use All World as a Dump," *Philadelphia Inquirer*, September 24, 1979, Senator H. John Heinz III collection, box 100, folder 2.

13. Sheila Rule, "Fire Breaks Out Amid Chemicals at Site in Jersey," *New York Times*, April 22, 1980, B3. See also "Earth Day Smoke Signal," *New York Times*, April 23, 1980, A26.

14. Josh Barbanel, "Runaway Chemical Reaction Releases Cloud of Toxic Fumes in Bayonne," *New York Times*, April 25, 1980, B2.

15. Josh Barbanel, "2 Hurt at Bayonne Chemical Plant," *New York Times*, May 8, 1980, B8.

16. "New Chemical Fire Flares in Jersey," *New York Times*, July 13, 1980, E6.

17. The Kin-Buc landfill received considerable media attention in the 1970s and early 1980s, but its place has faded from the environmental history of waste register. It receives passing reference in Brown, *Laying Waste*, 153–154; and Epstein, Brown, and Pope, *Hazardous Waste in America*, 171–173.

18. Nordland and Friedman, "Poison at Our Doorsteps."

19. Andrews, *Managing the Environment, Managing Ourselves,* 249. Andrews credits the Comprehensive Environmental Response, Compensation, and Liability Act—or Superfund—as a part of this generation of legislation tasked with better policing, managing, and remediating hazardous waste in the environment. (I discuss Superfund in chapter 4.) I would note here, too, the significance of the new vocabulary of waste, and the definition of "hazardous" as part of a project to develop a common language—legal and political—for its mitigation. Where that language also shaped local and grassroots efforts to understand and resolve contamination in communities during the 1980s, it might be possible to consider this lexicon as contributing to a more precise or concrete identification for heretofore vaguer environmental fears. My instinct, however, is that the abdication of government oversight during the early Reagan years undid much of the good work that these 1970s policies and initiatives imagined. Moreover, a more precise vocabulary permitted much of the informed, public participation that shaped many of the environmental struggles of the period. Further inquiry into the background of this question might begin with Boudia et al., *Residues*; and Moore, *Disrupting Science.*

20. Ann Hughey, "Poison Problem: Fearing New Love Canal, Chemical Firms Stress Safer Disposal of Hazardous Waste," *Wall Street Journal,* June 30, 1983, 58.

21. Fagin, *Toms River,* 176.

22. EPA, "Attack on Hazardous Waste: The Challenge of the 1980's" (Washington, D.C.: U.S. Environmental Protection Agency, February 1980), 6.

23. Magnuson et al., "Poisoning of America," 58.

24. W. L. Gaby, "Health Hazards Associated with Solid Waste Disposal," *Reviews on Environmental Health* 3, no. 3 (1981): 277–291.

25. Michael H. Brown, "New Jersey Cleans Up Its Pollution Act," *New York Times Saturday Magazine,* November 23, 1980, 36. For more on organized crime and waste disposal, see Block and Scarpitti, *Poisoning for Profit*; and Rebovich, *Dangerous Ground.* See also Epstein, Brown, and Pope, *Hazardous Waste in America,* 154–155.

26. Reflecting on a history of organized crime and hazardous waste disposal, Rebovich notes that "most commonly, the criminal dumper is an ordinary, profit motivated businessman who operates in a business where syndicate crime activity may be present but [is] by no means pervasive." Rebovich, *Dangerous Ground,* xiv. See also Zimring, *Clean and White.* Zimring touches on the stereotypes and associations between the dirty work of waste disposal and the dirty work of organized crime. See 179–181.

27. Shayna Panzer, "Toxic Task Force is Battling Dumpers," *New York Times,* January 6, 1980, NJ14.

28. Barbanel, "Explosive Fire in Jersey Causes a Night of Fear," B4.

29. "A N.J. 'Friend' of the Earth," *Philadelphia Inquirer,* September 24, 1979, Senator H. John Heinz III collection, box 100, folder 2.

30. Nordland and Friedman, "Poison at Our Doorsteps." Michael H. Brown recounts an almost identical quotation in *Laying Waste,* 255.

31. Nordland and Friedman, "Poison at Our Doorsteps."

32. Nordland and Friedman, "Poison at Our Doorsteps."

33. Nordland and Friedman, "Poison at Our Doorsteps."

34. "Where Perilous Chemicals Lie in Large Quantities," *Philadelphia Inquirer,* September 23, 1979, Senator H. John Heinz III collection, box 100, folder 2.

35. "Comprehensive Oil Pollution Liability and Compensation Act," Hearing Before the Subcommittee on Water Resources of the House of Representatives Committee on Public Works and Transportation, 96th Congress (September 26, 1979), 240. The real quantity was anybody's guess. The *Philadelphia Inquirer* reported on an estimate of 300,000 to 900,000 gallons of chemicals and oil during the same week. "Where Perilous Chemicals Lie in Large Quantities."

36. Lew Marcus, "Heinz—Pittston Tunnel Spill Worse Than TMI," *Scranton Tribune,* October 20, 1979, 3.

37. Donald Janson, "Toxic Waste: A Nightmare for New Jersey," *New York Times,* February 7, 1980, B5.

38. Janson, "Toxic Waste," B1.

39. Epstein, Brown, and Pope, *Hazardous Waste in America,* 160.

40. Martin Waldron, "Capital Report," *New York Times,* April 27, 1980, NJ10.

41. Joseph F. Sullivan, "Old Waste Dumps Now Haunt a Town," *New York Times,* May 9, 1980, B2.

42. Janson, "Toxic Waste," B5.

43. Janson, "Toxic Waste," B5.

44. Shayna Panzer, "Jackson Township Still Waits for Water," *New York Times,* June 22, 1980, NJ6–NJ7.

45. Michael Norman, "Landfill Decision Is Hailed in Jersey," *New York Times,* December 6, 1983, B2.

46. Panzer, "Jackson Township Still Waits for Water," NJ7. For more on fear, emotional and psychological distress, and the Legler case study, see Edelstein, *Contaminated Communities,* 17–42.

47. Leo H. Carney, "Dumped Plane Fuel at Lakehurst Stirs Water-Pollution Fear," *New York Times,* November 2, 1980, NJ1, NJ26.

48. On November 17, 1983, Legler residents were awarded $17.6 million from the township; $8.2 million was earmarked for a medical fund to test for future diseases as a result of their exposure. The court ruled that there was insufficient proof to make a causal connection between the contamination and the disturbing

number of diseases in the community. The rest was compensation for "reduced 'quality of life,' emotional distress, and miscellaneous costs" (Norman, "Landfill Decision Is Hailed in Jersey," B2). Legler residents' lawyer, Steven Phillips, stressed the importance of the case in setting a precedent for establishing "accountability for chemical wrongdoing" ("Jury Makes Award in Well Pollution," *New York Times*, November 18, 1983, B2). Hugh Kaufman, a pollution specialist in the Hazardous Site Control Division of the EPA, concurred: "It is something for citizens who live near the tens of thousands of sites all over the country to build on." Small consolation, perhaps, for the damage done. McCarthy was pleased with the verdict—he posted a hand-painted plywood sign on his front lawn that read "Legler beats Jackson Township"—but he still felt trapped. The decision did not compensate the plaintiffs for loss of property value. "We'd like to leave town and move to New Hampshire," McCarthy told the *New York Times* shortly after the decision. "But who wants to buy a house next to a contaminated dump?" (Norman, "Landfill Decision Is Hailed in New Jersey," B2.)

49. Nathaniel Sheppard Jr., "New Toxic Clouds Rise at Kentucky Derailment," *New York Times*, July 28, 1980, A12.

50. National Transportation Safety Board, *Seaboard System Railroad Freight Train FERHL Derailment and Fire, Marshville, North Carolina, April 10, 1984* (Washington, D.C.: National Transportation Safety Board, 1985).

51. National Transportation Safety Board, *Derailment of St. Louis Southwestern Railway Company (Cotton Belt) Freight Train Extra 4835 North and Release of Hazardous Materials Near Pine Bluff, Arkansas, June 9, 1985* (Washington, D.C.: National Transportation Safety Board, 1986).

52. National Transportation Safety Board, *Hazardous Materials Release Following the Derailment of Baltimore and Ohio Railroad Company Train No. SLFR, Miamisburg, Ohio, July 8, 1986* (Washington, D.C.: National Transportation Safety Board, 1987).

53. National Transportation Safety Board, *Hazardous Materials Release: Missouri Pacific Railroad Company's North Little Rock, Arkansas, Railroad Yard, December 31, 1984* (Washington, D.C.: National Transportation Safety Board, 1985), 1.

54. Keith Welks interview with Lester O. Brown, cited in Epstein, Brown, and Pope, *Hazardous Waste in America*, 174–175.

55. Nordland and Friedman, "Poison at Our Doorsteps."

56. McGurty, *Transforming Environmentalism*.

57. Taylor, *Toxic Communities*, 13–14.

58. Thornton, *Pandora's Poison*, 59.

59. Taylor, *Toxic Communities*, 14–15.

60. Hughey, "Poison Problem," 58. Landfilling in the 1980s predates most of the 1990s push to "resist garbage," and the slow and uneven practices and innovations-

"wasteways"—across American municipalities to rethink what Lily Baum Pollans calls the "weak recycling waste regime." See Pollans, *Resisting Garbage.*

61. Bullard, *Dumping in Dixie*, 30–32.

62. For more on the Southern Christian Leadership Conference and its intervention in Warren County, see Sellers, *Race and the Greening of Atlanta*, 240–242.

63. Urban Environment Conference, *Taking Back Our Health*, 38, quoted in Bullard, *Dumping in Dixie*, 31. Eileen McGurty reads the Warren County case as a watershed moment in the history of the movement for environmental justice. See McGurty, *Transforming Environmentalism.*

64. General Accounting Office, *Siting of Hazardous Waste Landfills and Their Correlation with Racial and Economic Status of Surrounding Communities* (Washington, D.C.: U.S. General Accounting Office, 1983).

65. Cole and Foster, *From the Ground Up*, 34–53.

66. Environmental justice case studies abound and proliferate. See, as overviews of this literature, Taylor, *Toxic Communities*; Spears, *Baptized in PCBs*; Cole and Foster, *From the Ground Up*; Roberts and Toffolon-Weiss, *Chronicles from the Environmental Justice Frontline*; LaDuke, *All Our Relations*; Camacho, *Environmental Injustices, Political Struggles*; Pulido, *Environmentalism and Economic Justice*; Bullard, *Confronting Environmental Racism*; and Bullard, *Dumping in Dixie.*

67. Bullard, *Dumping in Dixie*, 40.

68. "EPA Official Criticizes Landfill," *Winston-Salem Journal*, September 27, 1982, 7. Sanjour insisted that he was speaking in his capacity as a representative from Lois Gibbs's Citizens' Clearinghouse for Hazardous Waste.

69. Geiser and Waneck, "PCBs and Warren County," 17.

70. See also Shapiro, "Environmental Risk Assessment of Refuse Burning Incinerators."

71. For opposition to waste incineration and a case study on the Brooklyn Navy Yard incinerator, proposed in 1978, see, as an overview, Egan, *Barry Commoner and the Science of Survival*, 180–185.

72. Buell, "Toxic Discourse." In the immediacy of disaster, Buell writes, "not even the most humanistic intellectuals might agree with Emerson's dictum that the most abstract truth is the most practical," 640.

73. "Disasters Fast and Slow: Crafting a Multidisciplinary Research Agenda for Risk Reduction" (Session, American Historical Association annual conference, New York City, January 2, 2015), https://aha.confex.com/aha/2015/webprogram/Session12084.html.

74. Newman, *Love Canal.*

75. Nixon, *Slow Violence and the Environmentalism of the Poor.*

76. National Environmental Law Center and the United States Public Research Interest Group, *Chemical Releases Statistics* (Washington, D.C.: Associated Press International, 1994).

77. For Barry Commoner's Four Laws of Ecology, see Commoner, *Closing Circle*, 29–42. For further analysis, see Egan, "Social Significance of the Environmental Crisis."

Chapter Four. The Queer Part We Play

1. Kraft, "U.S. Environmental Policy and Politics," 27.

2. See, for example, Mirowski, *Never Let a Serious Crisis Go to Waste*, 325–358. I discuss the role of expertise, public chemical anxieties, and neoliberalism in chapter 7.

3. Freudenberg, *Lethal but Legal*, 80–82.

4. Michael Gordon, "Will Reagan 'Turn Business Loose' if Business Wants to Stay Regulated?," *National Journal*, January 3, 1981, 10.

5. Robert Bukowcyk, "State Units Said to Have a Three Mile Syndrome," *New York Times*, August 9, 1981, 30.

6. Hays, *Beauty, Health, and Permanence*, 498.

7. Ronald Reagan, Executive Order 12291—Federal Regulation, February 17, 1981.

8. Piasecki, "Politics of Toxic Wastes."

9. Hayward, *Age of Reagan*, 57–59.

10. Rushevsky, *Public Policy in the United States*, 226. See also Collin, *Environmental Protection Agency*, 279.

11. During the 1980s, the Office of Management and Budget wielded unprecedented powers. During the fall of 1981 Stockman imposed multiple and extensive cuts to the EPA budget that would reduce it to roughly half its size from when Reagan took office. New EPA director Anne Gorsuch managed to recoup some of these cuts in bitter debate, but at the expense of considerable political capital. The EPA proceeded on a significantly reduced budget. See Lash, Gillman, and Sheridan, *Season of Spoils*, 54–62; and Piasecki, "Politics of Toxic Wastes." For more, see Stockman, *Triumph of Politics*.

12. Proctor, *Cancer Wars*, 76–77.

13. Wilentz, *Age of Reagan*, 140.

14. James Nathan Miller, "What *Really* Happened at EPA," *Readers' Digest*, July 1983, 59–64, quotation from 60.

15. Andy Pasztor, "Cut Reagan Plans in Toxic-Waste Cleanup Meets Bipartisan Resistance in Congress," *Wall Street Journal*, February 5, 1981, 4.

16. Miller, "What *Really* Happened at EPA," 63–64.

17. Pasztor, "Revisionist Regulator: Political Realities Slow Up EPA's Chief, but She Still Manages to Jolt the Agency," *Wall Street Journal*, October 20, 1981, 56.

18. "Required Reading: A Sacred Cow," *New York Times*, October 21, 1981, A28. The full quotation: "Clean air happens to be one of the sacred cows of the American people, and the suspicion is afoot, however you slice it, that there are interests in the business community and among Republicans and some Democrats who want to keelhaul that legislation. And people are saying, 'Watch out. We will have your hide if you do it.' That is the only message that comes out of this as clearcut as anything I have ever seen in my professional career. All I can say to you is try it and you will see that you lose the '82 election."

19. Piasecki, "Politics of Toxic Wastes," 55. See also Lash, Gillman, and Sheridan, *Season of Spoils*, 103–104.

20. Vogel, *Fluctuating Fortunes*, 262–263. See also Foley, *Front Porch Politics*, 164.

21. Vogel, *Fluctuating Fortunes*, 265.

22. Daniel B. Moskowitz, "Disclosure Laws Gain as Chemical Companies Howl," *Washington Post*, September 19, 1983, WB15–WB16, quotation from WB16.

23. Leslie Maitland, "House Lawyer Says EPA Erred in Destroying Papers," *New York Times*, February 12, 1983, 9; Aaron Epstein, "Spectacle Engulfing EPA Obscuring Important Issues," *Philadelphia Inquirer*, February 20, 1983; Larry Mosier, "Behind the 'Scandal' at the Embattled EPA," *Los Angeles Times*, February 27, 1983, D1; Casey Bukro, "Mired in Dispute, EPA Superfund Moves to Clean Up Waste," *Chicago Tribune*, February 28, 1983, 4; and Dale Russakoff, "EPA Woes Dramatize the Struggle over Pollution Policy," *Washington Post*, March 6, 1983, A4.

24. Vogel, *Fluctuating Fortunes*, 266. James Watt would follow Gorsuch out of Washington before the end of the year.

25. Hays, *Beauty, Health, and Permanence*, 189.

26. See Lash, Gilman, and Sheridan, *Season of Spoils*, 103.

27. Brown, *Laying Waste*, 311.

28. Hays, *Beauty, Health, and Permanence*, 203.

29. Russell Train, quoted in U.S. Environmental Protection Agency, *Environmental News*, February 26, 1976. Train's remarks were subsequently added to the Toxic Substances Control Act, P.L. 94–469, Senate Report No. 94–698, Legislative History, March 16, 1976.

30. Asbestos constituted an important exception.

31. Magnuson et al., "Poisoning of America," 63–64.

32. Magnuson et al., "A Problem That Cannot Be Buried," *Time*, October 14, 1985, 76–84, see 77.

33. Michael Gorn, "William D. Ruckelshaus: Oral History Interview" (U.S. Environmental Protection Agency, January 1993), https://www.epa.gov/archive/epa/aboutepa/william-d-ruckelshaus-oral-history-interview.html.

34. Ruckelshaus, "Science, Risk, and Public Policy," 54. Ruckelshaus is quoted in Fischer, *Citizens, Experts, and the Environment*, 91. I pick up this thread on science, expertise, and risk in chapter 7.

35. Melinda Beck et al., "The Toxic-Waste Crisis," *Newsweek*, March 7, 1983, 24.

36. Norman Kempster, "Watchdogs Awash in Tide of Chemicals," *Los Angeles Times*, July 22, 1979.

37. John Filiatrean and Margot Hornblower, "Danger in the Valley of the Drums," *Boston Globe*, March 3, 1979, 3.

38. Debate over its renewal was contentious. The House proposal recommended $10 billion over five years, whereas the Reagan White House's number was $5.3 billion. "Meanwhile," *Time* reported, "fears about toxic wastes continue to grow." Magnuson et al., "A Problem That Cannot Be Buried," *Time*, October 14, 1985, 76.

39. Casey Bukro, "Overburdened Superfund Needs to Clean Up Its Act," *Chicago Tribune*, October 19, 1986, 1.

40. Philip Shabecoff, "Toxic Cleanup Delay Laid to 2 Ex-Aides," *New York Times*, April 9, 1983, 7.

41. "Spill at the Butler Tunnel in Pittston, Pa.," Hearing before the Subcommittee on Commerce, Transportation, and Tourism of the House of Representatives Committee on Energy and Commerce, 99th Congress (October 23, 1985), 1–2.

42. "Spill at the Butler Tunnel in Pittston, Pa.," 40–41, emphasis added.

43. "Spill at the Butler Tunnel in Pittston, Pa.," 27.

44. "Spill at the Butler Tunnel in Pittston, Pa.," 28.

45. "Spill at the Butler Tunnel in Pittston, Pa.," 6. In February 1985 Lee Thomas succeeded William Ruckelshaus as the head of the Environmental Protection Agency.

46. Cass Peterson, "Superfund Record Challenged," *Washington Post*, October 26, 1984, A3.

47. For a good, local overview of the Kepone case at Hopewell, see Wilson, *Poison Powder*; and Foster, "Kepone."

48. Plater, "Facing a Time of Counter-Revolution," 665.

49. Laura Kiernan, "Pesticide Plant Closed by Illnesses," *Washington Post*, August 13, 1975, B1, B4.

50. Sandra Sugawara, "10 Years After Kepone Dumping, Problems Persist," *Washington Post*, July 29, 1985, C1.

51. "Residents Criticize Carbide," *New York Times*, August 19, 1985, A17.

52. Bullard, *Dumping in Dixie*, 52–54.

53. According to a door-to-door survey taken by Representative Robert E. Wise Jr.'s staff on the evening after the accident, 144 out of 254 residents first knew of the leak by seeing, smelling, or feeling the gas, not by hearing the community alarm. "I was shocked that . . . they learned of the leak by actually being exposed to

it," Wise said. Franklin, "Federal Officials Question Credibility of Carbide," *New York Times*, August 14, 1985, A19.

54. Ben A. Franklin, "Toxic Cloud Leaks at Carbide Plant in West Virginia," *New York Times*, August 12, 1985, A1.

55. "Residents Criticize Carbide," A17. See also Bullard, *Dumping in Dixie*, 51–55. Bullard highlights the demographics of Institute, but notes that West Virginia State College, though founded as a Black college, began enrolling white students after the 1954 *Brown v. Board of Education* Supreme Court decision that read state segregation in public schools as an unconstitutional violation of the Fourteenth Amendment. By the 1980s, West Virginia State College's student body was largely composed of white students who commuted from nearby Charleston and other cities. The community, however, remained predominantly Black. In *Toxic Communities*, Dorceta E. Taylor raises Institute as one of many examples of polluting industries targeting established minority communities for the development of hazardous facilities. Taylor, *Toxic Communities*, 37–38. During the 1990s, an extended historiographic debate weighed the historical trajectory of industrial land use in minority communities across the United States. On the one hand, some scholars suggested that depreciating land values around polluting industries attracted poorer communities, predominantly of racial minorities, while others stressed the practice of sites being disproportionately located around existing disenfranchised minority communities such as Institute. For a brief summary of that debate, see Been, "Locally Undesirable Land Uses in Minority Neighborhoods"; and Pulido, "Critical Review." The welter of evidence since (Taylor's book is essential reading on this) is conclusive that noxious facilities have targeted and preyed upon minority communities across the United States.

56. Ben A. Franklin, "Federal Officials Question Credibility of Carbide," *New York Times*, August 14, 1985, A19.

57. David J. Sarokin and Warren R. Muir, "Too Little Toxic-Waste Data," *New York Times*, October 7, 1985, A31.

58. Agyeman, *Sustainable Communities and the Challenge of Environmental Justice*, 20. For analysis of the Toxics Release Inventory, see Lynn and Kartez, "Environmental Democracy in Action." See also Fung and O'Rourke, "Reinventing Environmental Regulation from the Grassroots Up." For access to information as a catalyst for environmental activism, see Egan, *Barry Commoner and the Science of Survival*, 47–78.

59. Virilio, *Original Accident*, 10.

60. Kai Erikson, "Contaminating the Countryside," *New York Times*, May 18, 1980, BR1. Erikson's piece was a review of Brown's *Laying Waste*, which I discussed in chapter 1.

61. Geiser, *Chemicals Without Harm*, 7.

62. Virilio, *Original Accident*, 3.

Chapter Five. Self-Awareness Raised to a Higher Level

1. Vyner, *Invisible Trauma*, 1.

2. See Ramadan and Shantz, "Phobic Constructions," 4.

3. Suzanne Charle, "And Now a Spate of Catastrophes Hits Homeowner," *New York Times*, June 22, 1980, R1.

4. NAIC Advisory Committee on Environmental Liability Insurance, *Environmental Liability Insurance* (September 1986), v-11, v-12.

5. NAIC Advisory Committee on Environmental Liability Insurance, *Environmental Liability Insurance* (September 1986), v-12.

6. "1980 Dioxin List Drew Little Action," *New York Times*, June 27, 1983, 13; Esposito, Tiernan, and Dryden, *Dioxins*.

7. "Court Rules 'Psychological Stress' Must Be Weighed at Three Mile Island," *New York Times*, May 15, 1982, 1.

8. "Cancer Clusters Prompt U.S. Study," *New York Times*, February 5, 1988, A11. See also Hartsough and Savitsky, "Three Mile Island."

9. March 28th Coalition, "Three Mile Island—One Year Later," call to action sent to antinuclear groups around the United States in 1980, quoted in Walsh, *Democracy in the Shadows*, 109. Also quoted in Zaretsky, *Radiation Nation*, 131.

10. Zaretsky, *Radiation Nation*, 129. For Three Mile Island and trauma, see 129–140.

11. Bourinski's testimony and the court findings are from *In re Three Mile Island Litigation*, 87 F.R.D. 433 (M.D. Pa. 1980), https://casetext.com/case/in-re-three-mile-island-litigation (last accessed April 24, 2019). Recent scientific evidence suggests that neighbors of the Three Mile Island site were exposed to more radiation than officials claimed. See Cindy Folkers, "Residents Around TMI Exposed to Far More Radiation Than Officials Claimed" (Beyond Nuclear International, March 24, 2019), https://beyondnuclearinternational.org/2019/03/24/residents-around-tmi-exposed-to-far-more-radiation-than-officials-claimed/ (last accessed April 24, 2019). In addition, twenty-five years after the accident, new findings suggested an alarming number of infant deaths in families living closest to the reactor. "In the six months after the accident, 31 infants living within 10 miles of the plant died, more than double the 14 deaths during the same six-month period the previous year." Mangano, "Three Mile Island," 32.

12. Langston, *Toxic Bodies*.

13. Podgers, "Toxic Time Bombs," 139.

14. "Toxic Time Bombs," *Newsweek*, September 6, 1982, 57. See also Warren Brown, "Manville Bankruptcy, Damages Cases Still Intertwined and Still Unresolved: Manville Insurance Agreement Clouds Fate of Future Asbestos Claimants," *Washington Post*, August 26, 1984, 169.

15. Podgers, "Toxic Time Bombs," 139.

16. "Toxic Time Bombs," *Newsweek*, September 6, 1982, 57.

17. Edelstein, *Contaminated Communities*, 162–163.

18. 274 Cal. Rptr. at 891, quoted in Marrs, "Mind Over Body," 6, emphasis added.

19. *Potter v. Firestone Tire & Rubber Co.* (1993), Justia, http://law.justia.com/cases/california/supreme-court/4th/6/965.html. For a summary of the case, see Fisher, "Potter v. Firestone and the Infliction of Emotional Distress." See also Kanner, "Tort Remedies and Litigation Strategies."

20. In the early 1980s, a series of cases raised the fear of cancer derived from exposure to diethylstilbestrol (DES), a drug given to women and that subsequently showed an elevated risk of cancer in their daughters. In the absence of physical cancer, these suits were uniformly unsuccessful. See Reaves, "Fear Not Enough."

21. The *Sterling v. Velsicol* case does not make reference to *Potter v. Firestone*, but in its 1993 appeal *Potter v. Firestone* cited *Sterling v. Velsicol*.

22. The discovery of the hazards and the subsequent negligence by state and federal officials is well recounted in Brown, *Laying Waste*, 121–131. For the court case, see *Sterling v. Velsicol Chemical Corp.* (1986), Justia, http://law.justia.com/cases/federal/district-courts/FSupp/647/303/2360375/.

23. *In re Moorenovich*, Leagle, http://www.leagle.com/decision/19861268634FSupp634_11174.xml/IN%20RE%20MOORENOVICH (last accessed October 14, 2025). See "Plaintiffs' Memorandum in Support of the Admissibility of Evidence Bearing Upon the Risk of Cancer," at 7.

24. Marrs, "Mind Over Body," 9.

25. *Jackson v. Johns-Manville Sales Corp., et al.*, Justia, https://law.justia.com/cases/federal/appellate-courts/F2/781/394/416068/ (last accessed October 14, 2025).

26. *Willmore*, supra, 3 Toxics L. Rptr. at p. 563, Justia, http://law.justia.com/cases/california/supreme-court/4th/6/965.html.

27. Phil Cha and Daniel Farino, "Handling Lawsuits for Fear of Cancer from Toxic Torts," Mondaq, March 7, 2014, http://www.mondaq.com/unitedstates/x/297932/Clean+Air+Pollution/Handling+Lawsuits+for+Fear+of+Cancer+From+Toxic+Torts.

28. Cha and Farino, "Handling Lawsuits for Fear of Cancer from Toxic Torts."

29. Cranor, *Toxic Torts*, 345–376.

30. E. Donald Elliott, "The Future of Toxic Torts: Of Chemophobia, Risk as a Compensable Injury and Hybrid Compensation Systems" (Faculty Scholarship Series, Paper 2199, 1988), http://digitalcommons.law.yale.edu/fss_papers/2199.

31. Thomas and Thomas, *Child in America*, 571–572.

32. "Missouri Said to Have World's Top Dioxin Levels," *St. Louis Post-Dispatch*, October 28, 1982, 1.

33. Quoted in Fortun, *Advocacy After Bhopal*, 70.

34. It needs to be stated clearly that the burden of stress was disproportionately imposed on marginalized communities and communities of color. In a history of toxic anxieties, environmental racism—the systemic imposition of harm on people of color—frequently takes a back seat to fear perceived as a universal quality. Especially in the 1980s, media attention (another aspect of systemic racism) gravitated toward white communities experiencing chemical harm. Three Mile Island, Love Canal, and Times Beach are examples of predominantly white communities receiving the concentration of national attention while diminishing other sites of contamination.

35. Button, "Popular Media Reframing of Man-Made Disasters."

36. Magnuson et al., "Poisoning of America," 58, 69.

37. "Cancer Scares," *Wall Street Journal*, July 27, 1979, 12.

38. Blum, *Love Canal Revisited*, 39.

39. Kruse and Zelizer, *Fault Lines*, 139–141.

40. Stallings, "Media Discourse and the Social Construction of Risk," 80.

41. Mazur, "Technical Risk in the Mass Media," 191, quoted in Friedman et al., "Alar and Apples," 3.

42. Friedman et al., "Alar and Apples," 3.

43. Natural Resources Defense Council, *Intolerable Risk: Pesticides in our Children's Food* (February 27, 1989), http://docs.nrdc.org/health/files/hea_11052401a.pdf (accessed May 6, 2015). "'A' Is for Apple" aired on *60 Minutes* on February 26, 1989.

44. Randolph, "Venture in Managing News Backfires," *Washington Post*, March 3, 1989, A17."

45. "An Unhappy Anniversary: The Alar 'Scare' Ten Years Later" (American Council on Science and Health, February 1, 1999), 1–4, http://acsh.org/1999/02/an-unhappy-anniversary-the-alar-scare-ten-years-later/ (accessed March 14, 2015). There is an important side note to this story around risk assessment and risk perception, which I will explore more thoroughly in chapter 7. The kind of public science conducted by the EPA and the USDA played a role in provoking fears in the Alar case. It seems to me that the science or language of chemical fear—and the evolution of technical language in public debate that evolved through the 1970s and 1980s—was at least inspired by this shared information. But the absence of public participation in these slow deliberations is what prompted social activism and exacerbated fears. For more on science information and public participation, see Egan, *Barry Commoner and the Science of Survival*.

46. Philip Shabecoff, "100 Chemicals for Apples Add Up to Enigma on Safety," *New York Times*, February 5, 1989, 22.

47. For more on the daminozide story, see Dunaway, *Seeing Green*, 208–222; and Jasanoff, *Fifth Branch*, 141–149. See also Egan, "Fear, Knowledge, and Activism," 190–194.

48. Glassner, *Culture of Fear*, xxi.

49. Darnton, "Writing News and Telling Stories," 192. Whereas Glassner remarked on media's power and potential for dramatizing every danger or disaster—a means of provoking and exacerbating fears—the historian Peter N. Stearns argues that the production of fear is a two-way street: "Media manipulation depends as well on audience, and an audience less ready to be disturbed by fear, less eager for risk-free assurances, would not have provided the climate for the media change." Further, there was no universal outlet for fostering fear through the media. In telling analysis, Stearns considers the lack of fear and hyperbole following the 2005 London subway bombings. If mainstream media plays a central and unilateral role in shaping fear, Stearns contends, then what do we make of the staid response to the terrorist attack, especially in comparison with 9/11, which had hardly dissipated from the public memory? "[The London attack] did not generate panic, for the most part—which means that either media themselves are partly shaped by dominant public emotional reactions, or that an insistently courageous public reaction can trump media manipulation, or both." See Stearns, "Fear and History," 23, 24.

50. Mirowski, "Postface," 417.

51. According to Cristina Rivera Garza, "the neoliberal state has established visceraless relationships with its citizens." These are "relationships without hearts or bones or innards. Disemboweled relationships." Rivera Garza examines the narco state in Mexico, but her treatment of neoliberalism is special for her determination to remove neoliberalism from the spreadsheet and infuse it with the disembodied horror of human experience. "If it is necessary to choose between profits and the body," she observes, "the final decision will always be for profit." Rivera Garza, *Grieving*, 22.

52. For a broader discussion of breeding public ignorance, see Proctor and Schiebinger, *Agnotology*; Michaels, *Doubt Is Their Product*; and Oreskes and Conway, *Merchants of Doubt*.

53. Mirowski, "Postface," 424.

54. Agis Salpukas, "A Three Mile Island for Chemicals," *New York Times*, December 16, 1984, F1.

55. Gary N. Dietrich, "EPA Is Doing—Not Undoing," *Washington Post*, November 20, 1981, A30.

56. Jerry Heston, "Dioxin Is Found in Southern Maryland," *Washington Post*, March 25, 1985, B7. "Not that it's something that you want to find," the newspaper felt compelled to add.

57. Dowie, *Losing Ground*, 70.

58. Taylor, *Toxic Communities*, 124–138.

59. "Networks," *Southern Action* 1 (1988): 3, Tufts University Digital Collection & Archives, MS001/008, box 13, folder 61.

60. Joseph Sjostrom and Terry Atlas, "Passion and Publicity—Tools of a New Crusade," *Chicago Tribune*, July 3, 1983, 1.

61. Polly Saltonstall, "Grassroots Movements Stir State Awareness," *Alabama: The Fading Beauty. Anniston Star Special Edition*, December 11–17, 1988, 7. The Center for Health, Environment, and Justice records at the Tufts University Digital Collections & Archives is a remarkable resource for identifying and tracing the number, variety, and lives of these grassroots organizations. Formerly the Citizens' Clearinghouse for Hazardous Waste, the Center for Health, Environment, and Justice connected with community reports and organizations all over the country, many of which reached out for advice when confronting government and industry obstacles to a clean environment.

62. See Wuthnow, *Be Very Afraid*; Maya Pines, "Psychological Times Bombs," *New York Times*, June 13, 1982, 10E; Taylor, "Adjustment to Threatening Events"; and Stone and Levine, "Reactions to Collective Stress," 174.

63. Linda Guillet to Joan Gipp, August 18, 1986, box 18, folder 31, MS65, Ecumenical Task Force of the Niagara Frontier Records, 1946–1995 (1978–1990 bulk), University Archives, State University of New York at Buffalo. See also Bruce D. Butterfield, "Living in Fear of Tainted Water," *Providence Journal-Bulletin* (n.d.), clipping in box 18, folder 31, MS65, Ecumenical Task Force of the Niagara Frontier Records.

64. "1986 Year End Report," Citizens' Clearinghouse for Hazardous Waste, 1, quoted in Zeff, "Not in My Backyard / Not in Anyone's Backyard," 81.

65. Martha McGranor, "Gibbs Did More Than Politicians," *Niagara Gazette*, June 1, 1980.

66. Edelstein, *Contaminated Communities*, 71.

67. Grace M. McCoulf, Senate Subcommittee on Toxic Substances and Chemical Wastes, April 5, 1979, 2–3, http://library.buffalo.edu/specialcollections/lovecanal/documents/pdfs/mccoulf.pdf (accessed July 17, 2017). See also Thomson, "Toxic Residents," 212; and Newman, *Love Canal*, 167. McCoulf worried about the dissolution of her family and community in the absence of government intervention. Her statement also included a slightly darker side of fear's American politics and its capacity to divide, especially within communities pressed up against hard financial times and further threats. McCoulf began by insisting that the federal government "perform its primary function—to serve the interest of the people." But her argument also included something of the fortress society mentality that inspired American populist politics, both recent and

historical. Too much money was being shipped overseas in foreign aid, she insisted. "The American people see only the billions shipped out to strangers and never see the aid given to the needy citizens who are the ones paying the taxes—the same taxes going overseas. Who needs it more?" McCoulf, Senate Subcommittee on Toxic Substances and Chemical Wastes, April 5, 1979, 1.

Chapter Six. Death Inside Me

1. DeLillo, *White Noise,* 127.
2. DeLillo, *White Noise,* 140–143.
3. Wilkinson, *Anxiety in a Risk Society.*
4. DeLillo, *White Noise,* 116.
5. DeLillo, *White Noise,* 280. There is an eerie echo in this exchange with the opening account of formaldehyde monitoring in Shapiro, Zakariya, and Roberts, "Wary Alliance."
6. Sunstein, *Worst-Case Scenarios,* 5.
7. "Cancer Had Many Causes," *Woburn Daily Times,* December 21, 1979, 1A.
8. Weart, *Rise of Nuclear Fear;* Egan, *Barry Commoner and the Science of Survival,* 47–78; and Masco, *Nuclear Borderlands.*
9. Carson, *Silent Spring.*
10. W. C. Hueper, "Environmental Cancer," Federal Security Agency, 1950, cited in Ross and Amter, *The Polluters,* 66. Hueper was one of the first to suggest that cancer was an environmental disease, but the idea had been percolating for quite some time. At the beginning of the eighteenth century, the Bolognese physician and "father of occupation medicine" Bernardino Ramazzini noted the near complete absence of cervical cancer but higher-than-expected incidences of breast cancer in local nuns, both of which he attributed to their celibacy. In 1775 Percival Pott, a London surgeon, observed a striking number of scrotal cancer cases among young men who had been chimney sweeps as boys.
11. World Health Organization, *Prevention of Cancer* (Geneva: World Health Organization, 1964), 4.
12. Cairns, "Cancer Problem," 64, quoted in Proctor, *Cancer Wars,* 55.
13. Charles C. Ryan, "Deaths from Cancer Increase in Woburn," *Woburn Daily Times,* December 6, 1979, 3A.
14. For more on the history of cancer, see Proctor, *Cancer Wars;* Davis, *Secret War on Cancer;* and Mukherjee, *Emperor of All Maladies.*
15. DiPerna, *Cluster Mystery,* 34.
16. The Department of Public Health's count was only twelve. But these discrepancies make up part of the story.

17. Essential reading on the Woburn cancer cluster consists of Brown and Mikkelsen, *No Safe Place*; and DiPerna, *Cluster Mystery*.

18. Irvin Molotsky, "Witnesses Tell Senators of Tainted Water's Perils," *New York Times*, June 7, 1980, 23.

19. "Pollution on Top of Pollution in River," *Woburn Daily Times*, February 11, 1972, 1. The reference desk at the Woburn Public Library contains scrapbooks of newspaper clippings pertaining to the Woburn case study.

20. "Mishawum Is Not a Rose," *Woburn Daily Times*, April 18, 1977, 1.

21. "Hazardous Material Found on MBTA Site," *Woburn Daily Times*, May 7, 1979, 1.

22. "City Water Emergency Declared," *Woburn Daily Times*, May 24, 1979, 1.

23. Charles C. Ryan, "Lagoon of Arsenic Discovered in N. Woburn," *Woburn Daily Times*, September 10, 1979, 1.

24. "Woburn Officials Upset No One Was Notified," *Woburn Daily Times*, September 11, 1979, 3A.

25. "Mark Phillip Says State Knew," *Woburn Daily Times*, September 11, 1979, 1.

26. "State Did Not Know of Arsenic Until Recently," *Woburn Daily Times*, September 12, 1979, 1. State records show, according to the newspaper article, that the DEQE was aware of the chromium pits, but there does not appear to be any indication of arsenic contamination.

27. "Find Some Answers," *Woburn Daily Times*, September 12, 1979, 1.

28. Ryan, "Lagoon of Arsenic Discovered in N. Woburn," 3A. Such a glib response—"out there" sounded like it came straight out of the horror movies of the time—was rarely a function of authorities masking the real risks; it stemmed from the fact that they didn't know what they were dealing with, were unprepared for such a disaster, and were understaffed.

29. Ryan, "DEQE Seeks Major Funds for Study," *Woburn Daily Times*, December 7, 1979, 1.

30. "City's Wells Safe," *Woburn Daily Times*, December 24, 1979, 1.

31. "Toxic Waste: Long Term Problem," *Woburn Daily Times*, December 20, 1979, 1.

32. "Cancer Has Many Causes," *Woburn Daily Times*, December 21, 1979, 1.

33. Richard A. Knox, "Cancer Probe in Woburn," *Boston Globe*, February 15, 1980, 17, 10.

34. "Employees Concerned Over Hazards," *Woburn Daily Times*, July 2, 1980, 1. See also Ryan, "Workers Near Toxic Wastes Show More Headaches, Fatigue," *Woburn Daily Times*, July 2, 1980, 1, 3.

35. "State Requests Federal Medical Study Here," *Woburn Daily Times*, April 2, 1980, 1. See also "Board of Health Confirms DPH Study," *Woburn Daily Times*, April 2, 1980, 4A.

36. "Daunting complexity" comes from Hanahan and Weinberg, "Hallmarks of Cancer."

37. DiPerna, *Cluster Mystery*, 17.

38. DiPerna, *Cluster Mystery*, 37.

39. "Higgins Blasts Impression City Not Concerned," *Woburn Daily Times*, December 20, 1979, 1.

40. Lawrence Ingrassia and Bryan Burrough, "Toxic Waste Scare 'Killed' Small Town, Its People Complain," *Wall Street Journal*, March 1, 1983, 1.

41. Melinda Beck et al., "The Toxic-Waste Crisis," *Newsweek*, March 7, 1983, 24.

42. Laffan, "Preface," in Laffan and Weiss, *Facing Fear*, vii.

43. DiPerna, *Cluster Mystery*, 14–15.

44. Brown, "Popular Epidemiology." See also Brown, "Popular Epidemiology Approach to Toxic Waste Contamination." In addition, see Clapp, "Popular Epidemiology in Three Contaminated Communities." Clapp cites Brown and Mikkelsen, *No Safe Place*.

45. Brown, "Popular Epidemiology Approach to Toxic Waste Contamination," 135. In addition to Brown and Mikkelsen's *No Safe Place*, see also Corburn, *Street Science*.

46. It is also worth noting that citizen action also served as a positive coping mechanism. Responding to the hazards in their community brought neighbors together and enabled a kind of social empowerment: a preparedness to confront authorities with data and science that they had been pivotal in collecting. On the subject of disease clusters at Love Canal, studies found that pregnant women who lived near the canal site suffered greater risks of miscarriage or of delivering babies with lower than normal birth weights. Proximity mattered: The women most susceptible to adverse effects lived immediately adjacent to the canal. Miscarriages reached their peak in the 1960s and 1970s. A further excess of birth defects—deemed by authorities not to be statistically significant—was also larger among the babies of mothers who lived closer to the canal, along 99th Street or in formerly wet areas nearby. *Habitability of the Love Canal Area: An Analysis of the Technical Basis for the Division on the Habitability of the Emergency Declaration Area—A Technical Memorandum* (Washington, D.C.: U.S. Congress, Office of Technology Assessment, OTA-TM-M-13, June 1983), 52.

47. The Rev. Bruce A. Young, "Leukemia," *Woburn Daily Times*, September 14, 1979, 3A.

48. Ryan, "Child Leukemia Answers," *Woburn Daily Times*, December 12, 1979, 1.

49. Young, "Leukemia," 3A.

50. Ryan, "Deaths from Cancer Increase in Woburn," *Woburn Daily Times*, December 6, 1979, 1.

51. This expression of citizen science through grassroots or community epidemiological research marks an important conceptual shift from the traditional,

one-way flow of expertise from experts to the public. One of the important and positive outcomes of this kind of venture, beyond the social and political empowerment associated with informed public participation, is the production of a vernacular science that speaks directly to a lay audience. I have written about the history of this public science in Egan, *Barry Commoner and the Science of Survival,* 47–78. For Woburn, see Clarke, *Acceptable Risk?* For the legal and administrative obstacles to assessing risk and mitigating chemical fear, see Hepler-Smith, "Molecular Bureaucracy"; and Jasanoff, "EPA's Regulation of Daminozide."

52. In April 1985, the plaintiffs added Unifirst to the suit. Unifirst countersued the families for libel two months later, but ultimately settled before trial in early October.

53. Lagakos, Wessen, and Zelen, "Analysis of Contaminated Well Water." For a summary, see Brown and Mikkelsen, *No Safe Place,* 23–26.

54. W. R. Grace Company had previously been implicated in the closing of wells in nearby Acton, Mass., in 1978. A slew of organic chemicals, including benzene and trichloroethylene, were found in the drinking water. Wells were in close proximity to the company's landfills and lagoons, which it used as disposal sites for its chemical effluent. Grace settled the case out of court. "Chemical Contamination of Water: The Case of Acton, Massachusetts" (Department of Urban and Environmental Policy, Tufts University, June 1981), Tufts University Digital Collections & Archives MS001.016, box 011, folder 00031.

55. Brown and Mikkelsen, *No Safe Place,* 30.

56. Quoted in DiPerna, *Cluster Mystery,* 155–161, cited in Brown and Mikkelsen, *No Safe Place,* 14.

57. "Industrial Hopewell: Hard Choices on Jobs, Environment," *Washington Post,* October 2, 1989, E39. The tension between jobs and health was hardly a theme isolated in the 1980s. "I'm not trying to put economy over health, but if DuPont would close, people will leave," Belpre, Ohio, Mayor Michael Lorentz told the *Washington Post* at the end of 2015 regarding lawsuits charging that the chemical company had poisoned local drinking water with perfluorooctanoic acid (C8), used in Teflon production. "With this C8 case, no one wins, everyone loses," Lorentz admonished. Kevin Williams, "Dupont Viewed as Savior and Sinner," *Washington Post,* December 13, 2015, A3.

58. Paula DiPerna, "Leukemia Strikes a Small Town," *New York Times Saturday Magazine,* December 2, 1984, 100–108.

59. For more on cancer cluster analysis, see Nash, *Inescapable Ecologies,* 196–201.

60. The Draft Summary is cited in Efron, *The Apocalyptics,* 437. See also Wildavsky, *But Is It True?,* 189.

61. Fagin, *Toms River,* 444. A 2014 survey of state and federal investigations into potential cancer clusters confirmed that finding causes for community cancer

clusters had been unsuccessful; their analysis found only one cluster over the preceding two decades. At the same time, the study concluded that "there are fundamental shortcomings to our current methods of investigating community cancer clusters." The authors' conclusions went on to recommend greater "multidisciplinary national dialog on creative, innovative approaches to understanding when and why cancer and other chronic diseases cluster in space and time." Goodman et al., "Cancer Clusters in the USA," 474. See also Goodman et al., "Cancer Cluster Investigations."

62. "Victims of Camp Lejeune Water Contamination Share Their Stories," *Wilmington Star News*, April 28, 2018, https://www.starnewsonline.com/news/20180428/victims-of-camp-lejeune-water-contamination-share-their-stories (last accessed March 20, 2019).

63. Paul Voosen, "Why Didn't Toxic Waste Cause a Cancer Epidemic, Like We Expected in the 1970s?," *National Geographic*, December 12, 2014, https://news.nationalgeographic.com/news/2014/12/141211-superfund-hazardous-waste-cancer-science-environment/ (last accessed March 20, 2019).

Chapter Seven. Securing Knowledge

1. Luhmann, "Modern Society Shocked by Its Risks," 4.
2. Beck, *Risk Society*.
3. Lupton, *Risk*, 31.
4. See, for example, Mohun, *Risk*.
5. Hacking, "Risk and Dirt."
6. Starr, "Social Benefit Versus Technological Risk," 1232. Another important avenue of inquiry for this question of expertise is its relationship to the instruments that measure invisible, insensible hazards. Much like the algorithms that determine, clinically, the minimum risk exposure, tools that conduct these measurements—pulsing stars and generating big numbers, in DeLillo's treatment—constitute another quantum leap between risk analysis and public fears. For an excellent discussion of instruments and invisible hazards, see Parr, *Sensing Changes*. See chapter 3, "Working Knowledge of the Insensible: Radiation Protection in Nuclear Power Plants, 1962–1992," 53–77, and esp. 68–71.
7. Implicit in this development in risk science is the entrenchment of legitimacy through quantification. Mary Poovey's now-classic analysis shows how early modern science established an objective reading of the physical world that made it possible to calculate the physical, social, and political worlds together. See Poovey, *History of the Modern Fact*. Porter's *Trust in Numbers* trains a similar lens on the modern world of science, and reflects on how quantification gained evermore

widespread traction across the sciences. But objectivity in the relationship between science and policy is a bit of a false flag. Writing in the 1980s about the precarious nature of what he called "crisis disciplines," emergencies that required rapid scientific and policy response—before all the facts were known—Michael Soulé outlined a changing scientific landscape that necessarily complicated the scientific expert's job in relaying reliable information and recommendations to policymakers. There was no definitive, objective knowledge, and if there was, there wasn't time to acquire it before acting. Soulé, "What is Conservation Biology?" Risk definitely qualified as a kind of crisis discipline. Indeed, underlying this chapter's tension between professional experts and lay publics and their incommensurable relationships with pollution risks is a history of the growing distrust of scientific expertise that manifested itself through the second half of the twentieth century. Chandra Mukerji traced the growing interdependence between science (and scientists) and policy (and power), where the objective science of experts funded by the state provided legitimacy to government policies. Mukerji, *Fragile Power.* Given the historical uncertainties around toxic hazards and their environmental impacts, it is worth noting Jerome Ravetz's observation that "hard" policy decisions were also inspired by "soft" scientific inputs (which is the wrong way around). Ravetz, "Post-normal Science." In my work on the biologist Barry Commoner, I followed Commoner's argument that scientific experts had no moral authority to determine what constituted acceptable risk to a larger public. To do otherwise was profoundly undemocratic. Egan, *Barry Commoner and the Science of Survival.* If there is a changing landscape in this debate over risk, expertise, and public participation from the works cited above, it might involve the manner in which neoliberal politics shifted the state's role in decision-making. Where Ravetz and Commoner, in particular, advocated greater public engagement and an expansion of the stakeholders in environmental policymaking, I would posit that the neoliberal project asserted an economic bottom line on how those more public engagements might go.

8. Clarke, *Acceptable Risk?*

9. Button, *Disaster Culture,* 147.

10. Jasanoff, "Political Science of Risk Perception," 91.

11. Recalling the opening to chapter 2, on toxic autobiography, I would hazard that that genre's popularity in the early 1980s came in some response to this tension between expertise and lived experience. In toxic autobiography, Lois Gibbs and other practitioners were able to tell their own story.

12. Otway and Winterfeldt, "Beyond Acceptable Risk," 252. My list as presented quotes an adaptation of Otway and Winterfeldt's list found in Pidgeon et al., "Risk Perception," 101.

13. National Academy of Sciences, *Risk Assessment in the Federal Government: Managing the Process* (Washington, D.C.: National Academy of Sciences, 1983), 9.

14. National Academy of Sciences, *Risk Assessment in the Federal Government*, 10.

15. Some of these egregious obfuscation of scientific findings or rejecting the science altogether in favor of more industrially expedient alternatives are covered in Demortain, *Science of Bureaucracy*. See esp. 119–121.

16. National Academy of Sciences, *Risk Assessment in the Federal Government*, 151.

17. For an excellent and comprehensive summary of the EPA's relationship with risk through the 1980s—a far more technical and complicated topic, much of which falls beyond the scope of a study of public fear—see Demortain, *Science of Bureaucracy*.

18. Demortain, *Science of Bureaucracy*, 27.

19. Garland, "Rise of Risk," 49.

20. For an important exception to this rule, see sociological work on "popular epidemiology." According to the sociologist Phil Brown, who coined the term, popular epidemiology "is the process by which lay persons gather scientific data and other information, and also direct and marshal the knowledge and resources of experts in order to understand the epidemiology of disease." Brown, "Popular Epidemiology Approach to Toxic Waste Contamination," 135. See also Brown and Mikkelsen, *No Safe Place*. For the relationship between toxic fear and popular epidemiology, see Michael Egan, "Fear, Knowledge, and Activism."

21. In her essay on risk, which draws parallels between the vulnerabilities associated with rising sea levels and the vulnerabilities associated with sexual assault, Elizabeth Rush observes that "to be 'at risk' means occupying the space of the threatened body, drawn close to danger. . . . From a distance, risk looks like something that can be managed, through informed decision making or insurance." Rush, *Rising*, 149.

22. In his analysis of risk as the defining aspect of the contemporary world, risk theorist David Garland playfully suggested that Beck could have written the publisher's blurb for *White Noise*. Garland, "Rise of Risk," see 79.

23. Beck, "Risk Society and the Provident State," 31.

24. In her work on early seismology, Deborah Coen reminds her readers that much of the nineteenth-century data that shaped earthquake epistemology came from lay observers—think citizen science in a 1980s context—before scientific data was reimagined as the domain of a professionalized and expert scientific order of practitioners. See Coen, *Earthquake Observers*. Coen also points to a necessary reversal of this trend, as evidenced in many of the community-based epidemiological projects offered in case studies through this work. For an insightful analysis of the politics of expertise, see Pamuk, *Politics and Expertise*.

25. "Cancer Scares," *Wall Street Journal*, July 27, 1979, 12.

26. Efron, *The Apocalyptics*, 474.

27. Quoted in Allitt, *Climate of Crisis*, 159.

28. On the rise of American conservatism/right, see McGirr, *Suburban Warriors*; Brennan, *Turning Right in the Sixties*; Berman, *America's Right Turn*; Robin, *Reactionary Mind*; Brick, *Age of Contradiction*; and Rodgers, *Age of Fracture*, 164–177.

29. Efron, *News Twisters*, quoted in Hemmer, "From 'Faith in Facts' to 'Fair and Balanced,'" 138.

30. Efron, *The Apocalyptics*, 474.

31. Efron, *The Apocalyptics*, 9.

32. Efron, *The Apocalyptics*, 21–23. See also Fagin, *Toms River*, 17.

33. Selikoff, "Perspectives in the Investigation of Health Hazards in the Chemical Industry," 79.

34. Richards, "U.S. Action Urged to Curb Cancer-Causing Agents," *Washington Post*, January 13, 1976, A2.

35. Efron, *The Apocalyptics*, 22.

36. Efron, *The Apocalyptics*, 23.

37. William Bennett, "Cancer and Its Causes: A Grim Debate," *Washington Post Book World* 14, no. 30 (July 22, 1984): 5. Bennett also condemned the book as "an unmodulated rant [of] nearly 500 pages."

38. Efron, *The Apocalyptics*, 14.

39. Whelan, *Toxic Terror*.

40. An important reminder, "The expert-lay dichotomy is false. Citizens who resist exposure to pollution are not isolated from expert opinion. They draw heavily on the expertise of environmental scientists." Tesh, *Uncertain Hazards*, 82. At the same time, it is critically important to recognize that environmental justice notes an unequal distribution not just of chemical harm but also, frequently, unequal access to that expertise.

41. This claim likely deserves more expansion and support than is provided here. While the rise of memberships in mainstream environmental groups and the emergence of the environmental justice movement suggest the 1980s constituted a period of environmental rejuvenation in the United States, it is also possible to argue that these positive developments marked an oppositional response to the decline of public environmental discourse, a drawing up of lines. A big part of the 1980s, outlined in the most cursory manner in this section, identifies the growth of agnotology, or doubt-making surrounding pollution. In framing cancer as the singular outcome of pollution—and debating those numbers—antienvironmental critics were effective in bounding the debate and shuttering effective dialog. For agnotology, see Proctor and Schiebinger, *Agnotology*; Michaels, *Doubt Is Their Product*; and Oreskes and Conway, *Merchants of Doubt*.

42. Starr, "Social Benefit Versus Technological Risk," 1237.

43. Sarewitz, "Science and Environmental Policy," 90.

44. Martha Shirk and Kathy Rogers, "Do Something About Dioxin, Residents Plead to Officials," *St. Louis Post-Dispatch*, November 18, 1982, 4.

45. Carson, *Silent Spring*, 15.

46. David Axelrod to Philip Handler, November 9, 1979, box 1, folder 4, 22/3F/634, Adeline Levine Love Canal research materials (pt. 1), 1953–1981 (1978–1981 bulk), University Archives, State University of New York at Buffalo.

47. Edelstein, *Contaminated Communities*, 11–12.

48. Nowotny et al., *Re-Thinking Science*, 37 and 182. Another takeaway is Aaron Wildavsky's observation that "fears are moral." In *Risk and Culture* (1982), Mary Douglas and Wildavsky posited that there was an intimate relationship between fear and values. People typically feared things that threatened to undermine their way of life. Wildavsky pursued that argument further in a later book, *But Is It True?*, which was published posthumously in 1995. After conducting a suite of studies, he reiterated his belief in the relationship between risk and culture: "Hierarchists fear social deviance, individualists fear regulation, and egalitarians fear technology." Wildavsky, *But Is It True?*, 440.

49. DeLillo, *White Noise*, 141.

50. P. M. Boffey, "Experts Showing Concern on Safety of Burying Toxic Wastes in Landfills," *New York Times*, March 16, 1983, A20.

51. Nixon, *Slow Violence and the Environmentalism of the Poor*, 2.

52. For the politics of "inviting apprehension," see Shapiro, Zakariya, and Roberts, "Wary Alliance." See also Boudia and Jas, *Powerless Science?* The essays in *Powerless Science?* examine the struggle for epistemic clarity surrounding health and toxicants when scientific knowledge, economic interests, and political imperatives collide.

53. Charles C. Ryan, "They Are Not Statistics," *Daily Times and Chronicle*, April 1, 1981.

54. Fagin, *Toms River*, 98.

55. Robert Bukowcyk, "State Units Said to Have a Three Mile Syndrome," *New York Times*, August 9, 1981, 30. The site was added to the Superfund program's National Priorities List in 1983.

56. Foley, *Front Porch Politics*.

57. Brown, "Popular Epidemiology Approach to Toxic Waste Contamination," 135.

58. Magnuson et al., "The Poisoning of America," 69. Shapiro's desire to move on from past disasters is a natural position for the transgressing industry, but it also constitutes another neoliberal tenet: No history is more powerful than the promise of future progress.

Conclusion. The Nature of Plots

1. In his work on existential fears surrounding nuclear radiation and climate change, Joseph Masco distinguishes between a planetary and a global imaginary, suggesting that the planetary epistemology is a recent product of the Cold War. See Masco, *Future of Fallout*, 17. For another good treatment of early climate fears, see Rich, *Losing Earth*. For a global account of air pollution, which I think helps to clarify the connection between toxic and climate fears, see Gardiner, *Choked*.

2. Jones, "Laboratory Study of Fear."

3. Chung and Hyland, *History and Philosophy of Psychology*, 284.

4. David S. Wilson, "Despite Boycott, Grape Sales Are Up," *New York Times*, November 27, 1988, 30.

5. Norgaard, *Living in Denial*.

6. Bourke, *Fear*, 34.

7. Toffler, *Future Shock*.

8. And the government, according to Ronald Reagan, who in 1986 famously asserted that "the nine most terrifying words in the English language are: 'I'm from the Government, and I'm here to help.'" Ronald Reagan, press conference, August 12, 1986, https://www.reaganfoundation.org/ronald-reagan/reagan-quotes-speeches/news-conference-1/.

9. See, for example, Wynne, "Public Engagement."

10. Berry, *Standing by Words*. Maybe I am also drawn to this idea for its proximity to Ursula K. Le Guin's "magic" in her *Earthsea* series of fantasy stories.

11. "TMI Anniversary Crowd Stern," *Harrisburg Patriot*, March 28, 1980, quoted in Zaretsky, *Radiation Nation*, 127.

12. See, for example, Irwin, "Risk, Science, and Public Communication."

13. Jarrige and Le Roux, *Contamination of the Earth*, 301.

14. Wassom, "Review of the Genetic Toxicology."

15. Radkau, *Age of Ecology*, 179.

16. Mizruchi, "Risk Theory and the Contemporary American Novel," 120. For reviews linking *White Noise* and Bhopal, see, for example, Johnson, "Conspirators"; and Janye Anne Phillips, "Crowding Out Death," *New York Times*, January 13, 1985.

17. Rosenblatt, "All the World Gasped," *Time*, December 17, 1984, 20.

18. Nixon, *Slow Violence and the Environmentalism of the Poor*, 63.

19. Fortun, *Advocacy After Bhopal*.

20. Bucquoy and Santi, *Mourir à Creys-Malville*.

21. For a summary of the French relationship with nuclear power, see Bess, *Light Green Society*.

22. Brown, *Manual for Survival*, 142. In a problematic, dismissive review of Brown's book in the *New York Times*, the philosopher Robert P. Crease suggested that Brown's epidemiological findings "are meaningful only within the tangled web of factors that radiation epidemiologists consider—including type and time-span of dose, pathways through the body, susceptibility of individual tissues and background radiation—as well as health issues like alcohol, obesity and stress." Curiously, Crease concludes his review with the assertion that the Chernobyl disaster was not really about nuclear power—no more than Bhopal was about pesticides—which seems a rather too-tidy categorization of technological failure as a function that pertains exclusively to engineering and industrial expertise. See Crease, "Looking Again at the Chernobyl Disaster," *New York Times*, April 3, 2019.

23. For a good survey of the international waste trade, see Clapp, *Toxic Exports*. See also O'Neill, "Out of the Backyard." See also O'Neill, *Waste*. For the *Khian Sea* story, see Müller, *Toxic Ship*. I am grateful to Kate O'Neill for recommendations from her work and to Simone Müller for sharing with me relevant portions of her bibliography on "Hazardous Travels: Ghost Acres and the Global Waste Economy."

24. Appadurai, *Future as Cultural Fact*, 3.

25. Buell, *Environmental Imagination*, 285.

26. For the environmental jeremiad, see Egan, *Barry Commoner and the Science of Survival*, 99–107. For the jeremiad in American rhetoric, see Bercovitch, *American Jeremiad*.

27. Colborn, Dumanoski, and Myers, *Our Stolen Future*, quoted in Buell, *From Apocalypse to Way of Life*, 112. See also Krimsky, *Hormonal Chaos*. Nancy Langston provides a terrific summary and explanation of endocrine disruption in *Toxic Bodies*. See esp. 6–12.

28. After Three Mile Island, where many men stayed behind, journalists coined the term "nuclear macho." Zaretsky, *Radiation Nation*, 226n98.

29. "Cancer Scares," *Wall Street Journal*, July 27, 1979, 12.

30. Gary Lee, "Dioxin: Hazard at Low Levels," *Washington Post*, May 12, 1994, A3.

31. For a good survey of dioxins in fetal development and body burdens, and for the debate over their toxicity, see Thornton, *Pandora's Poison*.

32. Bailey, *Ecoscam*, 3. For a lively and intelligent survey of the antienvironmental movement and strategy, see Buell, *From Apocalypse to Way of Life*, 3–37.

33. Showalter, *Hystories*, 8. See, as examples, Sykes, *Nation of Victims*; Hughes, *Culture of Complaint*; Kaminer, *I'm Dysfunctional, You're Dysfunctional*; and Dershowitz, *Abuse Excuse*.

34. Jim Inhofe, "The Facts and Science of Climate Change," Senate Floor Statement by James M. Inhofe (R-Okla.), Chairman, Committee on Environment and Public Works (July 28, 2003), http://www.epw.senate.gov/repwhitepapers/ClimateChange.pdf (accessed June 18, 2015).

35. Pynchon, *Gravity's Rainbow*, 251.

36. Vyner, *Invisible Trauma*, 13.

37. For an excellent history of bisphenol A, see Vogel, *Is It Safe?*

38. Mention of international conventions such as the Stockholm Convention on Persistent Organic Pollutants serves an important point to acknowledge that many scholars are also quick to note that the chemical coda to the 1980s is also intrinsically transnational; separating these concluding narratives threatens to confuse as much as clarify. Given chemicals' mobility in air and water, the disparate locations of their production consumption, and disposal, and the expansion of the global trade in hazardous wastes, it is important to consider the overlapping qualities in these conclusions. Woven into this history is an especially contentious reading of harm, both in its legal and in its medical designation. As a good entry into these questions, see Bohme, *Toxic Injustice*. See also Balayannis, "Following Pesticides in Disposal."

39. One of the most insightful and lyrical contemporary scholars and writers on plastics and toxics and the history and continuity of chemical contaminations is Rebecca Altman. See Altman, "Time-Bombing the Future." See also Altman, "American Petro-topia."

40. This count is from Barry Commoner, who shared this info at an event celebrating his ninetieth birthday in New York City. His count was inspired by Brody et al., "Environmental Pollutants, Diet, Physical Activity, Body Size, and Breast Cancer"; and Brody et al., "Environmental Pollutants and Breast Cancer." Drawing on this literature, Commoner checked the list of chemicals that caused breast cancer in laboratory animals against the Combined Chemical Dictionary. An unpublished letter to the editor of the *New York Times* was subsequently published online on June 27, 2007, on the public health blog *The Pump Handle*: Commoner, "Barry Commoner Responds to Attacks on Rachel Carson."

41. Vogel, *Is It Safe?*

42. President's Cancer Panel, "Reducing Environmental Risk: What We Can Do Now" (Washington, D.C.: U.S. Department of Health and Human Services, 2010).

43. Bullard, *Dumping in Dixie*.

44. Merchant, *Radical Ecology*, 169–176.

45. Michael Fellman argued that terrorism is something of an American institution, motivated by the rigid moral absolutism and self-righteousness that serve as

the core of American republicanism and Protestant Christianity. See Fellman, *In the Name of God and Country.*

46. Historian Peter N. Stearns draws on the experiences after and with 9/11 to tease out the manner in which American fears are distinctive from other disasters in other places. See Stearns, *American Fear,* 21–52.

47. Cindy Folkers, "Residents Around TMI Exposed to Far More Radiation than Officials Claimed" (Beyond Nuclear International, March 24, 2019), https://beyondnuclearinternational.org/2019/03/24/residents-around-tmi-exposed-to-far-more-radiation-than-officials-claimed/.

48. World Health Organization, "WHO Global Air Quality Guidelines: Particulate Matter (PM2.5 and PM10), Ozone, Nitrogen Dioxide, Sulfur Dioxide and Carbon Monoxide" (Geneva: WHO Press, 2021), https://iris.who.int/handle/10665/345329.

49. Milton Friedman, "Frustrating Drug Advancement," *Newsweek,* January 8, 1973, 49.

50. Carpenter, *Reputation and Power.* See also Cohen, *Pure Adulteration.*

51. Masco, *Future of Fallout,* 260.

52. Rodgers, *Age of Fracture,* 10.

53. See, for example, Gibson-Graham, "Rethinking the Economy." I should note, too, that in revisions to this project I was helped to reconsider the relationship between capitalism, neoliberalism, environmentalism, and power through feminist and colonial lenses. I am grateful to (and inspired by) Nevcihan Ozbilge's example in practice. See Ozbilge, "Refusal of State-Driven Northern Destiny." I am also indebted to guidance from such works as Liboiron, *Pollution Is Colonialism;* Voyles, *Wastelanding;* and Alaimo, *Bodily Natures.* These works reflect on the role of neoliberalism as a means to a colonial end.

54. Hofstadter, "Paranoid Style in American Politics," 77.

55. Hofstadter, "Paranoid Style in American Politics," 82.

56. Furedi, *Culture of Fear Revisited.*

57. Magnuson et al., "Poisoning of America," 64.

58. I am borrowing, not (I hope) stealing, "capitalist realism" from Fisher, *Capitalism Realism.*

59. For more, see Scott, *Seeing Like a State;* and Harvey, *Condition of Post-Modernity.*

60. Kovel, *Enemy of Nature.* For a survey of the histories of abundance and limits, see Worster, *Shrinking the Earth.*

61. Rodgers, *Age of Fracture,* 5.

62. This is a notion drawn from Helga Nowotny's work on rethinking uncertainty. See Nowotny, *Cunning of Uncertainty.*

63. MacKendrick, *Better Safe Than Sorry*, 27. For a good accounting of the precautionary principle, especially in the American context, see MacKendrick, *Better Safe Than Sorry*, 26–55.

Acknowledgments

1. I blogged about this teaching discovery here: https://eganhistory.wordpress.com/2014/10/31/the-80s-almost-killed-me-toxic-fear-in-america/ (last accessed June 6, 2025).

BIBLIOGRAPHY

Agyeman, Julian. *Sustainable Communities and the Challenge of Environmental Justice*. New York: New York University Press, 2005.

Alaimo, Stacy. *Bodily Natures: Science, Environment, and the Material Self.* Bloomington: Indiana University Press, 2010.

Alison, Jane. *Meander, Spiral, Explode: Design and Pattern in Narrative*. New York: Catapult, 2019.

Allitt, Patrick. *A Climate of Crisis: America in the Age of Environmentalism*. New York: Penguin, 2014.

Altman, Rebecca. "American Petro-topia." *Aeon*, March 11, 2015. https://aeon.co/essays/plastics-run-in-my-family-but-their-inheritance-is- in-us-all.

———. "Time-Bombing the Future." *Aeon*, January 2, 2019. https://aeon.co/essays/how-20th-century-synthetics-altered-the-very-fabric-of-us-all.

Andrew, Christopher M., and Vasili Mitrokhin. *The Sword and the Shield: The Mitrokhin Archive and the Secret History of the KGB*. New York: Basic Books, 1999.

Andrews, Richard N. L. *Managing the Environment, Managing Ourselves: A History of American Environmental Policy.* 2nd ed. New Haven, Conn.: Yale University Press, 2006.

Appadurai, Arjun. *The Future as Cultural Fact: Essays on the Global Condition*. London: Verso, 2013.

Aron, Raymond. *Main Currents in Sociological Thought I: Montesquieu, Comte, Marx, Tocqueville, the Sociologists of the Revolution of 1848*. Translated by Richard Howard and Helen Weaver. Garden City, N.Y.: Doubleday, 1968.

Azoulay, Ariella Aïsha. *Potential History: Unlearning Imperialism*. London: Verso, 2019.

Bailey, Ronald. *Ecoscam: The False Prophets of Ecological Apocalypse*. New York: St. Martin's, 1993.

Balayannis, Angeliki. "Following Pesticides in Disposal: A Chemical Geography." PhD dissertation, University of Melbourne, 2018.

Barca, Stefania. "Telling the Right Story: Environmental Violence and Liberation Narratives." *Environment and History* 20 (November 2014): 535–546.

Baricco, Alessandro. *The Barbarians: An Essay on the Mutation of Culture*. New York: Rizzoli Ex Libris, 2013.

Baum, Andrew, and India Fleming. "Implications of Psychological Research on Stress and Technological Accidents." *American Psychologist* 48 (June 1993): 665–672.

Beck, Ulrich. "Risk Society and the Provident State." In *Risk, Environment, and Modernity: Towards a New Ecology*, edited by Scott M. Lash, Bronislaw Szerszynski, and Brian Wynne, 27–43. London: Sage, 1996.

———. *Risk Society: Towards a New Modernity*. London: Sage, 1992.

———. *World Risk Society*. London: Polity, 1999.

Been, Vicki. "Locally Undesirable Land Uses in Minority Neighborhoods: Disproportionate Siting or Market Dynamics?" *Yale Law Journal* 103 (April 1994): 1383–1422.

Bercovitch, Sacvan. *The American Jeremiad*. Madison: University of Wisconsin Press, 1980.

Berman, William C. *America's Right Turn: From Nixon to Clinton*. 2nd ed. Baltimore: Johns Hopkins University Press, 1998.

Berry, Wendell. *Standing by Words*. Berkeley, Calif.: Counterpoint Press, 2011.

Bess, Michael. *The Light Green Society: Ecology and Technological Modernity in France, 1960–2000*. Chicago: University of Chicago Press, 2003.

Block, Alan A., and Frank R. Scarpitti. *Poisoning for Profit: The Mafia and Toxic Waste in America*. New York: William Morrow, 1985.

Blum, Elizabeth D. *Love Canal Revisited: Race, Class, and Gender in Environmental Activism*. Lawrence: University Press of Kansas, 2008.

Blumberg, Louis, and Robert Gottlieb. *War on Waste: Can America Win Its Battle with Garbage?* Washington, D.C.: Island Press, 1989.

Boddice, Rob. *The History of Emotions*. Manchester: Manchester University Press, 2018.

———. *A History of Feelings*. London: Reaktion Books, 2019.

Bohme, Susanna Rankin. *Toxic Injustice: A Transnational History of Exposure and Struggle*. Berkeley: University of California Press, 2015.

Boudia, Saroya, Angela Creager, Scott Frickel, et al. *Residues: Thinking Through Chemical Environments*. New Brunswick, N.J.: Rutgers University Press, 2022.

Boudia, Soraya, and Nathalie Jas, eds. *Powerless Science? Science and Politics in a Toxic World*. New York: Berghahn Books, 2014.

Bouk, Dan. *How Our Days Became Numbered: Risk and the Rise of the Statistical Individual*. Chicago: University of Chicago Press, 2015.

Bourke, Joanna. *Fear: A Cultural History*. London: Virago Press, 2005.

Bowser, Benjamin P. "Race Relations in the 1980s: The Case of the United States." *Journal of Black Studies* 15, no. 3 (March 1985): 307–324.

Boyer, Paul. *By the Bomb's Early Light: American Thought and Culture at the Dawn of the Atomic Age*. Chapel Hill: University of North Carolina Press, 1994.

Brennan, Mary C. *Turning Right in the Sixties.* Chapel Hill: University of North Carolina Press, 1995.

Brick, Howard. *Age of Contradiction: American Thought and Culture in the 1960s.* Ithaca, N.Y.: Cornell University Press, 2000.

Brody, Julia Green, et al. "Environmental Pollutants and Breast Cancer: Epidemiologic Studies." *Cancer* 109 (June 15, 2007): 2667–2711.

Brody, Julia Green, et al. "Environmental Pollutants, Diet, Physical Activity, Body Size, and Breast Cancer: Where Do We Stand in Research to Identify Opportunities for Prevention?" *Cancer* 109 (June 15, 2007): 2627–2634.

Brooks, Karl Boyd. *Before Earth Day: The Origins of American Environmental Law, 1945–1970.* Lawrence: University Press of Kansas, 2009.

Brown, Kate. *Manual for Survival: A Chernobyl Guide to the Future.* New York: Norton, 2019.

———. *Plutopia: Nuclear Families, Atomic Cities, and the Great Soviet and American Plutonium Disasters.* New York: Oxford University Press, 2015.

Brown, Michael. *Laying Waste: The Poisoning of America by Toxic Chemicals.* New York: Pantheon Books, 1979.

Brown, Phil. "The Popular Epidemiology Approach to Toxic Waste Contamination." In *Communities at Risk: Collective Responses to Technological Hazards,* edited by Stephen Robert Couch and J. Stephen Kroll-Smith, 133–155. New York: Peter Lang, 1991.

———. "Popular Epidemiology: Community Response to Toxic Waste-Induced Disease in Woburn, Massachusetts." *Science, Technology, and Human Values* 12 (July 1987): 78–85.

Brown, Phil, and Edwin J. Mikkelsen. *No Safe Place: Toxic Waste, Leukemia, and Community Action.* Berkeley: University of California Press, 1990.

Brown, Wendy. *Undoing the Demos: Neoliberalism's Stealth Revolution.* Cambridge, Mass.: Zone Books, 2015.

Bucquoy, Jan, and Jacques Santi. *Mourir à Creys-Malville.* Paris: Ansaldi, 1986.

Buell, Frederick. *From Apocalypse to Way of Life: Environmental Crisis in the American Century.* New York: Routledge, 2003.

Buell, Lawrence. *The Environmental Imagination: Thoreau, Nature Writing, and the Formation of American Culture.* Cambridge, Mass.: Harvard University Press, 1996.

———. "Toxic Discourse." *Critical Inquiry* 24 (Spring 1998): 639–665.

Bullard, Robert D., ed. *Confronting Environmental Racism: Voices from the Grassroots.* Boston: South End, 1993.

———. *Dumping in Dixie: Race, Class, and Environmental Quality.* Boulder, Colo.: Westview Press, 1990.

———, ed. *Unequal Protection: Environmental Justice and Communities of Color.* San Francisco: Sierra Club Books, 1994.

Burford, Anne M. *Are You Tough Enough? An Insider's View of Washington Power Politics.* New York: McGraw-Hill, 1986.

Button, Gregory. *Disaster Culture: Knowledge and Uncertainty in the Wake of Human and Environmental Catastrophe.* Walnut Creek, Calif.: Left Coast Press, 2010.

———. "Popular Media Reframing of Man-Made Disasters: A Cautionary Tale." In *Catastrophe and Culture: The Anthropology of Disaster,* edited by S. M. Hoffman and A. Oliver-Smith, 143–158. Santa Fe: School of American Research Press, 2002.

Cairns, John. "The Cancer Problem." *Scientific American,* November 1975, 64–78.

Camacho, David E., ed. *Environmental Injustices, Political Struggles: Race, Class, and the Environment.* Durham, N.C.: Duke University Press, 1998.

Čapek, Stella M. "The 'Environmental Justice' Frame: A Conceptual Discussion and an Application." *Social Problems* 40 (February 1993): 5–24.

Carpenter, Daniel. *Reputation and Power: Organizational Image and Pharmaceutical Regulation at the FDA.* Princeton, N.J.: Princeton University Press, 2010.

Carson, Rachel. *Silent Spring.* Boston: Houghton Mifflin, 1962.

Cavarero, Adriana. *Horrorism: Naming Contemporary Violence.* New York: Columbia University Press, 2011.

Chowkwanyun, Merlin. *All Health Politics Is Local: Community Battles for Medical Care and Environmental Health.* Chapel Hill: University of North Carolina Press, 2022.

Chung, Man Cheung, and Michael E. Hyland. *History and Philosophy of Psychology.* New York: Wiley, 2012.

Churchill, Ward, and Winona LaDuke. "Native North America: The Political Economy of Radioactive Colonialism." *Insurgent Sociologist* 13 (April 1986): 51–78.

Clapp, Jennifer. *Toxic Exports: The Transfer of Hazardous Wastes and Technologies from Rich to Poor Countries.* Ithaca, N.Y.: Cornell University Press, 2010.

Clapp, Richard W. "Popular Epidemiology in Three Contaminated Communities." *Annals of the American Academy of Political and Social Science* 584 (November 2002): 35–46.

Clarke, Lee. *Acceptable Risk? Making Decisions in a Toxic Environment.* Berkeley: University of California Press, 1989.

Coen, Deborah. *The Earthquake Observers: Disaster Science from Lisbon to Richter.* Chicago: University of Chicago Press, 2013.

Cohen, Benjamin R. *Pure Adulteration: Cheating on Nature in the Age of Manufactured Food.* Chicago: University of Chicago Press, 2019.

Colborn, Theo, Dianne Dumanoski, and John Peterson Myers. *Our Stolen Future.* New York: Plume Books, 1997.

Cole, Luke W., and Sheila R. Foster. *From the Ground Up: Environmental Racism and the Rise of the Environmental Justice Movement.* New York: New York University Press, 2001.

Collin, Robert W. *The Environmental Protection Agency: Cleaning Up America's Act.* Westport, Conn.: Greenwood, 2006.

Commoner, Barry. "Barry Commoner Responds to Attacks on Rachel Carson." *The Pump Handle,* June 27, 2007. https://thepumphandle.wordpress.com/2007/06/27/commoner-responds-to-attacks-on-carson/.

———. *The Closing Circle.* New York: Knopf, 1971.

Conis, Elena. *How to Sell a Poison: The Rise, Fall, and Toxic Return of DDT.* New York: Bold Type Books, 2022.

Corburn, Jason. *Street Science: Community Knowledge and Environmental Health Justice.* Cambridge, Mass.: MIT Press, 2005.

Craig, Brian. *Stringfellow Acid Pits: The Toxic and Legal Legacy.* Ann Arbor: University of Michigan Press, 2020.

Cranor, Carl F. *Toxic Torts: Science, Law and the Possibility of Justice.* 2nd ed. New York: Cambridge University Press, 2016.

Darnton, Robert. "Writing News and Telling Stories." *Daedalus* 104 (Spring 1975): 175–194.

Davies, William. *Nervous States: How Feeling Took Over the World.* London: Jonathan Cape, 2018.

Davis, Devra Lee. *The Secret War on Cancer.* New York: Basic Books, 2009.

Davis, Devra Lee, et al. "International Trends in Cancer Mortality in France, West Germany, Italy, Japan, England and Wales, and the USA." *The Lancet* 336 (August 1990): 474–481.

DeLillo, Don. *White Noise.* New York: Viking, 1985.

D'Emilio, John, and Estelle Freedman. *Intimate Matters: A History of Sexuality in America.* Chicago: University of Chicago Press, 1997.

Demortain, David. *The Science of Bureaucracy: Risk Decision-Making and the U.S. Environmental Protection Agency.* Cambridge, Mass.: MIT Press, 2020.

Dershowitz, Alan M. *The Abuse Excuse: And Other Cop-Outs, Sob Stories, and Evasions of Responsibility.* New York: Back Bay Books, 1995.

Di Chiro, Giovanna. "Living Environmentalisms: Coalition Politics, Social Reproduction, and Environmental Justice." *Environmental Politics* 17 (April 2008): 276–298.

DiPerna, Paula. *Cluster Mystery: Epidemic and the Children of Woburn, Mass.* St. Louis: C. V. Mosby, 1985.

Doctorow, E. L. "The State of Mind of the Union." *The Nation*, March 22, 1986.

Dowie, Mark. *Losing Ground: American Environmentalism at the Close of the Twentieth Century.* Cambridge, Mass.: MIT Press, 1995.

Doyle, Jack. *Trespass Against Us: Dow Chemical and the Toxic Century.* Monroe, Maine: Common Courage Press, 2004.

Dunaway, Finis. *Seeing Green: The Use and Abuse of American Environmental Images.* Chicago: University of Chicago Press, 2015.

Edelstein, Michael R. *Contaminated Communities: The Social and Psychological Impacts of Residential Toxic Exposure.* Boulder, Colo.: Westview Press, 1988.

Efron, Edith. *The Apocalyptics: How Environmental Politics Controls What We Know About Cancer.* New York: Simon & Schuster, 1984.

———. *The News Twisters.* Los Angeles: Nash, 1971.

Egan, Michael. *Barry Commoner and the Science of Survival: The Remaking of American Environmentalism.* Cambridge, Mass.: MIT Press, 2007.

———. "Fear, Knowledge, and Activism: Toxic Anxieties in the 1980s." In *The Nature of Hope: Grassroots Organizing, Environmental Justice, and Political Change*, edited by Char Miller and Jeff Crane, 182–201. Boulder: University Press of Colorado, 2018.

———. "The Social Significance of the Environmental Crisis: Barry Commoner's *The Closing Circle*." *Organization and Environment* 15 (December 2002): 443–457.

———. "Survival Science: Crisis Disciplines and the Shock of the Environment in the 1970s." *Centaurus* 59 (2017): 26–39.

Enders, Danielle. "The Rhetoric of Nuclear Colonialism: Rhetorical Exclusion of American Indian Arguments in the Yucca Mountain Nuclear Waste Siting Decision." *Communication and Critical/Cultural Studies* 6 (2009): 39–60.

Epstein, Samuel S., Lester O. Brown, and Carl Pope. *Hazardous Waste in America.* San Francisco: Sierra Club Books, 1982.

Ericson, Richard V. *Crime in an Insecure World.* Oxford: Polity, 2007.

Erikson, Kai. *A New Species of Trouble: Explorations in Disaster, Trauma, and Community.* New York: Norton, 1994.

Esposito, M. P., T. O. Tiernan, and Forrest E. Dryden. *Dioxins.* Washington, D.C.: Environmental Protection Agency, 1980.

Fagin, Dan. *Toms River: A Story of Science and Salvation.* New York: Bantam, 2013.

Farber, David. *Crack: Rock Cocaine, Street Capitalism, and the Decade of Greed.* New York: Cambridge University Press, 2019.

Fellman, Michael. *In the Name of God and Country: Reconsidering Terrorism in American History*. New Haven, Conn.: Yale University Press, 2010.

Fischer, Frank. *Citizens, Experts, and the Environment: The Politics of Local Knowledge*. Durham, N.C.: Duke University Press, 2000.

Fisher, Eric Scott. "Potter v. Firestone and the Infliction of Emotional Distress." *Tort & Insurance Law Journal* 30 (Summer 1995): 1071–1085.

Fisher, Mark. *Capitalism Realism: Is There No Alternative?* Winchester: Zero Books, 2014.

Foley, Michael Stewart. *Front Porch Politics: The Forgotten Heyday of American Activism in the 1970s and 1980s*. New York: Hill & Wang, 2013.

Fortun, Kim. *Advocacy After Bhopal: Environmentalism, Disaster, New Global Orders*. Chicago: University of Chicago Press, 2001.

Foster, Richard. "Kepone: The 'Flour' Factory." *Richmond Magazine*, July 8, 2005. http://richmondmagazine.com/news/kepone-disaster-pesticide/.

Frederickson, Leif. "The Age of Lead: Metropolitan Change, Environmental Health, and Inner City Underdevelopment." PhD dissertation, University of Virginia, 2017.

Freudenberg, Nicholas. *Lethal but Legal: Corporations, Consumption, and Practicing Public Health*. New York: Oxford University Press, 2014.

Friedman, Sharon M., et al. "Alar and Apples: Newspapers, Risk and Media Responsibility." *Public Understanding of Science* 5 (January 1996): 1–20.

Fung, Archon, and Dara O'Rourke. "Reinventing Environmental Regulation from the Grassroots Up: Explaining and Expanding the Success of the Toxics Release Inventory." *Environmental Management* 25 (February 2000): 115–127.

Furedi, Frank. *Culture of Fear Revisited*. London: Continuum, 2006.

Gaby, W. L. "Health Hazards Associated with Solid Waste Disposal." *Reviews on Environmental Health* 3, no. 3 (1981): 277–291.

Gardiner, Beth. *Choked: Life and Breath in the Age of Air Pollution*. Chicago: University of Chicago Press, 2019.

Garland, David. "The Rise of Risk." In *Risk and Morality*, edited by Richard V. Ericson and Aaron Doyle, 48–86. Toronto: University of Toronto Press, 2003.

Geiser, Ken. *Chemicals Without Harm: Policies for a Sustainable World*. Cambridge, Mass.: MIT Press, 2015.

Geiser, Ken, and Gerry Waneck. "PCBs and Warren County." *Science for the People* 15 (July/August 1983): 13–17.

Gensburg, Lenore J., et al. "Cancer Incidence Among Former Love Canal Residents." *Environmental Health Perspectives* 117 (August 2009): 1265–1271.

Gensburg, Lenore J., et al. "Mortality Among Former Love Canal Residents." *Environmental Health Perspectives* 117 (February 2009): 209–216.

Gerstle, Gary. *The Rise and Fall of the Neoliberal Order: America and the World in the Free Market Era*. New York: Oxford University Press, 2022.

Gibbs, Lois. *Love Canal: My Story*. Albany: State University of New York Press, 1982.

———. *Love Canal: The Story Continues....* Stony Creek, Conn.: New Society, 1998.

Gibson-Graham, J. K. "Rethinking the Economy with Thick Description and Weak Theory." *Current Anthropology* 55 (August 2014): s147–s153.

Glassner, Barry. *The Culture of Fear: Why Americans Are Afraid of the Wrong Things*. New York: Basic Books, 1999.

Goodman, Michael, et al. "Cancer Cluster Investigations: Review of the Past and Proposals for the Future." *International Journal of Environmental Research and Public Health* 11, no. 2 (2014): 1479–1499.

Goodman, Michael, et al. "Cancer Clusters in the USA: What Do the Last Twenty Years of State and Federal Investigations Tell Us?" *Critical Reviews in Toxicology* 42, no. 6 (2012): 474–490.

Grøn, Arne. *The Concept of Anxiety in Søren Kierkegaard*. Macon, Ga.: Mercer University Press, 2008.

Hacking, Ian. "Risk and Dirt." In *Risk and Morality*, edited by R. V. Ericson and A. Doyle, 22–47. Toronto: University of Toronto Press, 2003.

Hamilton, Cynthia. "Concerned Citizens of South Central Los Angeles." In *Unequal Protection: Environmental Justice and Communities of Color*, edited by Robert D. Bullard, 207–219. San Francisco: Sierra Club Books, 1994.

Hanahan, Douglas, and Robert A. Weinberg. "Hallmarks of Cancer: The Next Generation." *Cell* 144 (March 4, 2011): 646–674.

Hans, Joseph M., Jr., and Thomas C. Sell. *Evacuation Risks—An Evaluation*. Las Vegas: Environmental Protection Agency, 1974.

Hartsough, Don M., and Jeffrey C. Savitsky. "Three Mile Island: Psychology and Environmental Policy at a Crossroads." *American Psychologist* 39 (October 1984): 1113–1122.

Harvey, David. *A Brief History of Neoliberalism*. New York: Oxford University Press, 2005.

———. *The Condition of Post-Modernity: An Enquiry into the Origins of Social Change*. Oxford: Blackwell, 1989.

Hay, Amy M. *The Defoliation of America: Agent Orange Chemicals, Citizens, and Protests*. Tuscaloosa: University of Alabama Press, 2021.

———. "A New Earthly Vision: Religious Community Activism in the Love Canal Chemical Disaster." *Environmental History* 14 (July 2009): 502–526.

———. "Recipe for Disaster: Chemical Wastes, Community Activists, and Public Health at Love Canal, 1945–2000." PhD dissertation, Michigan State University, 2005.

———. "Recipe for Disaster: Motherhood and Citizenship at Love Canal." *Journal of Women's History* 21 (Spring 2009): 111–134.

Hays, Samuel P. *Beauty, Health, and Permanence: Environmental Politics in the United States, 1955–1985*. New York: Cambridge University Press, 1987.

Hayward, Steven F. *The Age of Reagan: The Conservative Counterrevolution, 1980–1989*. New York: Random House, 2009.

Heise, Ursula K. "Cultures of Risk and the Aesthetic of Uncertainty." In *Scientific Cultures–Technological Challenges: A Transatlantic Perspective*, edited by Klaus Benesch and Meike Zwingenberger, 17–44. Heidelberg: University of Heidelberg Press, 2009.

Hemmer, Nicole. "From 'Faith in Facts' to 'Fair and Balanced': Conservative Media, Liberal Bias, and the Origins of Balance." In *Media Nation: The Political History of News in Modern America*, edited by Bruce J. Schulman and Julian E. Zelizer. Philadelphia: University of Pennsylvania Press, 2017.

Hepler-Smith, Evan. "Molecular Bureaucracy: Toxicological Information and Environmental Protection." Environmental History 24, no. 3 (July 2019): 1–27.

Hernan, Robert Emmet. *This Borrowed Earth: Lessons from the Fifteen Worst Environmental Disasters Around the World*. New York: Palgrave Macmillan, 2010.

Hites, Ronald A. "Dioxins: An Overview and History." *Environmental Science & Technology* 45, no. 1 (2011): 16–20.

Hofstadter, Richard. "The Paranoid Style in American Politics." *Harper's*, November 1964, 77–86.

Holden, Constance. "Love Canal Residents Under Stress." *Science* 208 (June 13, 1980): 1242–1244.

Houser, Heather. *Ecosickness in Contemporary U.S. Fiction: Environment and Affect*. New York: Columbia University Press, 2014.

Houston, Donna. "Environmental Justice Storytelling: Angels and Isotopes at Yucca Mountain, Nevada." *Antipode* 45 (March 2013): 417–435.

Hughes, Robert. *The Culture of Complaint: The Fraying of America*. New York: Oxford University Press, 1993.

Irwin, Alan. "Risk, Science, and Public Communication: Third-Order Thinking about Scientific Culture." In *Handbook of Public Communication of Science and Technology*, edited by Massimiano Bucchi and Brian Trench, 199–212. New York: Rutledge, 2014.

Jarrige, François, and Thomas Le Roux. *The Contamination of the Earth: A History of Pollution in the Industrial Period*. Cambridge, Mass.: MIT Press, 2020.

Jasanoff, Sheila. "EPA's Regulation of Daminozide: Unscrambling the Messages of Risk." *Science, Technology, & Human Values* 12 (Summer/Fall 1987): 116–124.

———. *The Fifth Branch: Science Advisers as Policymakers*. Cambridge, Mass.: Harvard University Press, 1990.

———. "The Political Science of Risk Perception." *Reliability, Engineering, and System Safety* 59 (January 1998): 91–99.

Jelfs, Tim. *The Argument About Things in the 1980s: Goods and Garbage in an Age of Neoliberalism*. Morgantown: West Virginia University Press, 2018.

Jenkins, Philip. *Decade of Nightmares: The End of the Sixties and the Making of Eighties America*. New York: Oxford University Press, 2006.

Johnson, Diane. "Conspirators." *New York Review of Books*, March 14, 1985. https://www-nybooks-com.libaccess.lib.mcmaster.ca/articles/1985/03/14/conspirators/.

Jones, Mary Cover. "A Laboratory Study of Fear: The Case of Peter." *Pedagogical Seminary* 31, no. 4 (1924): 308–315.

Kagan, Jerome. *What Is Emotion? History, Measures, and Meanings*. New Haven, Conn.: Yale University Press, 2007.

Kaminer, Wendy. *I'm Dysfunctional, You're Dysfunctional*. New York: Vintage, 1993.

Kanner, Allan. "Tort Remedies and Litigation Strategies." In *The Law of Environmental Justice: Theories and Procedures to Address Disproportionate Risks*, 2nd ed., edited by Michael B. Gerrard and Sheila R. Foster, 667–712. Chicago: American Bar Association, 2008.

Kiechle, Melanie A. *Smell Detectives: An Olfactory History of Nineteenth-Century Urban America*. Seattle: University of Washington Press, 2017.

Kolata, Gina Bari. "Chromosome Damage: What It Is, What It Means." *Science* 208 (June 13, 1980): 1240.

———. "Love Canal: False Alarm Caused by Botched Study." *Science* 208 (June 13, 1980): 1239–1242.

Kovel, Joel. *The Enemy of Nature: The End of Capitalism or the End of the World?* London: Zed Books, 2002.

Kraft, Michael E. "U.S. Environmental Policy and Politics: From the 1960s to the 1990s." *Journal of Policy History* 12 (January 2000): 17–42.

Krimsky, Sheldon. *Hormonal Chaos: The Scientific and Social Origins of the Environmental Endocrine Hypothesis*. Baltimore: Johns Hopkins University Press, 2000.

Kruse, Kevin M., and Julian E. Zelizer. *Fault Lines: A History of the United States Since 1974*. New York: Norton, 2019.

Kuletz, Valerie. "Invisible Places, Violent Spaces: Cold War Nuclear and Militarized Landscapes." In *Violent Environments*, edited by Nancy Lee Peluso and Michael Watts. Ithaca, N.Y.: Cornell University Press, 2001.

———. *The Tainted Desert: Environmental and Social Ruin in the American West.* New York: Routledge, 1998.

Kummerer, Klaus. "The Ecological Impact of Time." *Time and Society* 5 (June 1996): 209–235.

LaDuke, Winona. *All Our Relations: Native Struggles for Land and Life.* Boston: South End, 1999.

Laffan, Michael, and Max Weiss, eds. *Facing Fear: The History of an Emotion in Global Perspective.* Princeton, N.J.: Princeton University Press, 2012.

Lagakos, Steven, Barbara J. Wessen, and Marvin Zelen. "An Analysis of Contaminated Well Water and Health Effects in Woburn, Massachusetts." *Journal of the American Statistical Association* 81 (September 1986): 583–596.

Langston, Nancy. *Toxic Bodies: Hormone Disruptors and the Legacy of DES.* New Haven, Conn.: Yale University Press, 2010.

Lash, Jonathan, Katherine Gillman, and David Sheridan. *A Season of Spoils: The Reagan Administration's Attack on the Environment.* New York: Pantheon Books, 1984.

Levine, Adeline Gordon. *Love Canal: Science, Politics, and People.* Lexington, Mass.: Lexington Books, 1982.

———. "Psychosocial Impact of Toxic Chemical Waste Dumps." *Environmental Health Perspectives* 48 (1983): 15–17.

Levy, Jonathan. *Freaks of Fortune: The Emerging World of Capitalism and Risk in America.* Cambridge, Mass.: Harvard University Press, 2012.

Liboiron, Max. *Pollution Is Colonialism.* Durham, N.C.: Duke University Press, 2021.

Lloyd-Smith, Mariann, and Bro Sheffield-Brotherton. "Children's Environmental Health: Intergenerational Equity in Action: A Civil Society Perspective." *Annals of the New York Academy of Science* 1140, no. 1 (October 2008): 190–200.

Luhmann, Niklas. "Modern Society Shocked by Its Risks." Social Sciences Research Center Occasional Paper 17, 1996.

Lupton, Deborah. *Risk.* New York: Routledge, 1999.

Lynn, Frances M., and Jack D. Kartez. "Environmental Democracy in Action: The Toxics Release Inventory." *Environmental Management* 18 (July 1994): 511–521.

MacKendrick, Norah. *Better Safe Than Sorry: How Consumers Navigate Exposure to Everyday Toxics.* Oakland: University of California Press, 2018.

Magnuson, Ed, et al. "The Poisoning of America." *Time,* September 22, 1980, 58–69.

Mangano, Joseph. "Three Mile Island: Health Study Meltdown." *Bulletin of the Atomic Scientists* 60 (September/October 2004): 30–35.

Markowitz, Gerald, and David Rosner. *Deceit and Denial: The Deadly Politics of Industrial Pollution*. Berkeley: University of California Press, 2002.

Marrs, Scott D. "Mind Over Body: Trends Regarding the Physical Injury Requirement in Negligent Infliction of Emotional Distress and 'Fear of Disease' Cases." *Tort & Insurance Law Journal* 28 (Fall 1992): 1–39.

Marshall, Eliot. "Experts Clash Over Cancer Data." *Science* 250 (November 16, 1990): 900–902.

Masco, Joseph. *The Future of Fallout, and Other Episodes in Radioactive World-Making*. Durham, N.C.: Duke University Press, 2020.

———. *Nuclear Borderlands: The Manhattan Project in Post–Cold War New Mexico*. Princeton, N.J.: Princeton University Press, 2006.

———. *The Theater of Operations: National Security Affect from the Cold War to the War on Terror*. Durham, N.C.: Duke University Press, 2014.

Mazur, Allan. *A Hazardous Inquiry: The Rashomon Effect at Love Canal*. Cambridge, Mass.: Harvard University Press, 1998.

———. "Technical Risk in the Mass Media." *Risk: Health, Safety & Environment* 189 (June 1994): 191.

McGirr, Lisa. *Suburban Warriors: The Origins of the New American Right*. Princeton, N.J.: Princeton University Press, 2002.

McGurty, Eileen. *Transforming Environmentalism: Warren County, PCBs, and the Origins of Environmental Justice*. New Brunswick, N.J.: Rutgers University Press, 2007.

Merchant, Carolyn. *Radical Ecology: The Search for a Livable World*. New York: Routledge, 2012.

Michaels, David. *Doubt Is Their Product: How Industry's Assault on Science Threatens Your Health*. New York: Oxford University Press, 2008.

Milazzo, Paul Charles. *Unlikely Environmentalists: Congress and Clean Water, 1945–1972*. Lawrence: University Press of Kansas, 2006.

Mirowski, Philip. *Never Let a Serious Crisis Go to Waste: How Neoliberalism Survived the Financial Meltdown*. London: Verso, 2013.

———. "Postface: Defining Neoliberalism." In *The Road from Mont Pèlerin: The Making of the Neoliberal Thought Collective*, edited by Philip Mirowski and Dieter Plehwe, 417–455. Cambridge, Mass.: Harvard University Press, 2015.

Mitman, Gregg, Michelle Murphy, and Christopher Sellers. "Introduction: A Cloud over History." In *Landscapes of Exposure: Knowledge and Illness in Modern Environments*, edited by Mitman, Murphy, and Sellers. Chicago: University of Chicago Press, 2004.

Mizruchi, Susan. "Risk Theory and the Contemporary American Novel." *American Literary History* 22 (Spring 2010): 109–135.

Mohun, Arwen. *Risk: Negotiating Safety in American Society*. Baltimore: Johns Hopkins University Press, 2012.

Monbiot, George, and Peter Hutchison. *Invisible Doctrine: The Secret History of Neoliberalism*. London: Allen Lane, 2024.

Moore, Kelly. *Disrupting Science: Social Movements, American Scientists, and the Politics of the Military, 1945–1975*. Princeton, N.J.: Princeton University Press, 2008.

Mukerji, Chandra. *A Fragile Power: Scientists and the State*. Princeton, N.J.: Princeton University Press, 1989.

Mukherjee, Siddhartha. *The Emperor of All Maladies: A Biography of Cancer*. New York: Scribner, 2011.

Müller, Simone M. *The Toxic Ship: The Voyage of the* Khan Sea *and the Global Waste Trade*. Seattle: University of Washington Press, 2023.

Nahr, Sybille, ed. *Poison Fire, Sacred Earth: Testimonies, Lectures, Conclusions: The World Uranium Hearing, Salzburg, 1992*. Salzburg: World Uranium Hearing, 1993.

Nash, Linda. *Inescapable Ecologies: A History of Environment, Disease, and Knowledge*. Berkeley: University of California Press, 2006.

Newman, Richard. "Darker Shades of Green: Love Canal, Toxic Autobiography, and American Environmental Writing." In *Histories of the Dustheap: Waste, Material Cultures, Social Justice*, edited by Stephanie Foote and Elizabeth Mazzolini. Cambridge, Mass.: MIT Press, 2012.

———. *Love Canal: A Toxic History from Colonial Times to the Present*. New York: Oxford University Press, 2016.

Nixon, Rob. *Slow Violence and the Environmentalism of the Poor*. Cambridge, Mass.: Harvard University Press, 2011.

Norgaard, Kari Marie. *Living in Denial: Climate Change, Emotions, and Everyday Life*. Cambridge, Mass.: MIT Press, 2011.

Nowotny, Helga. *The Cunning of Uncertainty*. Cambridge: Polity, 2016.

Nowotny, Helga, Peter Scott, and Michael Gibbon, eds. *Re-Thinking Science: Knowledge and the Public in an Age of Uncertainty*. Cambridge: Polity, 2001.

O'Neill, Kate. "Out of the Backyard: The Problems of Hazardous Waste Management at a Global Level." *Journal of Environment & Development* 7, no 2 (1998): 138–163.

———. *Waste*. Cambridge: Polity, 2019.

Oreskes, Naomi, and Erik M. Conway. *Merchants of Doubt: How a Handful of Scientists Obscured the Truth on Issues from Tobacco Smoke to Global Warming*. New York: Bloomsbury, 2010.

Otway, Harry J., and Detlof von Winterfeldt. "Beyond Acceptable Risk: On the Social Acceptability of Technologies." *Policy Sciences* 14 (June 1982): 247–256.

Ozbilge, Nevcihan. "A Refusal of State-Driven Northern Destiny: Deconstructing the Mackenzie Valley Pipeline Inquiry Hearings." PhD dissertation, McMaster University, 2022.

Pamuk, Zeynep. *Politics and Expertise: How to Use Science in a Democratic Society.* Princeton, N.J.: Princeton University Press, 2021.

Parr, Joy. *Sensing Changes: Technologies, Environment, and the Everyday, 1953–2003.* Vancouver: University of British Columbia Press, 2010.

Patterson, James T. *Restless Giant: The United States from Watergate to Bush v. Gore.* New York: Oxford University Press, 2005.

Piasecki, Bruce, ed. *Beyond Dumping: New Strategies for Controlling Toxic Contamination.* Westport, Conn.: Quorum Books, 1984.

———. "The Politics of Toxic Wastes: Why the OMB Weakens EPA Programs." In *Beyond Dumping: New Strategies for Controlling Toxic Contamination,* edited by Bruce Piasecki, 53–68. Westport, Conn.: Quorum Books, 1984.

Pidgeon, Nick, et al. "Risk Perception." In *Risk: Analysis, Perception and Management.* London: Royal Society, 1992.

Pietruska, Jamie. *Looking Forward: Prediction and Uncertainty in Modern America.* Chicago: University of Chicago Press, 2017.

Plamper, Jan. *The History of Emotions: An Introduction.* Oxford: Oxford University Press, 2015.

Plamper, Jan, and Benjamin Lazier. "Introduction: The Phobic Regimes of Modernity." *Representations* 110 (Spring 2010): 58–65.

Plater, Zygmunt J. B. "Facing a Time of Counter-Revolution: The Kepone Incident and a Review of First Principles." *University of Richmond Law Review* 29 (1995): 657–713.

Podgers, James. "Toxic Time Bombs: Say Latent Disease Suits Will Be Key Battleground in '80s." *American Bar Association Journal* 67 (February 1981): 139–142.

Pollans, Lily Baum. *Resisting Garbage: The Politics of Waste Management in American Cities.* Austin: University of Texas Press, 2021.

Poovey, Mary. *A History of the Modern Fact: Problems of Knowledge in the Sciences of Wealth and Society.* Chicago: University of Chicago Press, 1998.

Porter, Theodore M. *Trust in Numbers: The Pursuit of Objectivity in Science and Public Life.* Princeton, N.J.: Princeton University Press, 1996.

Proctor, Robert N. *Cancer Wars: How Politics Shapes What We Know and Don't Know About Cancer.* New York: Basic Books, 1995.

Proctor, Robert N., and Londa Schiebinger, eds. *Agnotology: The Making and Unmaking of Ignorance.* Stanford, Calif.: Stanford University Press, 2008.

Pulido, Laura. "A Critical Review of the Methodology of Environmental Racism Research." *Antipode* 28 (April 1996): 142–159.

———. *Environmentalism and Economic Justice: Two Chicano Struggles in the Southwest*. Tucson: University of Arizona Press, 1996.

Pynchon, Thomas. *Gravity's Rainbow*. New York: Viking, 1973.

Radkau, Joachim. *The Age of Ecology*. Cambridge: Polity, 2014.

Ramadan, Hisham, and Jeff Shantz, eds. *Manufacturing Phobias: The Political Production of Fear in Theory and Practice*. Toronto: University of Toronto Press, 2016.

———. "Phobic Constructions: An Introduction." In *Manufacturing Phobias: The Political Production of Fear in Theory and Practice*, edited by Hisham Ramadan and Jeff Shantz, 3–14. Toronto: University of Toronto Press, 2016.

Ravetz, Jerome. "Post-normal Science—An Insight Now Maturing." *Futures* 31, no. 7 (1999): 641–646.

Reaves, Lynne. "Fear Not Enough: Noncancer DES Case Fails." *American Bar Association*, June 1983, 725–726.

Rebovich, Donald J. *Dangerous Ground: The World of Hazardous Waste Crime*. New Brunswick, N.J.: Transaction, 1992.

Reddy, William M. *The Navigation of Feeling: A Framework for the History of Emotions*. Cambridge: Cambridge University Press, 2001.

Rich, Nathaniel. *Losing Earth: A Recent History*. New York: Farrar, Straus and Giroux, 2019.

Riismandel, Kyle. *Neighborhood of Fear: The Suburban Crisis in American Culture, 1975–2001*. Baltimore: Johns Hopkins University Press, 2020.

Rivera Garza, Cristina. *Grieving: Dispatches from a Wounded Country*. New York: Feminist Press, 2020.

Roberts, J. Timmons, and Melissa Toffolon-Weiss. *Chronicles from the Environmental Justice Frontline*. New York: Cambridge University Press, 2001.

Robin, Corey. *Fear: The History of a Political Idea*. New York: Oxford University Press, 2004.

———. *The Reactionary Mind: Conservatism from Edmund Burke to Sarah Palin*. New York: Oxford University Press, 2011.

Robinson, Marilynne. "Fear." *New York Review of Books*, September 24, 2015. https://www.nybooks.com/articles/2015/09/24/marilynne-robinson-fear/.

Rodgers, Daniel T. *Age of Fracture*. Cambridge, Mass.: Harvard University Press, 2011.

Rome, Adam. "What Really Matters in History? Environmental Perspectives on Modern America." *Environmental History* 7 (April 2002): 303–318.

Rose, Deborah Bird. *Reports from a Wild Country: Ethics for Decolonisation*. Sydney: University of New South Wales Press, 2004.

Rosenwein, Barbara H. *Emotional Communities in the Early Middle Ages*. Ithaca, N.Y.: Cornell University Press, 2006.

———. "Worrying about Emotions in History." *American Historical Review* 107 (June 2002): 821–845.

Rosenwein, Barbara H., and Riccardo Cristiani. *What Is the History of Emotions?* London: Polity, 2018.

Ross, Benjamin, and Steven Amter. *The Polluters: The Making of Our Chemically Altered Environment*. New York: Oxford University Press, 2010.

Ruckelshaus, William D. "Science, Risk, and Public Policy." In *Taking Sides: Clashing Views on Controversial Environmental Issues*, 4th ed., edited by Theodore D. Goldfarb. Guilford, Conn.: Dushkin, 1991.

Rush, Elizabeth. *Rising: Dispatches from the New American Shore*. Minneapolis: Milkweed Editions, 2018.

Rushevsky, Mark. *Public Policy in the United States*. 5th ed. New York: M. E. Sharpe, 2013.

Sarathy, Brenda, Vivien Hamilton, and Janet Farrell Brodie, eds. *Inevitably Toxic: Historical Perspectives on Contamination, Exposure, and Expertise*. Pittsburgh: University of Pittsburgh Press, 2018.

Sarewitz, Daniel. "Science and Environmental Policy: An Excess of Objectivity." In *Earth Matters: The Earth Sciences, Philosophy, and the Claims of Community*, edited by Robert Frodeman. New York: Prentice Hall, 2000.

Schrader-Frechette, Kristin. *Burying Uncertainty: Risk and the Case Against Geologic Disposal of Nuclear Waste*. Berkeley: University of California Press, 1993.

Schulman, Sarah. *Let the Record Show: A Political History of Act Up New York, 1987–1993*. New York: Farrar, Straus and Giroux, 2021.

Schwab, Gabriele. *Radioactive Ghosts*. Minneapolis: University of Minnesota Press, 2020.

Schwetz, B. A., et al. "Toxicology of Chlorinated Dibenzo-*p*-dioxins." *Advanced Chemistry* 120 (1973): 55–69.

Scott, James C. *Seeing Like a State: How Certain Schemes to Improve the Human Condition Have Failed*. New Haven, Conn.: Yale University Press, 1998.

Selikoff, Irving J. "Perspectives in the Investigation of Health Hazards in the Chemical Industry." Meeting of the Scientific Committee on Occupational Medicine, Milan, December 12, 1975.

Sellers, Christopher C. *Crabgrass Crucible: Suburban Nature and the Rise of Environmentalism in Twentieth-Century America*. Chapel Hill: University of North Carolina Press, 2012.

———. *Hazards of the Job: From Industrial Disease to Environmental Health Science*. Chapel Hill: University of North Carolina Press, 1997.

———. *Race and the Greening of Atlanta: Inequality, Democracy, and Environmental Politics in an Ascendant Metropolis*. Athens: University of Georgia Press, 2023.

Sellers, Christopher, and Joseph Melling. "Towards a Transnational Industrial Hazard History: Charting the Circulation of Workplace Dangers, Debates, and Expertise." *British Journal for the History of Science* 45 (September 2012): 401–424.

Shapiro, Karen. "Environmental Risk Assessment of Refuse Burning Incinerators." Unpublished manuscript.

Shapiro, Nick, Nasser Zakariya, and Jody A. Roberts. "A Wary Alliance: From Enumerating the Environment to Inviting Apprehension." *Engaging Science, Technology, and Society* 3 (2017): 575–602.

Shilts, Randy. *And the Band Played On: Politics, People, and the AIDS Epidemic.* New York: St. Martin's, 2007.

Showalter, Elaine. *Hystories: Hysterical Epidemics and Modern Media.* New York: Columbia University Press, 1997.

Slovic, Paul. "Perception of Risk." *Science* 236 (April 17, 1987): 280–285.

Solnit, Rebecca. *Hope in the Dark: Untold Histories, Wild Possibilities.* New York: Nation Books, 2004.

———. *Savage Dreams: A Journey into the Hidden Wars of the American West.* San Francisco: Sierra Club Books, 2000.

Soulé, Michael. "What Is Conservation Biology?" *Bioscience* 35, no. 11 (1985): 727–734.

Spears, Ellen Griffith. *Baptized in PCBs: Race, Pollution, and Justice in an All-American Town.* Chapel Hill: University of North Carolina Press, 2014.

Stallings, Robert A. "Media Discourse and the Social Construction of Risk." *Social Problems* 37 (February 1990): 80–95.

Starr, Chauncey. "Social Benefit Versus Technological Risk." *Science* 165, no. 3899 (1969): 1232–1238.

Stearns, Peter N. *American Fear: The Causes and Consequences of High Anxiety.* New York: Routledge, 2006.

———. *Anxious Parents: A History of Modern Childrearing in America.* New York: New York University Press, 2003.

———. "Fear and History." *Historein* 8 (2008): 17–28.

Stearns, Peter N., and Carol Z. Stearns. "Emotionology: Clarifying the History of Emotions and Emotional Standards." *American Historical Review* 90 (October 1985): 813–836.

Steinberg, Ted. *Acts of God: The Unnatural History of Natural Disaster in America.* New York: Oxford University Press, 2000.

Stockman, David A. *The Triumph of Politics: Why the Reagan Revolution Failed.* New York: Harper & Row, 1986.

Stoffle, Richard W., and Richard Arnold. "Confronting the Angry Rock: American Indian's Situated Risks from Radioactivity." *Ethnos* 68 (2003): 230–248.

Stone, Russell A., and Adeline G. Levine. "Reactions to Collective Stress: Correlates of Active Citizen Participation at Love Canal." In *Beyond the Individual: Environmental Approaches and Prevention*, edited by Abraham Wandersman and Robert Hess, 153–177. New York: Haworth Press, 1985.

Stone-Mediatore, Shari. *Reading Across Borders: Storytelling and Knowledges of Resistance*. New York: Palgrave Macmillan, 2003.

Sunstein, Cass R. *Worst-Case Scenarios*. Cambridge, Mass.: Harvard University Press, 2007.

Sutter, Paul S. "The World with Us: The State of American Environmental History." *Journal of American History* 100 (June 2013): 94–119.

Sykes, Charles J. *A Nation of Victims: The Decay of the American Character*. New York: St. Martin's, 1993.

Szasz, Andrew. *Shopping Our Way to Safety: How We Changed from Protecting the Environment to Protecting Ourselves*. Minneapolis: University of Minnesota Press, 2007.

Taylor, Dorceta E. *Toxic Communities: Environmental Racism, Industrial Pollution, and Residential Mobility*. New York: New York University Press, 2014.

Taylor, Shelley E. "Adjustment to Threatening Events: A Theory of Cognitive Adaptation." *American Psychologist* 38 (November 1983): 1161–1173.

Tesh, Sylvia Noble. *Uncertain Hazards: Environmental Activists and Scientific Proof*. Ithaca, N.Y.: Cornell University Press, 2000.

Thomas, W. I., and Dorothy Swaine Thomas. *The Child in America: Behavior Problems and Programs*. New York: Knopf, 1928.

Thomson, Jennifer. "Toxic Residents: Health and Citizenship at Love Canal." *Journal of Social History* 50, no. 1 (2016): 204–223.

———. *The Wild and the Toxic: American Environmentalism and the Politics of Health*. Chapel Hill: University of North Carolina Press, 2019.

Thornton, Joe. *Pandora's Poison: Chlorine, Health, and New Environmental Strategy*. Cambridge, Mass.: MIT Press, 2000.

Toffler, Alvin. *Future Shock*. New York: Random House, 1970.

Trouillot, Michel-Rolph. *Silencing the Past: Power and the Production of History*. Boston: Beacon, 1995.

Tversky, Amos, and Daniel Kahneman. "Availability: A Heuristic for Judging Relevancy and Probability." *Cognitive Psychology* 4 (1973): 207–232.

Urban Environment Conference. *Taking Back Our Health: An Institute on Surviving the Toxic Threat to Minority Communities*. Washington, D.C.: Urban Environment Conference, 1985.

Van Horssen, Jessica. *A Town Called Asbestos: Environmental Contamination, Health, and Resilience in a Resource Community*. Vancouver: University of British Columbia Press, 2016.

Virilio, Paul. *The Original Accident*. London: Polity, 2007.

Vogel, David. *Fluctuating Fortunes: The Political Power of Business in America*. New York: Basic Books, 1989.

Vogel, Sarah A. *Is It Safe? BPA and the Struggle to Define the Safety of Chemicals*. Berkeley: University of California Press, 2013.

Voyles, Traci Brynne. *Wastelanding: Legacies of Uranium Mining in Navajo Country*. Minneapolis: University of Minnesota Press, 2015.

Vyner, Henry M. *Invisible Trauma: The Psychosocial Effects of Invisible Environmental Contaminants*. Lexington, Mass.: Lexington Books, 1988.

Walker, J. Samuel. *The Road to Yucca Mountain: The Development of Radioactive Waste Policy in the United States*. Berkeley: University of California Press, 2009.

Walsh, Edward J. *Democracy in the Shadows: Citizen Mobilization in the Wake of the Accident at Three Mile Island*. Westport, Conn.: Greenwood, 1988.

Walsh, Edward J., Rex Warland, and D. Clayton Smith. *Don't Burn It Here: Grassroots Challenges to Trash Incinerators*. University Park: Pennsylvania State University Press, 1997.

Warren, Christian. *Brush with Death: A Social History of Lead Poisoning*. Baltimore: Johns Hopkins University Press, 2001.

Wassom, J. S. "A Review of the Genetic Toxicology of Chlorinated Dibenzo-*p*-dioxins." *Mutation Research* 47 (1977–1978): 141–160.

Weart, Spencer R. *The Rise of Nuclear Fear*. Cambridge, Mass.: Harvard University Press, 2012.

Weinberg, Alvin M. "Science and Trans-Science." *Minerva* 10 (April 1972): 209–222.

Wellum, Caleb. *Energizing Neoliberalism: The 1970s Energy Crisis and the Making of Modern America*. Baltimore: Johns Hopkins University Press, 2023.

Whelan, Elizabeth M. *Toxic Terror: The Truth Behind the Cancer Scares*. Ottawa, Ill.: Jameson Books, 1985.

Wildavsky, Aaron. *But Is It True? A Citizen's Guide to Environmental Health and Safety Issues*. Cambridge, Mass.: Harvard University Press, 1995.

Wilentz, Sean. *The Age of Reagan: A History, 1974–2008*. New York: Harper, 2008.

Wilkinson, Iain. *Anxiety in a Risk Society*. New York: Routledge, 2001.

Wilson, Gregory S. *Poison Powder: The Kepone Disaster in Virginia and Its Legacy*. Athens: University of Georgia Press, 2023.

Worster, Donald. *Shrinking the Earth: The Rise and Decline of American Abundance*. New York: Oxford University Press, 2016.

Wuthnow, Robert. *Be Very Afraid: The Cultural Response to Terror, Pandemics, Environmental Devastation, Nuclear Annihilation, and Other Threats*. New York: Oxford University Press, 2010.

Wynne, Brian. "Public Engagement as a Means of Restoring Public Trust in Science—Hitting the Notes, but Missing the Music?" *Community Genetics* 9 (May 2006): 211–220.

Zahara, Alex. "Against Risk Perception: The Deficit Model and Public Understandings of Risk." *Discard Studies*, October 1, 2018. https://discardstudies.com/2018/10/01/against-risk-perception-the-deficit-model-and-public-understandings-of-risk/.

Zaretsky, Natasha. *Radiation Nation: Three Mile Island and the Political Transformation of the 1970s*. New York: Columbia University Press, 2018.

Zeff, Robbin Lee. "Not in My Backyard / Not in Anyone's Backyard: A Folkloristic Examination of the American Grassroots Movement for Environmental Justice." PhD dissertation, Indiana University, 1990.

Zeigler, Donald J., Stanley D. Brunn, and James H. Johnson Jr. "Evacuation from a Nuclear Technological Disaster." *Geographical Review* 71 (January 1981): 1–16.

Zimring, Carl A. *Clean and White: A History of Environmental Racism*. New York: New York University Press, 2016.

INDEX

SINCE 1970: HISTORIES OF CONTEMPORARY AMERICA

Jimmy Carter, the Politics of Family, and the Rise of the Religious Right
by J. Brooks Flippen

Rumor, Repression, and Racial Politics: How the Harassment of Black Elected Officials Shaped Post–Civil Rights America
by George Derek Musgrove

Doing Recent History: On Privacy, Copyright, Video Games, Institutional Review Boards, Activist Scholarship, and History That Talks Back
edited by Claire Bond Potter and Renee C. Romano

The Dinner Party: Judy Chicago and the Power of Popular Feminism, 1970–2007
by Jane F. Gerhard

Reconsidering Roots: Race, Politics, and Memory
edited by Erica L. Ball and Kellie Carter Jackson

Liberation in Print: Feminist Periodicals and Social Movement Identity
by Agatha Beins

Pushing Back: Women of Color–Led Grassroots Activism in New York City
by Ariella Rotramel

Remaking Radicalism: A Grassroots Documentary Reader of the United States, 1973–2001
edited by Dan Berger and Emily K. Hobson

Deep Cut: Science, Power, and the Unbuilt Interoceanic Canal
by Christine Keiner

America's Other Automakers: A History of the Foreign-Owned Automotive Sector in the United States
by Timothy J. Minchin

Public Religions in the Future World: Postsecularism and Utopia
by David Morris

Goldwater Girls to Reagan Women: Gender, Georgia, and the Growth of the New Right
by Robin M. Morris

Here Are My People: LGBT College Student Organizing in California
by David A. Reichard

Black Revolutionaries: A History of the Black Panther Party
by Joe Street

Toxic Fear: Pollution Anxieties in the American 1980s
by Michael Egan